THE FALASHAS

The
Falashas

A Short History of the Ethiopian Jews

DAVID KESSLER

FRANK CASS
LONDON • PORTLAND, OR.

First edition published in 1982 by Allen & Unwin
Reprinted in 1982 by Africana Publishing Co. (Holmes and Meier)
Second edition published in 1985 by Schocken Books
This third revised edition published in 1996 in Great Britain by
FRANK CASS & CO. LTD
Newbury House, 900 Eastern Avenue, London IG2 7HH

and in the United States of America by
FRANK CASS
c/o 5804 N.E. Hassalo Street, Portland, Oregon 97213-3644

Copyright © 1996 David Kessler

British Library Cataloguing in Publication Data

Kessler, David
    Falashas:Short History of the Ethiopian
    Jews. – 3Rev.ed
    I. Title
    296.8

Library of Congress Cataloging-in-Publication Data

Kessler, David.
    The Falashas : a short history of the Ethiopian Jews / David
Kessler. — 3rd rev. ed.
        p. cm.
    Rev. ed. of: The Falashas : the forgotten Jews of Ethiopia.
    Includes bibliographical references and index.
    ISBN 0-7146-4646-6 (hbk.). — ISBN 0-7146-4170-7 (pbk.)
    1. Jews—Ethiopia—History. 2. Ethiopia—Ethnic relations.
I. Title.
DS135.E75K47 1996
963'.004924—dc20   95-38181
                                                          CIP

ISBN 0 7146 4646 6 (cloth)
ISBN 0 7146 4170 7 (paper)

Printed and bound in Great Britain by
Bookcraft (Bath) Ltd., Midsomer Norton, Somerset

Contents

In Memoriam
Mary Matilda
1915–1990
Norman Bentwich
1883–1971

List of Illustrations

between pages 86 and 87

List of Abbreviations

Alliance (A.I.U.)	Alliance Israélite Universelle
AJDC	American Joint Distribution Committee (Joint)
C.M.J.	Church Mission to the Jews
C.M.S.	Church Missionary Society
Enc. Brit.	*Encyclopaedia Britannica*
Enc. Jud.	*Encyclopaedia Judaica*
F.W.A.	Falasha Welfare Association, subsequently merged with World Jewish Relief (CBF)
J.C.A.	Jewish Colonisation Association
J.C.	*Jewish Chronicle*
J.J.S.	*Journal of Jewish Studies*
J.S.S.	*Journal of Semitic Studies*
N.E.B.	*New English Bible*
ORT	Organisation for Rehabilitation through Training
OSE	British OSE Society for Medical Aid
S.O.A.S.	School of Oriental and African Studies, London University
W.J.C.	World Jewish Congress

Preface to Second Edition

Although the situation of the Ethiopian Jews, usually known as Falashas, has altered dramatically since the first edition of this book was published in 1982, I have not found that anything but superficial changes in the original text were required. The story remains, by any standard, a remarkable, if not unique example of Jewish survival in the face of almost overwhelming odds.

The drastic change in the situation has, of course, been provided by the airlift to Israel, code named 'Operation Moses', which followed directly from the rapidly deteriorating conditions in the Horn of Africa affecting all those inhabitants caught up in the apparently never-ending crisis of famine and civil wars. Ethiopian Jews represented one of the more vulnerable minorities, innocent victims of this immense tale of suffering.

The lifeline which had been thrown to the Falashas in the form of the aid and rehabilitation programme operated by the World ORT Union, described in the Postscript, was peremptorily closed down by the Ethiopian Government in October 1981. At first there were some hopes that the authorities could be persuaded to reverse their decision, and efforts were made to this end, but without avail. The Falashas found themselves, once again, on their own, although a few had managed, by various means, to reach Israel. By the end of 1981 it was estimated by the American Association for Ethiopian Jews, which had been instrumental in helping a number of them, that not more than 1,500 had arrived. A year later that figure had grown to 2,500 with another 3,000 who had arrived in refugee camps in the Sudan. Impatient at the slow rate of immigration and desperate to be reunited with their families, many of those Ethiopian Jews who had reached Israel staged rowdy demonstrations outside the Knesset (Parliament) and the Prime Minister's home in Jerusalem in an attempt to induce the government to take steps to increase the flow of immigration.

The Government, under the leadership of Menachem Begin, was not unsympathetic to the Falasha cause – indeed, it was a great deal more favourable than the previous Labour-led coalition – but it was in a difficult position. It was, on the whole, anxious to assist *aliyah*, immigration, but it had to move extremely warily in order not to alarm either the Ethiopian or Sudanese governments. Israel had no official relations with either of these countries, both of which looked with disfavour on the Jewish State and could easily, if they wished, jeopardise the position of the Jews within their borders. While some of the pro-Falasha organisations found it difficult to accept the argument for quiet diplomacy and expressed their own views loudly, the Israeli authorities were perhaps unduly cautious in explaining their intentions, even though they could not, for obvious reasons, disclose their precise plans. This led to a somewhat critical attitude towards the friendly and constructive intervention of Mr. Malcolm Rifkind, the Minister of State at the British Foreign Office, when he returned from an official visit to Addis Ababa in July 1984. The Minister reported that he had been told by members of the government that 'the Falashas are treated in the same way as other Ethiopians who want to migrate. In principle this means that they are free to leave, subject to the usual formalities'. It was unclear as to what precise formalities were required, but the significance of this statement was interpreted to mean that while the Ethiopian authorities admitted that 'there had been problems in the past' they did not intend to place 'impediments in the way of members of the community emigrating to Israel'.[1] The publication of this report naturally created widespread interest and brought renewed pressure on the Israeli authorities to increase the momentum of their immigration programme. It was, moreover, the first time that the British Government had officially intervened in this question.

Meanwhile the situation in Africa continued to deteriorate. Drought and famine were spreading in Ethiopia, the wars in Eritrea and Tigrai were bringing increasing misery in their train, and the refugee camps across the border in Sudan administered by the United Nations High Commission for Refugees (UNHCR) were obliged to give food and shelter to ever-growing numbers of fugitives. Famine was spreading throughout the sub-Saharan Sahel region and the situation in Sudan was becoming as desperate as in Ethiopia.

The authorities in Addis Ababa could no longer control their frontiers, and many of the Jews from Gondar followed the example of those from Tigrai who had fled earlier and had undertaken the arduous and hazardous journey on foot to gain relative safety and endure the rigours of a refugee camp while awaiting rescue by one of the clandestine agencies. The conditions were severe: shortage of food and water, excessive heat in the plains, the danger of attacks by *shiftas* or bandits, en route, illness, often fatal, caused or accentuated by malnutrition and, finally, in the camps, discrimination at the hands of non-Jewish refugees. The old, infirm and mothers with very young children were left behind to fend for themselves and await reunification with their families as and when it could be arranged.

[1]Letters dated 2 August 1984 and 15 October 1984 to Falasha Welfare Association.

When the news of Operation Moses, the code name for the secret Israeli-organised air and sea rescue, broke in the first week of January 1985 it was estimated that the Ethiopian Jewish population in Israel had reached 15,000, or just over half the total community. Another 5,000 were probably still in the camps, leaving some 8,000 in Ethiopia.

Operation Moses was a triumph for the State of Israel and for the Jewish spirit but it was tragic that the news was divulged before the operation was completed, for it gave the governments of both Sudan and Ethiopia – who knew but would not admit that the exodus was taking place – the excuse to declare that it had to cease forthwith. Fortunately, the Sudanese soon recognised (possibly with Western encouragement) that it was better to let a few thousand miserable refugees escape than to keep them indefinitely in camps at public expense. On 21 January 1985 President Nimeiry announced that the Jews were free to leave Sudan provided that they did not go directly to Israel. The Ethiopian authorities huffed and puffed but there was little they could do to halt the traffic across their frontier.

The intense interest created by news of Operation Moses took observers by surprise. Suddenly, this little-known, almost forgotten tribe of black Jews became famous. Newspapers, television services and radio networks throughout the world vied with one another for information to satisfy public curiosity. Jewish organisations in Israel and abroad hastily arranged fund-raising campaigns to aid their Ethiopian co-religionists and to help pay for the enormous cost of the transport and resettlement.

Basking in the somewhat unwonted approbation, at least of the Western world, for their bold and original humanitarian endeavour, the Israelis rose to the occasion in welcoming the new arrivals. In the Knesset on 8 January 1985 Shimon Peres, the Prime Minister, made a stirring speech in which he proclaimed that 'immigration is continuing and it will continue. . . . Neither economic difficulty, nor internal distress, nor geographical distance, nor political obstacles', he declared, 'shall halt or postpone the rescue and immigration effort, enwrapped in ancient splendour and enveloped in secret heroism. . . . The Government of Israel has acted and will continue to act within the range of its ability and even beyond it, in order to complete the mission which is so humane and so Jewish – until the last Ethiopian Jew reaches his homeland.

'With all modesty and humility, it may be said that this is one of the most daring and wonderful acts of self-redemption that our country, and not only our country, has ever known. . . . Now, more than ever, we are called upon to devote ourselves to a dignified and serious absorption process and to demonstrate an ancient truth in our lives. For even with the difference in origin and location, even with the difference in shade and emphasis, we are one people, tied to an ancient and splendid faith, and no physical force and no external difference can divide us. For we are one people, there are no black Jews and white Jews: there are Jews. History and faith bind us together forever'.

Then, as leader of the government of national unity, he paid a generous tribute to his predecessor. 'This is also the right time', he said, 'to discharge a debt of honour to Menachem Begin, whose government invested efforts and resourcefulness to make possible the first hidden trickles which have blazed a trail. This is also the time to state, on behalf of the Government I have the honour of heading, that the tremendous effort already begun will not be stopped'.

At long last, it seemed, the struggle for recognition had been truly and finally won. The whole country and the Diaspora, embracing all shades of opinion, rallied behind the Prime Minister of Israel in his determination to ensure the success of Operation Moses – the twentieth-century Exodus from the land of bondage. The first phase was moving forward but the next step was the integration and absorption of the newcomers into the life of Israel. Few who have had experience of Ethiopian Jews doubt that with sympathy and goodwill they will relatively soon settle into their new homeland, despite the enormous difference between the culture they have left behind and the culture they have entered and to which they have their own valuable contribution to offer.

But even in the moment of euphoria a small, dark cloud was discernable on the horizon. Serious differences of opinion were expressed by various branches of the rabbinate in Israel as to the precise religious status of the immigrants. Were they to be regarded as full Jews or must they first undergo a symbolic religious conversion to establish their authenticity? The rabbis wavered. At first they insisted on the ritual *Hattafat Dam Brit* (token circumcision for males) and *Mikveh* (immersion). The immigrants, however, were loud in their protests, declaring that the rabbis' demands were an insult and degrading. 'Our worst enemies', they said, 'never imagined such a painful way to hurt us as the wound inflicted by our own brethren'.[2] By the end of February 1985, however, the rabbis, led by Ovadia Yossef and Shlomo Goren, the two former Sephardi and Ashkenazi chief rabbis of Israel, had relented, and the previous decision was reversed.

A word of explanation is required for the use of the word *Falasha* throughout this volume. Since this book was first published it has become usual to avoid the name *Falasha* for Ethiopian Jews on the grounds that it is a pejorative term which the people themselves dislike. This is justified up to a point.

[2] *J. C.* 15 February 1985.

The word *Falasha* is derived from an ancient Ethiopic, or Ge'ez term meaning an exile or a stranger.[3] It is difficult to know when it was first introduced, though it has certainly been in use for many centuries. The Falashas themselves used to employ the word *Kayla* when they still spoke the Agau language,[4] while more recently many have preferred the term *Beta Israel* (House of Israel). I am not convinced that the word *Falasha* is necessarily derogatory, believing that it becomes offensive only when it is used as an insult in much the same way as the word *Jew* can have an unpleasant connotation if the speaker intends it in that sense. The original meaning of Falasha, implying the idea of exile, cannot be considered derogatory inasmuch as Ethiopian Jews themselves, like observant Jews in other parts of the Diaspora, acknowledged that they were living in *Galut* or Exile from the Promised Land and were waiting for the coming of the Messiah to redeem them. For those who have reached the shores of Israel the name is clearly not appropriate.

The uncertainty surrounding the implications of the word *Falasha* is indicative of the need for much more research into the Ethiopian Jewish way of life and culture for which I pleaded in the first edition of this work. There can be little doubt that academic circles in Israel will seize the unique opportunity presented by the current wave of immigration to further the cause of Ethiopian Jewish studies.

In conclusion, I venture to express the hope that this edition will offer a wider public the opportunity to become acquainted with the extraordinary story of a heroic, long-suffering and loyal branch of the Jewish people whose exile is in the process of ending with its redemption in circumstances which could not have been foreseen when this book first appeared three years ago.

March 1985

Preface to Third, Revised, Edition

Some readers may find it easier to follow the story and argument of this book if they return to this preface after reading the main text.

The earlier editions of this book bore the subtitle 'The Forgotten Jews of Ethiopia'. It is a mark of the success which has crowned the Falashas' struggle for recognition that a change is now necessary, for the former subtitle is now obsolete and is replaced by 'A Short History of the Ethiopian Jews'.

The significance of this change is basic to an understanding of the Falashas' position in society. Their situation has been totally transformed. From a sorely disadvantaged minority in their own country, isolated from and sometimes even spurned by their white co-religionists, they have seen the realisation of their age-old hopes and aspirations. Virtually the entire community has been transferred to Israel where the Falashas take their place as equal members of a free society, occupying a unique position as the only homogeneous group of black immigrants from Africa and bringing with them a religious tradition of extraordinary value.

The first edition of this book appeared in 1982 and the second edition was published in the United States three years later just after Operation Moses, the code name for the first mass airlift of Ethiopian Jews to Israel, which was followed in 1991 by Operation Solomon. The first airlift had brought the number of Ethiopian Jews in Israel to approximately 15,000. The second had added about 14,500 while the total population of Ethiopian Jews now in Israel is between 50,000 and 55,000, leaving only a numerically insignificant remnant in Ethiopia. The discrepancy between this total and the previous estimate of about 30,000 for the Falasha population is due to several factors. The previous figure, mentioned in the preface to the second edition, was never more than a guess based on data which had been difficult to collect and it failed to include people living in distant regions whose existence, in many cases, was unknown to the Falasha Welfare Association which had been responsible for the first census. The news of an organised emigration to Israel inevitably brought out many people anxious to take advantage of the new situation, while natural increase has also added to the population, which includes 8,200 children born in Israel between 1977 and 1992.[1] It should be mentioned, apropos the figures included on p. 9, that the total population of Ethiopia, including Eritrea, which gained its independence in 1993, was estimated by the United Nations in 1991 at 50 million of whom approximately 45 per cent were Muslim and 40 per cent Christian.

Much has happened since 1991 but this edition, like its predecessors, traces the remarkable story of the Ethiopian Jews from the earliest times until their redemption by the State of Israel. I leave it to others, better qualified than I am, to describe in detail the situation in which these people now find themselves and, in particular, to deal with the sociological and psychological problems which they face in their totally new surroundings. Once more I concentrate on the challenge thrown down by Professor Wolf Leslau, some 45 years ago, to unravel the mystery of the origin of the Jews of Ethiopia for what he said then remains valid: 'the problem still awaits final solution'.

We shall not understand the Ethiopian Jews and they themselves will have difficulty in defining their self-identity if the problem is not tackled in a scientific spirit and free from the contentions which have marred much of the discussion in academic circles. We must also recognise that there has been a tendency to underrate the significance of the impact of ancient Egypt and of Nubia or Meroë, which lay within Egypt's cultural and religious sphere, on the development of the Horn of Africa. The importance of the Nile Valley and the Red Sea as channels of communication and, in general, the nature of the spread of ideas from one centre of civilisation to another, deserve greater attention. Stuart Monro-Hay suggested that 'virtually nothing is known of what sort of contacts Axum had with ... the kingdom of Meroë or Kasu and its large but probably loosely controlled area of more or less effective influence'.[2] Nevertheless, he has shown that the use of the Greek language for royal inscriptions and on coins before and after the adoption of Christianity by the Axumite kingdom in the fourth century indicates that Ptolemaic influences, spreading from Egypt via Meroë, must have been of great importance in ancient Ethiopia.

The first edition of this book was generally well received for breaking new ground and it has been followed by a considerable number of books and articles about Ethiopian Jews. In discussing a subject which is so meagre in solid historical evidence there is

[1] See S. Kaplan in *ISSR Journal*, vol. 10, no. 2 (1995), p. 22.
[2] Stuart Munro-Hay, *Aksum* (1991), p. 54.

ample scope for various interpretations not to say speculations with some of which I find myself in strong disagreement. For example, Professor Simon Hopkins, then at the University of Cape Town and now at the Hebrew University in Jerusalem, questioned my subtitle on the grounds that I had not proved the Falashas were Jews notwithstanding that the Government of Israel was at that moment admitting them in considerable numbers under the Law of Return.[1] Another academic at the Hebrew university, who seems to have had difficulty in distinguishing between the classical and modern Ethiopias, accused me and others of overlooking the great distance which separates Upper Egypt from Abyssinia which would preclude Judaism from reaching Axum from Elephantine.[2] Other scholars have joined in the argument. A writer from the School of Oriental and African Studies has deplored the 'personal convictions and prejudices [of writers] as to the alleged [sic!] Judaic origins of the people' and asserted 'that, although the widely canvassed Egyptian origin (Elephantine) undoubtedly commands the least scholarly support in terms of the scant evidence available to us now, even the alleged South Arabian provenance for the supposed Jewish groups in the Axumite Empire in ancient times is largely founded on an *argumentum e silentio*[3] but he did not suggest a solution to the problem. Nevertheless, Quirin quotes from a genealogy of the Emperor Takla Haymanot who claimed that his ancestors 'came forth from Egypt with Israel into the land of Ethiopia',[4] showing that this tradition was deep-seated even if historically unproven.

Professor Christopher Clapham, of the University of Lancaster, wrote that 'it is extremely doubtful whether the Beta Israel can be regarded either as descendants of any part of the Jewish diaspora, or even as authentically Jewish converts' and added that 'it is hard to avoid the conclusion that the Beta Israel *aliyah* of 1985–91 was derived from assumptions that historical research has now shown to be mistaken'.[5] It seems more probable that the historical research mentioned, far from being conclusive, was seriously flawed.

Indeed, the historical research has led Kaplan, who seems to think that the Ethiopian Jews were 'invented' by Christian monks, to the conclusion 'that the Beta Israel must be understood as the product of processes that took place in Ethiopia between the 14th

---

[1] *J.J.S.* XXXIV no. 2 (Autumn 1983), p. 228.
[2] S. Kaplan, *Les Falashas*, p. 17.
[3] A. K. Irvine, *Bulletin of the School of Oriental and African Studies*, vol. vii, pt. 2 (1994), p 385.
[4] J. Quirin, *The Evolution of the Ethiopian Jews*, p. 222 n. 79.
[5] *Times Literary Supplement*, 10 September, 1993.

and 16th century.'[1] This theory, according to Quirin's explanation, 'emphasises ... the significance of the Christian influences on the development [of the Falashas' religion and culture] and even postulates a Christian origin of the Beta Israel'.[2]

Pursuing a similar line of thought, Professor Kay Kaufman Shelemay, who has undertaken very valuable research on Falasha music in Ethiopia, explained that 'it was in the new studies of Ethiopian history and literature that I found the final key to understanding how the Beta Israel might have come to perpetuate a Judaic tradition that apparently was brought to them by Ethiopian Christian monks. This seeming paradox was actually quite consistent with the religious history of the country. While the source of the early Jewish influence on Ethiopian Christianity remains an enigma, I now had compelling evidence dating the Beta Israel liturgical tradition to the fifteenth century.'[3]

The theory of a Christian origin is based on the story of Abba Saga, the son of King Zar'a Ya'qob (1434–68), who rebelled against his father, adopted the Jewish religion and, in collaboration with a monk called Abba Sabra, variously described as a Falasha or a Christian, allegedly set about introducing radical reforms to Jewish practices including the liturgy, sacred music and literature and establishing monasticism. An elaborate theory has been developed around this story which credits the schismatic Christian sect, which the two men apparently initiated, with being the origin of the Falasha community. It cannot be altogether a coincidence that this movement arose at approximately the same time as European Jesuit missionaries were beginning to exert pressure on the Ethiopian Orthodox church with the aim of bringing it within the orbit of Rome, thereby provoking a strong anti-clerical reaction.

A twofold difficulty is presented by this theory, which, because the movement was founded by Christians who rebelled against their Church, Quirin has designated the 'Rebel Perspective'.[4] Firstly, it fails to indicate how the Jewish influences reached Abyssinia in the first place and, secondly, it does not explain how the Christian monks could have acquired such a detailed knowledge of Judaism, including pre-rabbinic doctrines largely based on the Books of Jubilees and Enoch, unless there was an existing Jewish presence in the country from whom they could learn as they were completely isolated from other Jewish communities.

[1]S. Kaplan, *The Beta Israel (Falasha) in Ethiopia*, p. 73.
[2]J. Quirin, op. cit., p. 10.
[3]K. K. Shelemay, *A Song of Longing*, pp. 143, 145.
[4]J. Quirin, op. cit., p. 10 and p. 66 *et seq.*

Indeed, Quirin admits that 'here is persuasive evidence that the "Hebraic-Judaic" element in Ethiopian Christianity must have been due to a pre-Christian Jewish presence in Aksum ... whether brought by a so-called Lost Tribe or more likely a group of Agaw converts to Judaism ...' He suggests that 'at various historical periods of intensive Christian proselytisation some of these Jews ... refused to go along with the new conversion effort and reinforced instead the *ayhud* or Gedewonite content of their society. As can be seen in the better documented period beginning in the fourteenth century, this group was also reinforced by dissident or rebelling Christians who joined them, bringing important new religious and literary elements. This dialectical process, whose origins date to ancient Axum, continued in the new "Solomonic" dynasty after 1270, as the *ayhud-falasha-beta esra'el* identity continued to evolve.'[1]

While stressing the significance of the 'rebel perspective', Quirin tends to confuse the basic tenets of the Beta Israeli Falashas with the rites and forms of their practices. He does not appreciate that the religion 'as it has come down to us'[2] in essence means a belief in the oneness of the Almighty, based on the teachings of the Torah (*Orit*), and a faith in the coming of the Messiah. These religious desiderata do not date 'mainly to this critical period ... in the mid-fifteenth century' for they were always present. They, more than ritual differences – important though they are – distinguish Judaism from Christianity and could not conceivably have been invented by the rebel monks.

Evidence of an ancient Jewish presence can also be seen in the existence of a small number of Aramaic loan words in the Ge'ez version of the Septuagint, which is accepted by both Falashas and Orthodox Christians, and presupposes that a Jewish hand probably played a part in the translation process well before the sixth century when Christian tradition claims that the translation was undertaken by nine Syrian saints.

It may be, as Quirin has suggested, that the Beta Israel liturgy, literature and calendar 'were received through the filter of Ethiopian Christianity' but that filter could not have existed had it not been founded on a Jewish base. From the end of the Axumite kingdom, in about the seventh century, until the arrival of the Zagwe dynasty in the twelfth, Ethiopia passed through a Dark Age which, inevitably, affected the Jewish population. A serious weakening of Beta Israel religious and intellectual conviction may have

[1] Quirin, op. cit., pp. 18, 26, 27.
[2] ibid., p. 68.

followed leaving the community exposed to the attentions of Christian monks anxious to bolster the pristine religion of their country which has always been held in high esteem. The recognition of the Christian influences does not infer that there was a break in the continuity of the Jewish presence nor that the latter emerged as a consequence of inverted proselytising activities.

If the form of certain Jewish practices owes something to Christian influences how much greater is the debt of the daughter religion to its parent? Writing of the observance by Christian Ethiopians of the Saturday Sabbath, Quirin quotes Gatatchew Haile, a leading Christian Ethiopian scholar, who has written:

> Only the Christianity of a nation or community which first practised Judaism would incorporate Jewish religious practices and make the effort to convince its faithful to observe Sunday like Saturday. In short, the Jewish influence in Ethiopian Christianity seems to originate from those who received Christianity and not from those who introduced it. The Hebraic-Jewish elements were part of the indigenous Aksumite culture adopted into Ethiopian Christianity.[1]

I have found myself under a strong obligation to enter this argument because I deemed it necessary to try to mitigate the damage which could be done to the Falashas' reputation and the cause of historical truth as well as to their own pride in their origins from what would appear to be a serious error of scholarly judgement. Indeed, it is difficult not to sympathise with the comment of Fiona MacCarthy, a well-known biographer, that 'history is too important to be left to academics.'[2] An obligation surely rests on those who have regard for Ethiopian Jewish studies to proclaim the historical truth as we see it.

It is probable, and not surprising, considering the close proximity of the two communities, that some of the Falashas' customs, music and 'literature have been influenced by their neighbours, especially in the development of the monastic life on which the advocates of this model place great importance. Nevertheless, the latter appear to ignore that the origin of Christian monasticism in the East is itself derived from the Jewish sect of the Theraputae (physicians) about whom Philo wrote in the first century BC when the sect was already old. This religious movement seems to have been the precursor of the Essenes – whose name also means

[1] ibid., p. 18.
[2] *The Observer Review*, 12 February 1995, p. 17.

healers – and of the Qumran community and 'affords evidence of the existence of the monastic system long before the Christian era.'[1] It is possible that the system could have lapsed among the Falashas in the Dark Ages and that they reintroduced it under the influence of the Christians in the fifteenth century. Some scholars have assumed that those Falasha practices which are similar to those of the Orthodox Church must have been acquired from the Christians whereas it is more probable, on the contrary, that they were original Jewish practices adopted by the Church. Such observances as the dietary laws, circumcision, Saturday as a day of rest, liturgical music and church design were manifestly taken from Jewish practices while others, such as the laws concerning ritual purity, animal sacrifice, avoidance of travel on the Sabbath and many others largely inspired by the Books of Jubilees and Enoch, which moreover are included in the Christian Ethiopian canon, were omitted from the Orthodox rite. As regards church practices, Antoine d'Abbadie was quite clear that the sistrum and all the customs of the Christian Church, with the exception of the cross, were borrowed from the Falashas, while Munro-Hay observes that 'Ethiopian church ritual today contains many extra-ordinary features, which may well date even to pre-Aksumite times. There is also a strong Jewish element, owing to Jewish influences received, it seems, before the introduction of Christianity.'[2]

The Beta Israel religious ceremony of *Seged* is unique to them and is the community's only approximation to a pilgrimage. Since the transfer of the population to Israel it has developed almost into an Ethiopian Jewish national festival.[3] Shelemay has drawn attention to its similarities with the Christian Orthodox ceremony of *Mehlella*[4] which is precisely the same name by which *Seged* was, until recently, known. The Beta Israel celebration which is held on 29 Cheswan (about November) is based on the passage in the Book of Ezra[5] in which the prophet inveighs against mixed marriages and urges the people to make confession. The word *mehlella* means supplication or entreaty and the Christian form, says Shelemay, is 'almost certainly related to the rogation ceremony', whose name is derived from the Latin *rogare*, to beseech, and is, therefore, equivalent to the Ge'ez *mehlella*. What-ever may be its origins – and we cannot at present say when or

[1] *Enc. Brit.*, eleventh ed., vol. 26, p. 793 and see W. H. C. Frend, *The Early Church*, p. 188.
[2] Munro-Hay, op. cit., p. 208.
[3] J. Abbink 'Seged Celebration in Ethiopia and Israel', *Anthropos*, vol. 78 (1983).
[4] Shelemay, *Music, Ritual and Falasha History*, p. 48.
[5] Ezra 10: 10–12.

where it originated – *Seged* bears the hallmark of a Hebraic
ceremony. Shoshana Ben-Dor sees in it a similarity with a ceremony
described in the Community Rule of the Qumran sect[1] which also
emphasises the importance of confession.[2] The principal feature of
the festival is a procession (sometimes referred to as a pilgrimage) up
a hill or mountain led by Beta Israel priests. 'All the people, men,
women and children', wrote Leslau after a visit to Ethiopia in 1947,[3]
'carry stones on their shoulders to a hill outside the village.[4] There
they put the stones in a circle around the priests who recite prayers
in which all the people participate. This custom of carrying stones
is probably to be interpreted, as it is among the Ethiopians, as an
act of submission. Various prayers are recited throughout the day
and lessons from the Commandments of the Sabbath, the Book of
Ezra, and some prophets are read. Three times on that day, at
nine, twelve and three o'clock, they perform the *emen* (a word of
Cushitic origin meaning reminder). The *emen* consists in putting a
handful of millet on stones and leaving it there for the birds in order
to commemorate the dead.' After descending from the hill, 'as at
all the important festivals and fasts, bread and beer are brought to
the synagogue to be blessed by the priests.' Shelemay adds that 'as
the priests approach the prayerhouse, one brings the *nagarit* (drum)
and they sing and dance with the *Orit* (Torah) uplifted.'[5]

Though the Jewish and Christian festivals share a common
name (much like Passover (Pesach) and Easter (Paques) or Pentecost) they celebrate different episodes. The Jewish *Seged* festival
recalls the actions of Ezra and Nehemiah in rejuvenating Judaism
after the trauma of the Babylonian exile, which were seen as 'a
great national confession of guilt and a solemn undertaking to
observe the new covenant.'[6] The Christian ceremony, however,
is related to the Rogation Days and is associated with Ascension
Day, forty days after Easter. The Rogation festival, instituted in
511, was marked by the chanting of litanies in procession (*rogationes*
entreaties) and to that extent it resembled the *Seged* ceremonial
from which it could have borrowed both its Ethiopic name and
ritual. According to Bernard Velat the Christian *Mehlella* prayers
include some which are similar to Rogations prescribed by the

[1] 'The Religious Background of Beta Israel' in *Saga of Aliyah* (Jerusalem 1993).
[2] G. Vermes, *The Dead Sea Scrolls in English*, fourth ed., p. 71.
[3] Leslau, *Falasha Anthology*, pp. XXXIV/V.
[4] This might be inspired by the Book of Nehemiah which describes how 'the
Israelites assembled for a fast clothed in sackcloth and with earth on their heads
... and confessed their sins and the iniquities of their forefathers'. Ch. 9, 1–2
(NEB).
[5] Shelemay, op. cit., p. 50.
[6] *Enc. Brit.*, eleventh ed., vol. 10, p. 108.

liturgy. The supplication and penitential prayers are marked by processions around the church with each participant carrying a stone around his neck and the congregation chanting 'Lord have mercy on us.'[1] A parallel could also be drawn with the annual penitential pilgrimage to Croagh Patrick in western Ireland which was marked by the carrying of stones to the summit to be used for building the chapel dedicated to St Patrick who is credited with having banished from there all noxious reptiles in the island. The ceremony is believed to be of pagan origin and was adapted by the Christian Church for its own purposes.

If this analysis is correct – and clearly there is ample room for further research as to the origin of the Beta Israel festival – similar examples could follow in respect of other ceremonies and we may be drawing closer to reaching a consensus on who borrowed what from whom. In other words, it may be that the Christians were more indebted to the Jews than *vice versa* and the claim of the Beta Israel to a religious continuum from ancient times until the present would be vindicated.

It is stretching credulity almost to the limit to believe that practices (with the possible exception of monasticism) which were recognised at the time of the Second Temple and some of which became obsolete in normative Judaism could have been resurrected by former Christian monks and passed on by them to a sect whom they are alleged to have converted to Judaism. The only plausible explanation for the Falashas' steadfast adherence to these practices is that the community, which followed the precepts of the Torah (*Orit*) before the coming of Christianity, continued to observe them in their original form in an unbroken sequence from their first arrival in the highlands of Ethiopia. The idea of continuity (to employ the fashionable term) is further reinforced by popular local legend among both Jews and Christians, including the tradition that some members of the Zagwe dynasty who ruled from the tenth to the thirteenth century, as well as the renowned Queen Judith, were Jews. In addition, we should not disregard the travellers' reports, not only of Eldad ha-Dani in the ninth century, but also of Benjamin of Tudela in the twelfth, Marco Polo in the thirteenth and Elia of Ferrara in the first half of the fifteenth, all of whom reported tales of a Jewish presence in Abyssinia well before the didactic activities of Abba Sabra.

More than one critic has expressed surprise that people so few in numbers should have attracted so much attention and been

[1]'Me'eraf Commun de l'Office Divin Ethiopien pour Toute l'Annee' (Louvain 1961).

the object of so much controversy. But the Falashas' tenacity in maintaining their religious faith in the face of great opposition and hardships for some 2,000 years has provided an example of Jewish survival which stands comparison with that of any other Jewish community in the world, while their numbers were not always so small nor their influence so slight as the following pages will demonstrate.

The Falashas' unique achievement in preserving a form of early Judaism (not a 'fossilised relic' as it was once described) presents the world of scholarship with an opportunity – which so far it does not appear to have fully seized – to study in depth certain practices which could shed a useful light on the development of the Jewish religion. It also enables a useful comparison to be drawn with the two other non-rabbanite branches of Jewry, the Samaritans and the Karaites which, for different reasons, do not accept the *Halachah* which many people regard as the touchstone of Jewish identity. Owing to the paucity of epigraphic evidence scholars have been reluctant to undertake research into the pre-mediaeval period whereas in the later period they can make use of royal chronicles and other Christian sources which, however, can hardly be considered impartial when recording the behaviour of the sometimes rebellious and 'heretical' Beta Israel. Dependence on legend, tradition and the books of the Bible has also inhibited research into ancient history as some historians are not prepared to face the criticism of those who dismiss Biblical evidence, contained in such books as Isaiah and Zephaniah, or the Acts of the Apostles, as 'folklore or moral tales'. If historians recognise only the contemporary written record as evidence – though inscriptions and chronicles, too, can falsify history – we shall make slow progress in research. Tradition, legend and oral history have a role which must not be ignored. This is clearly relevant to Ethiopia/ Abyssinia where the paramount importance of the Solomon-Sheba legend assumed such a significant place in the life of the country, at least until the overthrow of the monarchy in 1974.

While it is difficult to accept all of Graham Hancock's imaginative reconstruction in tracing the adventures of the Ark of the Covenant from Solomon's Jerusalem to Sheba's and Haile Selassie's Axum, his book[1] raises the issue of why the legend achieved such importance in the Christian Ethiopian empire. As the Biblical story leaves the exact location of the Land of Sheba in doubt, the answer must surely be found in the pre-Christian tradition that the Queen's country should be identified with Ethiopia meaning

[1]Hancock, *The Sign and the Seal* (1992).

either Cush, according to Josephus, or the Axumite kingdom as claimed by the *Kebra Nagast* but not Arabia as Islamic tradition maintains. It is likely that the story found its way to Axum at the same time as the Septuagint was introduced and, amply embroidered by the Christian scribes, became the foundation of Ethiopia's great national epic. The idea was nurtured that Ethiopia had taken the place of Israel as the new Zion and its cathedral of St Mary of Zion at Axum eventually became the alleged final resting-place of the Ark of the Covenant which Menelik I was said to have surreptitiously removed from the Temple at Jerusalem. The Ethiopians assumed the role of the new Israelites, their religion was seen as the logical extension of Judaism and their monarchs claimed to be the lineal descendants of Solomon and Sheba and took the title of 'Conquering Lion of the Tribe of Judah'. The tradition that half the country was Jewish when it adopted Christianity became firmly established. Professor D. Crummey, of the University of Illinois, has confirmed that 'influences derived from the Hebrew scriptures had a profound effect on the moulding of a variety of religious cultures in Ethiopia, principally that of the Ethiopian Orthodox Church, and secondarily of the Falashas and of the Qemant.' He does not explain how these Hebrew influences arrived, but insists that the idea of an 'early Jewish presence in Ethiopia prior to that country's adoption of Christianity' is devoid of 'historical, literary, epigraphic or archaeological evidence.'[1] While this sweeping generalisation ignores the weight of tradition, the most likely explanation would seem to be that the Hebrew influences had been brought by people who practised the Jewish religion but were not necessarily so-called ethnic Jews such as the Ethiopian eunuch mentioned in the Acts of the Apostles. The notion of a Jewish racial group has long been regarded by anthropologists as a myth, though the idea that Judaism can be spread only by a movement of people and not by dissemination and conversion dies hard. If it is acknowledged, as Salo Baron has written (see p. 47 below), that proselytism in the Roman period 'must have been a tremendous force in Jewish life' Hebrew influences could have spread into Axum in the Ptolemaic period and led to the conversion of a substantial section of the indigenous Agaw population. The absence of written evidence does not prove that it did not happen.

While epigraphic evidence to prove the existence of a Jewish substratum in ancient Axum is certainly lacking, Professor Ullendorff has observed, in this context, that 'the absence of relevant and reliable historical sources is, however, compensated

[1] *Journal of African History*, vol. 35, no. 2 (1994), p. 314.

for, at least in part, by fairly numerous threads of indirect evidence which, in their cumulative effect, present an impressive array.'[1] It has been my aim to gather such indirect evidence as I can and to show that there has existed a continuous thread of Jewish history in the Horn of Africa from the earliest times to the present day. The suggestion that the Falashas are descended from Christian converts to Judaism runs counter to all Jewish historical experience. It presupposes an influential movement – as distinct from individual cases – forsaking Christianity in favour of Judaism which, if it were authenticated, would be a unique and most surprising phenomenon. There would seem to be no known record of any significant group conversion of this kind with the solitary exception, recalled by Friedmann,[2] of the pathetic little community of San Nicandro, in Southern Italy, which, after the Second World War, invited an Italian rabbi to convert them. Numbering some fifty persons, they departed for Israel in 1949 where they attempted, unsuccessfully, to establish an agricultural settlement. The conversion of the Khazars in the eighth century, like other early examples, was not, of course, comparable as it was not a conversion from the Christian religion. Some of the opinions cited in these pages suggest a tendency to denigrate or underestimate the antiquity and significance of the Falasha people which could owe more to the field of psychological than historical studies.

In order to keep this preface within reasonable limits I have relegated some additional thoughts on Falasha origins to an Afterword beginning on p. 172. Apart from the revision of demographic statistics made necessary by the transfer of the population to Israel, a significant change in this edition has been the emphasis which I have now given in the Afterword to the Eldad ha-Dani story. I have revised my assessment of its importance and now attempt to make good the deficiency notwithstanding its dismissal by one scholar as 'mythic or legendary tale' for which 'there appears little if any basis ... as the solution to the riddle of the origins of the Beta Israel.'[3]

With their mass immigration accomplished, the Ethiopian Jews' long cherished hopes for recognition have been fulfilled. As I approach the end of my ninth decade I shall lay down my pen, after nearly thirty years' endeavour, content in the knowledge that the Beta Israel have eventually attained their goal, eager, if ill-prepared, to meet the challenges of their new life in the Promised Land.

[1] Ullendorf, *Ethiopia and the Bible*, p. 24.
[2] D. Friedmann, *Les Enfants de la Reine de Saba*, p. 341 and *Enc. Jud.*, vol. 14, col. 844.
[3] S. Kaplan, *The Beta Israel*, p. 26.

★ ★ ★ ★ ★

The second edition of this book touched on Operation Moses which lasted from the middle of November 1984 until 5 January 1985, and rescued about 7,000 Falashas from the refugee camps in Sudan before a breach of the security arrangements brought it to a sudden halt. Three months later, thanks to the intervention of George Bush, then Vice-President of the United States, another 500 immigrants, who had been left behind, were transported by US airforce planes to Israel under the code-name Operation Sheba. Both Ethiopia and Sudan were determined to prevent a repetition of these events and placed a total ban on the emigration of the remaining Jewish population. Some 15,000 people found themselves trapped inside Ethiopia. Anticipating, mistakenly, that they would soon be able to travel to Israel and rejoin their families and friends, several thousand abandoned their villages and made their way to Addis Ababa where they endured many months of waiting in conditions of great hardship and poverty until the Israeli embassy was reopened and some assistance could be provided for them.

By the end of 1989 the tyrannical Marxist dictatorship of Mengistu Haile Mariam was under severe pressure and was rapidly losing control of those areas in the north which were occupied by the rebel armies advancing from Eritrea, Tigrai and Begemder. The government no longer enjoyed the massive assistance of the Soviet Union whose support had been withdrawn early in the 1990s and it was urgently in need of both financial and military aid. Perhaps it was in desperation that it turned to Israel, which had been such a staunch friend in the days of Haile Selassie.

Negotiations between the two countries started early in 1990. Israel saw this as an opportunity to reopen the question of the emigration of the Ethiopian Jews while at the same time recognising that there was a strategic interest due to Ethiopia's geographical position adjoining the western coast of the Red Sea. The talks succeeded in restoring diplomatic relations and in reopening the Israel embassy after a lapse of sixteen years. In return for a supply of arms and money the Ethiopian government allowed a few hundred Jews to leave every month on condition that Israel provided the necessary travel documents and that transport would be supplied by Ethiopian Airways whose flights would be routed via Rome where the passengers would be transferred to Israeli planes.

By February 1991 rebel forces had reached Gondar and the Israelis recognised that the fall of Addis Ababa could not be long delayed. Understandably, they feared that a rebel occupation of the capital might spell disaster for the approximately 20,000 Jews who by then were concentrated in the city. Observing the example of the chaotic situation which had developed in neighbouring Somaliland and appreciating that Israel might be accused of supporting the hated Mengistu regime, with dire consequences for their protégés when the rebels arrived, swift action was imperative. A military mission was despatched in March led by Brigadier General (now Major General) Meir Dagan with Lt Col Amir Maimon (later Second Secretary at the Embassy in London) as second-in-command and including Uri Lubrani, a senior diplomat, as chief negotiator. Their brief was to plan and organise the evacuation of as many Falashas as could be identified. Negotiations lasted about two months. Meanwhile, rebel forces continued their advance and, on 23 May, when they were already closing in on the capital, it was decided to activate Operation Solomon. At this point the intervention of the USA chargé d'affaires proved vital as Itzhak Shamir, then Israeli Prime Minister, declared. The Americans persuaded the commander of the rebel army to keep his troops outside Addis Ababa for 72 hours while the airlift was in progress. The start of the operation was signalled by the arrival of two unmarked Israeli transport planes at the International Airport at 10.00 a.m. on Friday, 24 May. By 11 o'clock the following day the evacuation was completed and over 14,400 Ethiopian Jews had been transported on 41 military and civilian flights taking an astonished world completely by surprise. The ambassador and five members of his staff alone remained. Three days later Addis Ababa fell. Mengistu fled and a new government was soon in place. The worst fears for the safety of the civilian population, fortunately, were not realised and a comparatively peaceful transfer of power ensued.

Relations with Israel rapidly improved and the new foreign minister, in striking contrast to the official attitude after Operation Moses, expressed the wish that those Ethiopians who had departed would, in time, serve as a bridge between his country and Israel. On the initiative of the new Ambassador, Haim Divon, Israel became the first nation to offer technical, not military, aid and a fresh chapter in the relationship between the two countries was opened.

With the resumption of diplomatic relations, Jewish relief organisations were again permitted to operate and both the Jewish Agency and the American Joint Distribution Committee (AJDC) and the North American Conference on Ethiopian Jewry (NACOEJ) despatched representatives to Ethiopia who stayed after the airlift to attend to those who had, for one reason or another, been left behind. In the following twelve months approximately another 3,000 Beta Israel were assisted to travel to Israel, including some 2,500 from the distant Agau-speaking Kwara region who had been isolated from the main body of the community.

The Israeli immigration and absorption authorities, for their part, were faced with a daunting task. Unluckily for them, the immigration from Ethiopia coincided with an even greater influx of new settlers from the former Soviet Union, likewise demanding housing and all the other needs of an immigrating population. The African newcomers, like those who had arrived earlier, were obliged to cope with the difficulties of adjustment in a new and very strange society, including the need to learn Hebrew. There were also psychological stresses arising from the trauma caused by the hardships and frustrations encountered on their journey from their homes and depression created by family separations and casualties. Many of the earlier settlers were also subject to anxiety caused by the demands of the orthodox rabbinate which, in many cases, refused to recognise them as Jews unless they underwent a token conversion ceremony – which has since been modified – and which they considered both shameful and insulting. Some also suffered, for the first time, the humiliation of discrimination due to skin colouring to say nothing of the discovery that not everything in the Holy Land, including the Sabbath, was holy. As always, in such situations, the older people have had more difficulty in adjusting than the younger ones but, at the time of their arrival, 80 per cent were under 35 and 60 per cent under 18 years of age.[1]

The Israeli government agencies are, no doubt, open to some criticism for their policy of concentrating the immigrants in absorption centres which, planned as temporary accommodation, in many places turned into permanent homes.[2] It was also a mistake, in the view of some observers, not to have taken greater advantage of the immigrants' skills as artisans and as agricultural people to settle them in rural areas instead of in crowded urban centres where they encountered great difficulty in finding work. Bureaucratic and planning errors, though regrettable, were perhaps to be expected but both government and the general population of Israel on the whole displayed a generosity of spirit in doing their best to welcome the Beta Israel and make them feel at home. If it had been possible to spend more time preparing for

[1]Gadi Ben-Ezer, 'Ethiopian Jews encounter Israel' in *International Yearbook of Oral History and Life Studies*, vol. III (1994), p. 101.
[2]ibid., p. 112.

the operation a smoother transfer could have been achieved but events moved too fast and the Israeli government was under severe pressure to take advantage of a window of opportunity while it existed.

There is no exact parallel with the Ethiopian *aliyah*. Perhaps the nearest example was the arrival of the Yemeni Jews in 1948/9, under Operation Magic Carpet, 'on the wings of eagles', and similar movements from other Arab countries when the impetus came largely from political considerations. I recall watching the dramatic arrival of the Kurdish Jews of Iraq at Lydda airport in 1951 which brought tears to the eyes of Malcolm Muggeridge, a hard-headed, experienced journalist and broadcaster. An analogy might be drawn with the Pilgrim Fathers, voluntary refugees seeking a new home from religious persecution in the New World or the Russian and German Jews seeking freedom from tyranny. The Ethiopian experience contains something of all these examples but what differentiates it is that it represents, above all, the fulfilment of an age-old longing, far stronger than in the other examples, to bring the exile to an end. Although the Beta Israel were not inspired by a charismatic leader, their movement was dominated by religious conviction. Doubtless political, economic and sociological factors also played a part for their conditions were miserable even by Ethiopian standards. Unlike other immigrants to Israel they had been isolated in distant villages where the Zionist philosophy had only touched the fringe of the community and had not penetrated as it did, for example, in the Arab countries. It is this religious urge, directly inspired by the Bible, which many Gentile and some Jewish observers have found difficult to grasp and which has led to considerable misunderstanding.

During Operation Solomon a new, intractable problem came to light which, if the authorities had been better prepared, would not have taken them by surprise. The new immigrants began to enquire after the relatives they had left behind and it gradually transpired that there was a large number, running to at least 30,000, of Christian Ethiopians who claimed to be the relatives of Beta Israel admitted under the Law of Return and who wished to be reunited with them. These people, called 'Falashmura' in Israel (though the origin of the name is obscure) had either been converted relatively recently by European, mainly Protestant, missionaries or had chosen to join the Orthodox Church or were the descendants of such converts and had remained in contact with their Falasha relatives and suffered some degree of discrimination from both Jews and Christians. The Israeli government was faced with a dilemma. On humanitarian grounds it was inclined to accept them in response to the cry for reunification of families. On legal grounds, however, they were excluded as, not being Jews by religion, the authorities considered they were under no obligation to admit them to full citizenship. After much deliberation and in spite of some opposition it was decided that, under the supervision of the spiritual leadership of the Ethiopian priests, the *Qesotch*, they should be accepted provided that they could prove that they were the genuine first degree relatives (parents, children, spouses and siblings) of Jewish immigrants, and a continuing controlled immigration was put into operation. Nearly 1,000 arrived in the twelve months from the summer of 1993, and were granted Israeli citizenship and received the same treatment as other new arrivals.[1] It is considered most likely that in a short time they will return to the faith of their ancestors and will be absorbed fully into Israeli society. Ethiopian Jews already established in Israel have themselves expressed the opinion that 'experience has shown that the Falashmura, having reached the Promised Land, have reverted to Judaism.'[2]

The problems of adjustment will not be easily solved but, with the determination and goodwill which the people and government have displayed, the Ethiopian Jews (their preferred name) will surely become an integral and valuable component of the complex and varied human tapestry which is Israel. Not only the educational, religious and social elements but also the army play a determining role in this developing process, and colour prejudice, though not completely eliminated, has been kept well within bounds and Israel could serve as an example in this respect to other countries.

In the introduction to the first and second editions I acknowledged with gratitude the assistance I received from a number of scholars and friends. In the preparation of this edition I was given most valuable help and advice by Professor Ruth Finnegan of the Open University as well as by Professor Hugh Williamson of Oxford, Dr John Ray and Dr David Phillipson of Cambridge, Dr J. H. Taylor of the British Museum, Mr Amir Maimon, Dr Francis Clark and Peter Salinger. To Professor Alan Crown A.M. of Sydney I am especially indebted for he has been most generous in giving of his time and sharing his knowledge and I am again most grateful to Dr Tessa Rajak for her helpful advice. It goes without saying that the full responsibility for any inadvertent errors of fact or judgment in this work is entirely mine.

October 1995

[1] D. Friedmann, op. cit., p. 115.   [2] Ibid., op. cit., p. 114.

Introduction

I am black, but comely, O ye
daughters of Jerusalem, as
the tents of Kedar, as the
curtains of Solomon.
                    The Song of Songs

MANY inconclusive theories have been advanced to explain the origin of the Falashas, the black Jews of Ethiopia, and my investigation into their history has led into a number of unexpected paths. From time to time tentative and sometimes conflicting suggestions have been propounded by scholars while the Falashas themselves have relied on picturesque legends and tradition. The story of this unique tribe is both heroic and pathetic. It runs like a continuous thread through the whole length of Ethiopian history and at the same time illuminates the practices of pre-Exilic Judaism and the development of Ethiopian Christianity. The question to be answered is not so much how the Falashas reached Ethiopia as how Judaism got there. Framed in this way the problem appears less intractable. People do not ask how Christians reached England but how Christianity came to these shores. The same may be said of other religious ideas which have spread from country to country, such as Hellenism or Buddhism or Islam.

King Solomon and the Queen of Sheba were bound to play an important part in unravelling the story but I had not anticipated that this would lead to the hypothesis that the Bible story represents an historical 'slippage' of some two centuries, nor that the queen, though an historical personage, was not to be identified, as she usually is, with the land of the Sabaeans in south-west Arabia but more probably with ancient Meroë – a civilisation of which only a few people are aware. This led to a glimpse of ancient Egyptian history and, in particular, of the pharaohs of the twenty-fifth, or so-called Ethiopian, dynasty, the 'broken reed' against which the Assyrians warned King Hezekiah. These were Meroïtic kings who came from the country known to the Old Testament writers by the Egyptian name Cush which was called Ethiopia by the Greeks and today forms part of northern Sudan.

Then the trail led to the New Testament story of St Philip and the Ethiopian eunuch who was treasurer to Queen Candace. From the queen's name it was clear that her treasurer was a high official of the court of Meroë. He had come to Jerusalem to worship and, since he practised the Jewish religion, it was unlikely that he practised it in isolation. Did this represent the missing link which connected the present-day Jews of Abyssinia, the Falashas, with the Ethiopia of old?

Jews had been established in Upper Egypt – the biblical Pathros – since before the fall of the First Temple in 586 BC and at Elephantine, the great ivory market on the southern frontier of that country, the Jews had a Temple which for centuries remained independent of the hierarchy in Jerusalem. It was not until the time of the Ptolemies that they abandoned it and apparently moved south up the Nile into the kingdom of Meroë.

As the story developed, it led into the fields of Gentile–Jewish relations, of ethnicity, linguistics, African history, the Inquisition and an armed Jewish struggle for freedom. It has been said that the best way to learn history is to write it. I have found it a rewarding experience, and in this book I have attempted to pass on something of this knowledge of a subject which has been unwarrantably neglected.

The cause of the neglect may perhaps be traceable to the prevalence of the traditional view that all Jews belong to the same race or, in other words, are descendants of the same ethnic stock which originated in ancient Palestine. Jews who were black did not fit into this picture. While they undoubtedly share a common religious and cultural heritage, the notion that Jews from the Mediterranean, from the Slav and Teuton countries, from India, Yemen and Ethiopia all share a common ancestral origin is clearly open to serious doubt. If that were accepted the Jewish communities in various parts of the world must all be the product of migration, as they were, for example, in the United States or South Africa. But this was not always the case. Before the rise of Christianity and Islam, the Jewish religion spread widely as a result of the distribution of ideas in the same way as Christianity or Buddhism.

Peoples migrate under political, economic or military pressure and take ideas with them but, equally, culture is disseminated by small groups such as traders, missionaries, adventurers or conquerors and by intermarriage. Christianity did not envelop the western world at the time of Constantine the Great as a result of a migration any more than Buddhism reached to the farthest corners of southern Asia or the English language and British culture spread to a vast area over which the sun never set.

Similarly, Judaism had reached many countries, especially around the Mediterranean Sea, long before the destruction of Jerusalem by the Romans. The spread of their religion depended partly on the migration of ethnic Jews but also on the distribution of their ideas. The conversion of the Khazars in the eighth century AD is only a later and more impressive example of this process. It is, however, unjustifiable to say, as some do, that if the Jews are not racially homogeneous they can lay no claim to the territorial state of Israel. The concepts of nation and race are not interchangeable. That the Jews as a people, of whatever ethnic origin, have a religious and historic connection with Israel is not open to dispute, and no section of the people has a stronger attachment to the Holy Land than the Jews of Ethiopia. It is estimated that in the days of Philo of Alexandria, in the first century BC, there were one million Jews in each of Syria, Egypt, Babylonia and Asia Minor and that the Diaspora outnumbered the Jews of Palestine by three to one.[1] A total Jewish population which then numbered some eight million could only have been the result of conversion due to the spread of ideas. Judaism was a religion which appealed to those who sought an alternative to the polytheism of Greece and Rome. According to Ethiopian tradition half the population was Jewish before the country was converted to Christianity in the fourth century.

The Jewish religion penetrated to the limits of the Graeco-Roman world and beyond, into countries where the strangers in their midst were readily absorbed into existing small Jewish communities. No penalty attached to those who were converted such as was later imposed on apostates both by Christian and Muslim rulers; and the rabbis did not discourage proselytism as, subsequently, they were obliged to do largely as a measure of self-protection for the community.

Nor was separation from the Holy Land and Jerusalem, following the Roman conquest, an insuperable obstacle to the coherence of the scattered settlements, which displayed an astonishing resilience in the face of disaster. Exile, as Professor Elie Kedourie has insisted, 'figures from the earliest times as a *leit motiv* in the Jewish self-view. Following the destruction of the Second Temple and the ending of Jewish autonomy, the fact, and the consciousness, of exile naturally became even more prominent. Through their own sins, successive generations of Jews were taught, they had brought this punishment on themselves. But God

[1] S. W. Baron, *A Social and Religious History of the Jews*, vol. 1, pp. 170f.

is a merciful God, they were also taught, who will in his own time send the Messiah to redeem them and restore them to the Holy Land.'[1] This belief sustained Jews in the Diaspora – whether they were exiles from Palestine or descendants of proselytes – for over two thousand years. It is, perhaps, not surprising that the word 'Falasha' means emigrant or exile and it is not impossible that the Jews of Ethiopia themselves originally adopted this term to indicate that they were exiles from the Holy Land into which, when the Messiah came, they would be gathered. Such an explanation of its meaning would place a different interpretation on the name from the usual one, which supposes that it was coined by gentiles and used pejoratively to denote an alien. A study of Falasha culture presents a fresh insight to the meaning of Exile (Golah) and the Return to Zion; one which is less historico-political and more religio-spiritual than the western conception.

The history of the Jews is the history of a people following the Jewish religion and linked indissolubly with the land of Israel. The long-drawn-out argument as to whether the Falashas are Jews has in the last few years been settled affirmatively first by the rabbis and later by the government in Israel. This has cleared away many misconceptions and made it easier to see the story of Ethiopian Jewry in the perspective both of the history of the Jewish people and of the country in which they live. From the days of the early Axumite Empire, reaching back perhaps to the time when it fell within the sphere of influence of the Ptolemaic pharaohs, two hundred years before the Christian era, to the present day the Falashas have shown a determination to remain a separate identifiable group. Their fortitude in the face of apparently overwhelming odds can stand comparison with the Jewish record anywhere. This is all the more remarkable since they follow a form of the Jewish religion which is pre-rabbinic and, therefore, depends entirely on the Written Law, without support from the Oral Law codified in the Talmud. Further, the Jews of Ethiopia appear never to have used Hebrew in their liturgy, which is also commonly believed to be an essential ingredient and binding force. In this respect they may be contrasted with the now extinct Chinese Jews of Kaifeng-Fu, whose holy books were written in Hebrew. When, due to their isolation, they forgot that language, they were bereft of religious literature and their religion gradually dissolved in ignorance. The Falashas maintained their faith intact because they could read the sacred texts in Ge'ez, the local liturgical tongue.

[1] Elie Kedourie (ed.), *The Jewish World*, p. 10.

Coming from the Agau tribe, of Hamito-Cushitic stock, the Falashas can lay no more claim to being semites or ethnic Jews than the converted Jews of Khazaria. They illustrate Professor H. W. F. Saggs's observation that in ancient times there was an absence of ethnic exclusiveness among Jews which persisted until after the Exile, for 'the Israelites did not think of themselves as ethnically distant in origin from their neighbours'.[1] Despite their almost total isolation, which denied the Jews of Ethiopia the opportunity to bring their religion into line with the ideas developed in the rest of the Jewish world, and which has laid them open to the reproach of fossilisation, they displayed a remarkable loyalty to their faith. Faced with the alternatives of death or conversion they followed the example of the defenders of Masada and chose mass suicide or execution.

It might be supposed that with a record as heroic and as remarkable as that of the Falashas, western Jewry would have wished to make contact with their African brethren as soon as their existence became generally known. That did not occur and it is one of the ironies of Jewish history that the isolation of the Falashas has continued almost until the present day. Ever since they lost their independence in the seventeenth century – they were the last segment of the Jewish people to surrender their autonomy – their numbers have been eroded by assimilation into the surrounding society and this remains today the greatest threat to their survival.

Oblique references to Jews in Cush occur in several places in the Old Testament and the fact that St Philip in the New Testament story apparently evinced no surprise at meeting an Ethiopian who had come to Jerusalem to worship suggests that the existence of a Jewish community in the Horn of Africa was known at that time. Subsequently, Jewish travellers from at least the ninth century AD reported that there was a Jewish kingdom in Abyssinia (modern Ethiopia) and the Portuguese adventurers were well aware of a Jewish population in the country in the sixteenth century. First-hand and far more detailed information was made available by James Bruce when he published his five-volume *Travels to Discover the Source of the Nile* in 1790; this was studied by Jewish writers like M. L. Marcus in France and Filosseno Luzzatto in Italy in the second quarter of the nineteenth century. The Jewish press had called attention to the existence of Falashas by 1847 in England and four years later in France, while gentile publications and Christian missionaries had taken cognisance of them many

[1]ibid., p. 40.

years earlier. Nevertheless, neither orthodox nor reform Jews displayed much interest in their plight, and they failed to take the opportunity to demonstrate that Judaism was impervious to colour prejudice.

It was not until 1867, when General Napier was preparing his assault on Emperor Theodore's fortress at Magdala to rescue the British hostages, that the first emissary, Joseph Halévy, was commissioned by western Jewry to make contact with the Falashas. Thereafter, nothing further was done for the best part of thirty years until Jacques Faitlovitch took up the theme and fought almost alone to bring succour to his neglected co-religionists. Even ten years ago Norman Bentwich was constrained to protest that 'the Jewish neglect of the Falashas for one hundred and fifty years is not credible'.

It is to Bentwich that I owe my initiation into the problem of the Ethiopian Jews. As we walked together across the Bloomsbury squares late one night in 1967 after attending a lecture he turned to me and asked what he should do about the Falashas. I was at a loss for an answer as I was ignorant of the subject but I agreed to join the committee over which he presided.

This book is the indirect outcome of that encounter and aims to fill a gap which has existed for too long. It would probably not have come into existence but for the interest displayed by Max Braude, the former Director-General of World ORT Union, whose support and encouragement converted an idea into reality. I am therefore pleased to have this opportunity to record both my gratitude for his help in bringing this project to fruition and my admiration for his ability and dedication in leading his organisation to the unchallenged position it now occupies in the field of technical education in many parts of the world. His enthusiastic adoption of the Falasha cause brought to its side at a critical moment the full weight of his prestigious Organisation for Rehabilitation through Training (ORT).[1]

I am only too well aware of many deficiencies caused by attempting to cover a very big subject in a relatively small compass and I sometimes marvel at my temerity. However, I believe there is a need to piece together the scanty references which have survived (there can be little doubt that in the course of time much written evidence has been destroyed) and to try to present a balanced account from the earliest times to today. While this endeavour aims to lift the veil which has covered a remote corner

[1]The initials are derived from the Russian name of the original Society for Handicrafts and Agricultural Work among the Jews of Russia which was founded in 1880 at St Petersburg (see L. Shapiro, *The History of ORT*).

of Jewish and African history, I hope that it will also stimulate further research into this little-explored field. Each chapter could provide the framework for a book of its own. I have naturally relied heavily on published material but I have essayed to draw conclusions from existing data which are sometimes radically at variance with established lines of thought.

An inevitable result of the neglect from which Falasha studies have suffered is that this forgotten tribe has been either omitted or only cursorily mentioned in most of the standard Jewish histories and texts. From the Talmud to Graetz, Dubnow or Roth, the Falashas are fortunate if they receive so much as a passing reference. Even Salo Baron's great *Social and Religious History of the Jews* is only slightly more generous. Nevertheless, a study of the Falashas has many lessons to teach in the fields of Jewish history and religion as well as in the phenomenon of Jewish survival.

A further consequence of the paucity of reliable material has been the appearance, in various publications and reports, particularly in the United States, of contributions which have been more remarkable for their inaccuracy and tendentiousness than for truth and objectivity. The purpose of this book will be served if it helps to put the record straight and if it encourages future historians to assign to the Falashas the position they merit. They may not have produced a Maimonides or an Ibn Gabirol but they have placed us all in their debt by their example and their courage in testifying to the message of the Mosaic laws while withstanding for centuries the forces of intolerance and prejudice. Such a people have earned the right to survive not as an ecologist's exhibit in a museum but because the world would be a poorer place without them.

A word is necessary about spelling. I have tried to be consistent in the transcription of foreign names and have relied as far as possible on the experts. Since they frequently differ I have, when in doubt, chosen the spelling which will be most easily understood as, for example, Theodore, not Tewodorus, or Theodorus, Axum not Aksum, Tigrai not Tigre, Semien, not Simien etc.

The biblical quotations have been taken from the Revised Version. Page references to Bruce's *Travels* are to the first edition (Edinburgh, 1790). I make no apology for the inclusion of footnotes on a fairly generous scale as I believe that they serve a useful purpose in assisting those readers who wish either to check my statements or to enlarge their own knowledge.

Any work such as this, which aims to present for the first time in outline the consecutive story of Ethiopian Judaism from the earliest times to today, must inevitably depend heavily on existing published material. Unhesitatingly, I acknowledge my debt to those scholars who have delved in this field before me and to none do I owe a greater debt than to Professor Edward Ullendorff. Though I make bold to dissent from some of his conclusions it would be ungracious not to pay tribute to his profound knowledge of Ethiopia which has found expression in numerous writings on which I have drawn freely.

My deep sense of gratitude extends especially to Professor Richard Pankhurst and Rabbi David Goldberg, both of whom have been good enough to read the whole text and have made most valuable suggestions, thus symbolising the fusion of Ethiopian and Jewish studies. I am also indebted to the following for their help and for their advice and kindness in various capacities, but I hasten to add that I accept sole responsibility for any errors of commission or omission which may inadvertently have crept into this book: David Appleyard, Professor A. F. L. Beeston, Batya Bier, Yona Bogale, John Bright-Holmes, Alan Crown, Charles Cotter, Itzhak Grinfeld, Ena Halmos, Arthur Irvine, Julian Kay, Sir Laurence Kirwan, Arthur Levinson, Hyam Maccoby, Professor Roland Oliver, Professor Chaim Rabin, Tessa Rajak and Professor J. B. Segal. In addition, I am most grateful to the librarians and staff of various institutions who have readily given me their assistance, especially the School of Oriental and African Studies (University of London) and also the Alliance Israélite Universelle in Paris, the Board of Deputies of British Jews, the *Jewish Chronicle*, Jews' College, the Wiener Library, the Office of the Chief Rabbi, University College London, and World ORT Union. Finally, I must thank Hilda Alberg for her expertise in preparing the typescript.

1

Strangers in the Midst

THE state of Socialist Ethiopia, the successor since 1974 to the empire of Haile Selassie I, holds a unique position on the African continent. It is the only African state which has never succumbed to foreign rule, if we exclude the five years of Italian occupation, and the only country of black Africa to develop its own written language. The pattern of its history is shot through with legend and romance. Even today, as it struggles to find its destiny in a new world, an air of mystery attaches to the country with its superb mountain scenery and fascinating arch-aeological sites. In Byzantine times it was at one period rated the third most important power in the world. Hamito–Semitic or Afro–Asian, by language and culture, and basically a product of the civilisations of the Nile and the Red Sea, it shows a closer affinity with the Middle East than with sub–Saharan Africa. Hebraic traditions run deep in the only country of its continent which can claim that its rulers have always been Christian since the fourth century.

Ethiopia is a state composed of many peoples, many languages and several religions. Accurate statistics are hard to come by but it is estimated that of the present population of about 32 million, Christians of the Orthodox Coptic Church represent 60 per cent, Sunni Muslims 25 per cent, and others, including Jews, 15 per cent. There is a homogeneity in the appearance of most of the population. With the exception of small numbers of people of negroid stock along the southern and south-western borders and of Arabs on the Red Sea littoral the majority are a brown-skinned people of 'Caucasian' stock with a slight admixture of negro blood which has darkened their colour. Their features tend to be regular, many of them are tall and well built and both men and women are often strikingly handsome. The main languages of the country can be roughly divided between those of the older Hamitic or Cushitic family and those of the relatively more recent Semitic group. The latter are today the dominant tongues and are divided between Amharic, the official language of Ethiopia; Tigrinya, prevalent in Tigrai Province and the central highlands of Eritrea; and Tigre, spoken in northern Eritrea. The principal languages of the Cushitic group are Galla (or Oromo), Somali, Afar and Agau. Numerically, the two language groups are approximately equal and their members display a common range of physical characteristics. The country is overwhelmingly agricultural and exports considerable quantities of coffee, hides and skins, pulses and oilseeds. The rate of literacy in 1970 was only 8·1 per cent and the G.N.P. in 1972 stood as low as US $80 per capita.

This is the home of the Falashas, the indigenous Jews who still practise a pre-rabbinic form of Judaism. Their presence in the country pre-dates both the Christians and Muslims and their origin has for long been a subject for speculation. Their small clan, numbering today probably fewer than 30,000 souls, represents the relic of a tribe which has behind it a record of courage and endurance in the face of adversity which bears comparison with any other section of the Jewish people. They played a significant role in the formative period of the Ethiopian variety of Christianity, and for over a thousand years they maintained their independence, at one time, it is said, even overthrowing the paramount power of the Amhara kings.

The name Falasha derives from an ancient Ethiopic, or Ge'ez word, meaning to emigrate[1] and hence signifies an exile, immigrant or stranger. It is sometimes used pejoratively, much as the word Jew is in English. Some Falashas prefer to call themselves Beta Israel (House of Israel) or else they use the more ancient Agau term *kayla*. Their original language is a dialect of Agau known as Kwarinya which is now almost extinct, having been replaced by Amharic or Tigrinya.

The Falashas, unlike their co-religionists in almost every other country of the Diaspora, are primarily agriculturists. Until the socialist revolution in 1974, when the land was nationalised, they were nearly all tenants of mostly rapacious landlords, though a few owned their own smallholdings. They live in scattered, primitive villages principally in the highlands of the north-west of the country in the neighbourhood of Lake Tana, in the Semien mountains further north, in Lasta and in Tigrai provinces and in small groups elsewhere.[2] In common with their gentile neighbours they lead a life which is simple in the extreme and can have altered

[1] Leslau, *Falasha Anthology*, p. ix.
[2] Including Kwara.

little in 2,000 years. In the remote districts, scarcely touched by western progress, they still live virtually an Iron Age existence. Their standard of living is among the lowest in the world and over the years the central government has done little to improve their lot.

They are undistinguished by their dress, and the visitor would not be able to differentiate an Ethiopian Jew from his fellow countryman any more than he could readily recognise a European Jew in the streets of Europe or America, unless it be for that slightly apologetic mien worn the world over by persecuted minorities which it takes several generations of freedom to lose. They grow the same crops, raise the same cattle and farm the land in the same way as their neighbours. An important difference is that in addition to being cultivators they are also artisans. They work as blacksmiths, weavers and tanners, while the women are the potters and basket-makers for the district and sometimes travel considerable distances to sell their wares. They used to be stonemasons but with the general decline of the country the craft has largely fallen into disuse and today masons are hard to find. It is said by the villagers of Aba Entonis and Tedda that as a reward for their work as craftsmen in building the castles and churches in neighbouring Gondar, two hundred and fifty years ago, King Fasilidas gave them land some of which they still own.

The smiths journey from village to village making plough-shares and other simple implements for the farmers, and the Falasha women may be seen in many a market selling their pots and pitchers and gaily coloured basket-ware. But there is a penalty attached to the pursuit of these handicrafts. The proud Amharas, the Christian ruling caste, like the Arabs on the other side of the Red Sea, hold handiwork and craftsmen in contempt. They associate the blacksmith, in particular, with the evil eye and regard his products as the work of the devil. The new regime is attempting to eradicate these traditional superstitions and, at a recent government-sponsored exhibition in Gondar, a sign was erected by the Falasha exhibitors reading (in translation): 'There is no despised or unworthy craft and we are proud of our calling.' In recent years factory-manufactured metalwork and utensils have tended to displace the village-made articles, thus producing additional economic hardship for the villagers.

Living cheek by jowl with their neighbours in the pre-dominantly Christian areas of the country, the Falashas are tolerated but unloved. Their groups of mostly round, thatched dwellings are separated from the other huts but share a common village with the Christians something like the ghettos of mediaeval Europe or the *mellahs* of Muslim countries. In some respects they can be compared with the outcasts of India though with the important distinction that for the observant Falasha it is as improper to touch a gentile as to be touched by him. As in India, so too in Ethiopia these expressions of untouchability are rapidly disappearing. The suspicions and superstitions, however, after so many centuries and among a population which is approximately 90 per cent illiterate die hard. The Falashas complain bitterly that their neighbours ascribe to them occult and evil powers, called *buda*, and accuse them of turning themselves at night into hyenas and of raiding the Christian homes and committing monstrous crimes.

Added to the disadvantages which they have suffered in common with other Ethiopian minority communities (such as the Kemant and Agaus, and pagans like the Shangellas), the Falashas have also had to bear the stigma of deicide, the doctrine that their forebears killed Christ. Not only are they reviled for this deed in the liturgy of the Ethiopian Coptic Church, the established religion, but in the *Kebra Nagast*, the book of the Glory of Kings, the great national epic, they are stigmatised as 'enemies of God'[1] and their extermination is foretold. This kind of teaching is scarcely calculated to endear the Jews to their neighbours, despite the strong influence exercised by the Mosaic religion on the monophysite version of Christianity practised in the country and notwithstanding the weight of Hebraic-inspired traditions which colour Ethiopian life and culture.

The Bible is greatly venerated by the Christians and the story of King Solomon and the visit paid to him by the Queen of Sheba has been elaborated and virtually appropriated by them. In Ethiopian tradition it is axiomatic that the Queen of Sheba was an Ethiopian monarch. The *Kebra Nagast* relates how, by a ruse, King Solomon inveigled the queen into sharing his bed with the result that she bore a son named Menelik, who in due course became king or negus of Ethiopia. The queen was so deeply impressed by her visit to the Holy Land that, according to the *Kebra Nagast*, she adopted the Jewish religion. When Menelik grew up he visited his royal father and (perhaps in retaliation for the deceit practised on his mother) surreptitiously transferred the Ark of the Covenant from Jerusalem to his capital at Axum. Thereafter the role of the chosen people was assumed by the Ethiopians as, they said, the Jews had forfeited the honour. Such myths, which have all the force of religious dogma, have helped to accentuate the suspicion felt

[1]Budge, *The Queen of Sheba and her only son Menyelek*, p. 225.

for the 'unbelieving' Falashas by their simple fellow countrymen. Christianity was proclaimed the official religion of Abyssinia, with its capital at Axum, in the reign of King Ezana, about the middle of the fourth century, when the new church placed itself under the patronage of the Patriarchate of Alexandria, at that time the centre of the Christian world. When the Coptic Church in Egypt refused to accept the doctrines proposed by the Oecumenical Council of Chalcedon in the year 451, the Ethiopian Church followed the Copts, in company with the Armenians and the Jacobites of Syria, to form the monophysite branch of Christianity. Briefly, its doctrine maintains 'that Christ was one person with one nature which was made up of the indissoluble union of a divine and a human nature'.[1] This may be contrasted with the Chalcedonian definition, which declared 'that Christ was consubstantial with the Father as touching his Godhead and consubstantial with us as touching his manhood, and that the two natures concur in one person, without confusion, without change, without division, and without separation'.[2] A fine distinction, one might say, more suited to the expert than the layman. The Council of Chalcedon marked the end of the supremacy of Alexandria and its place was taken by Constantinople.

Although the Ethiopian Church continued until 1951 to look to the Coptic hierarchy of Alexandria to supply it with its Patriarch, or Abuna, after Chalcedon the ties with Egypt gradually weakened, and the Church became increasingly isolated from the outside world. It is a characteristic of Coptic Christianity that it incorporates a greater measure of Jewish practices, including circumcision, than other denominations, but the Ethiopians went even further than the Egyptians in this respect. It seems likely that the retention of many Mosaic ordinances was a consequence partly of the isolation of the country, which provided a relative immunity from European influences, and partly of the conviction that the people, having inherited the biblical responsibilities of the chosen people, were under an obligation to adhere strictly to Old Testament precepts. This conviction was no doubt reinforced by their position as subjects of a monarch who claimed direct descent from King Solomon and whose supposed emblem, the double triangle or Star of David, was until recently much in evidence on the uniforms of the Imperial Guard. Besides circumcision, which is performed, as with Jews, on the eighth day after birth, Ethiopian Christianity also observes the Mosaic dietary laws, with special

[1]*Enc. Brit.*, eleventh edn, vol. 7.
[2]R. M. French, *The Eastern Orthodox Church*, p. 27.

emphasis on the ban on pork, recognises the Sabbath in addition to
Sunday as the day of rest, and incorporates – in theory at least –
many other Jewish rituals, including those dealing with personal
cleanliness. Little wonder that visitors are often struck by the Old
Testament atmosphere which pervades much of Ethiopian life.
Female circumcision (or excision), which is widely practised in
Ethiopia by Jews as well as by other groups, is an African custom
without justification in Scripture. Just as Ethiopian Orthodoxy
can no doubt tell us much about early Christianity before it was
subjected to Greek and Roman and other influences, so too the
Falasha brand of Judaism, cut off at a very early date from the
mainstream of Jewish thought, can throw much light on the
Jewish religion before it developed under the impact of rabbinic
teaching. In both areas there is still plenty of room for research. If
the two religions have become 'fossilised', as is often said, as the
result of their isolation from the centres of civilisation, it can be
argued that fossils have much to teach the inquiring mind.

The unique way in which Jewish customs have influenced
Ethiopian Christianity seems to attest, as Joseph Halévy suggested
– and Donald Levine among others has agreed[1] – to the probable
presence of Jews in the early days of the spread of Christianity.
Indeed, the Jewish religion appears to have been widely adopted
and, in Professor A. H. M. Jones's opinion, it was the conversion
of the royal house to Christianity which 'prevented Judaism from
becoming the official religion of the Abyssinian Kingdom, but
was not in time to prevent the conversion of various independent
Agau tribes to Judaism, nor the adoption by the Abyssinians of
certain Jewish practices'.[2] Professor Edward Ullendorff,[3] more
cautiously, states that 'Old Testament influences and reflections
had probably reached Ethiopia even before the introduction of
Christianity in the fourth century and before the translation of the
Bible'. In these circumstances, it is a little surprising that as most
contemporary Jewish communities received some attention in the
Talmud there is no mention in it of Jews living in Ethiopia, though
its few references to the country itself are friendly. For example, in
the discussion of the nations offering gifts to the Messiah, Ethiopia
is praised for never having been Israel's taskmaster, and there is a
tradition that Dan, one of the lost ten tribes, had migrated to Cush,
that is to say Ethiopia, and made its home there.[4]

While the strength of Jewish practices in the Ethiopian Church

[1]*Greater Ethiopia*, p. 32.
[2]Jones and Monroe, *A History of Ethiopia*, p. 42.
[3]*Ethiopia and the Bible*, p. 15.
[4]Pesachim, 118b; Ginzberg, *The Legends of the Jews*, vol. 3, pp. 166–7.

has given rise to controversy and even hostility within Christendom, the origin and credentials of the Falashas have likewise occasioned considerable argument in Jewish circles. The question has frequently been asked whether the Falashas are Jews and whence they came. It is largely the doubts and uncertainties aroused by these questions, coupled with their remoteness, that have resulted in the long separation of the Falashas from the rest of world Jewry, condemning them to fight their battle for recognition ill equipped and almost single-handed.

Two hundred years ago, Gibbon epitomised the isolation of the country when he wrote how, 'encompassed by the enemies of their religion, the Ethiopians slept for near a thousand years, forgetful of the world by whom they were forgotten', and added that 'they were awakened by the Portuguese, who, turning the southern promontory of Africa, appeared in India and the Red Sea, as if they had descended through the air from a distant planet'. If that lapidary phrase represented a somewhat exaggerated view when applied to the nation as a whole, it was, nevertheless, broadly applicable to the Jewish section of the population. When the Falashas were first visited by European Jews in the nineteenth and early twentieth centuries they were surprised to find that they were not the only Jews left in the world.

Gibbon's comment appeared in *The Decline and Fall of the Roman Empire*[1] at about the time that a pioneering work was being written by another very remarkable author. James Bruce's *Travels to Discover the Source of the Nile*, first published in 1790, described his adventures in Abyssinia during the years from 1769 to 1771. The Scottish explorer had brought back with him to Europe not only a thrilling tale but also a vast collection of documents and pictures dealing with the history, customs, languages, religions and natural history of Ethiopia. Never before had so much information about this distant land been made available for study by the scholarly world. Gibbon and Bruce may not have met but they moved in similar social circles and the historian would almost certainly have heard of the explorer's travels.

Bruce's five volumes also contained the first eyewitness account of the Falashas since a few stray references to them had appeared in the reports of Portuguese and Spanish soldiers and missionaries in the sixteenth and seventeenth centuries. His description of their history, language and religion was fuller and more objective than anything which had previously appeared and he had no doubt that he had observed and talked to members of a once-powerful Jewish

[1]Vol. 2, ch. 47.

sect. His writings aroused much interest and no little controversy; three editions were published in Great Britain and translations appeared in French and German. When the revelation that indigenous Jews living in east-central Africa was eventually comprehended by English churchmen and by Protestants in Germany and Switzerland, they realised that there were prospects for proselytisation which were not to be missed. By 1838 the London Society for Promoting Christianity amongst the Jews began to think of establishing a mission in Ethiopia, though it took another eighteen years before the intention was translated into reality.

A different picture was presented by the Jewish world, at that time comprising many individual communities with no co-ordinating international institutions, which evinced remarkably little interest in their long-lost brethren. Despite the circulation of the early reports it was not until the 1840s that Jewish organisations began to express any concern and then on a most modest scale, being motivated principally by a desire to counteract the threat from the missionaries.

While the Christian evangelists were convinced that they had discovered a long-lost branch of the Jewish faith and that it was their duty to bring the Falashas into their fold, the Jewish world remained sceptical and it took many years before they fully recognised the validity of the Falashas' demand to be joined to the wider community. Their claim was based on their strict adherence to the teachings of the Torah, the five books of Moses, as well as their acceptance of all the other books of the Old Testament. Falashas reject the New Testament and the Koran. Their Bible, which, excluding the New Testament, they share with the Christians, is written in Ge'ez, the ancient Ethiopic language which is now 'dead' and used only for liturgical purposes both in synagogues and churches. A few Hebrew and Aramaic words have found their way into the Ge'ez Bible, which is a translation from the Greek Septuagint, itself a translation from Hebrew made, it is said, by seventy-two Jewish scholars in Egypt at the instance of King Ptolemy II, Philadelphus, in the third century BC. A knowledge of the Hebrew language appears to have completely bypassed the Ethiopian Jews. Orthodox rabbis have questioned the authenticity of their attachment to the Jewish religion because they do not follow the precepts of the Halachah, or Oral Law, as distinct from the Torah or Written Law which they scrupulously follow. However, as the codification of the Oral Law, known as the Talmud, was not completed until about AD 500, at a time when the Jews of Ethiopia were already cut off from their co-religionists in the rest of the world, it is hardly surprising that they had no knowledge of its contents. Their position was different from that of the Karaite and Samaritan sects which positively rejected the Halachah and rabbinic authority as a matter of principle.

It was a poor reward, after zealously maintaining their loyalty to the teachings of Moses and heroically withstanding persecution for something like 2,000 years, to be told by western rabbis, even after the establishment of the State of Israel, that they could not be recognised as members of the Jewish brotherhood and to be rejected by leading Jewish scholars.

Conflicting opinions as to their origin also caused difficulties. Whatever records may once have existed have long since disappeared in the upheavals which have beset the country. Neither the Falashas themselves nor foreign scholars have been able to explain with certainty how a Jewish community came to exist in such a remote area and, because of the colour of their skin, they did not conform to the conventional idea that all Jews belonged to the same race, originated from Palestine, and were dispersed over the earth as a result of the Assyrian, Babylonian or Roman conquests.

The notion that the Jews are a race, in the anthropological sense, has frequently been questioned by scholars, notably by Julian Huxley in his book *We Europeans*, written in reply to the Nazi theories current in the 1930s. More recently, Arthur Koestler in *The Thirteenth Tribe* has demonstrated how, with the conversion of the Khazars of Russia, a people of Turkish stock, the Jewish people successfully absorbed foreign racial elements on a considerable scale, while the geneticists continue to express grave doubts about a common Jewish ancestral origin.[1] Race, after all, as we have been reminded by a cultural anthropologist, 'is largely in the eye of the beholder; it is more a matter of social ascription than biology'.[2] It is ironical that the Israelis, who themselves have created a melting-pot of different ethnic groups united by a common religious and historical consciousness, should have been among those showing the greatest reluctance to acknowledge the Falasha claim.

The older generation of Falashas, and those who have had little contact with western thought, accept the tradition that their ancestors came to Ethiopia with Menelik, the son of Solomon and Sheba, at Solomon's behest, in the role of a bodyguard of Israelites to escort the prince on his return to his country after visiting Jerusalem. Others, as Wolf Leslau has written, 'say that they have

[1]See, for example, G. Brown, in *Journal of Jewish Studies*, vol. 31, no. 1, p. 130.
[2]W. Y. Adams, *Nubia*, p. 8.

descended from Jews who came after the destruction of the First or the Second Temple'. He continues:

> Very few of the western scholars who have dealt with the problem of the Falashas are of the opinion that they are ethnically Jews. Most of them think that they are a segment of the indigenous Agau population which was converted to Judaism. How and when they were converted is a problem for which historical evidence is lacking. It has been argued that the Jews of Egypt – we know of the existence of a Jewish community in Elephantine in the fifth century BC – or the Jews of Yemen may have sent forth missionaries who converted these African tribes to Judaism. There seems to be more historical evidence for contact between Yemen and Ethiopia than between Egypt and Ethiopia, and I would therefore be inclined to think, with some others, that the conversion came from the Jews of Yemen. It must be conceded, however, that nearly all the proofs in favour of this view are indirect rather than direct. The problem still awaits final solution.[1]

It will be among the aims of this book to meet this challenge.

The view that the Jewish religion reached the Axumite kingdom of Ethiopia by way of the Yemen has had many advocates. A Jewish settlement was established in south-west Arabia – the *Arabia Felix* of Roman geographers – following the destruction of the Second Temple in AD 70 and the renewed dispersion of the Jewish population of Palestine. It is reasonable to suppose, therefore, that some Jews made the short sea-crossing to the African coast where the port of Adulis was already an important trading centre. Moreover, many links of religion, language and commerce connected the two coasts of the Red Sea.

Alternatively, it is at least equally likely that Jewish influences reached Axum by way of the Nile Valley. There had been Jewish settlements in Egypt and Upper Egypt for centuries before there were similar outposts in southern Arabia. Between Egypt and Axum lay the kingdom of Meroë in what we now know as northern Sudan. There is evidence, in both the Old and New Testaments, to show that Jews could have settled there. From Meroë, following the valley of the Nile or one of its tributaries, it is no great distance, and not an unduly hazardous journey, to Axum.

The fact that the Bible was translated into Ethiopic (or Ge'ez) from the Greek Septuagint and not from the Hebrew text, which

[1]*Falasha Anthology*, p. xliii.

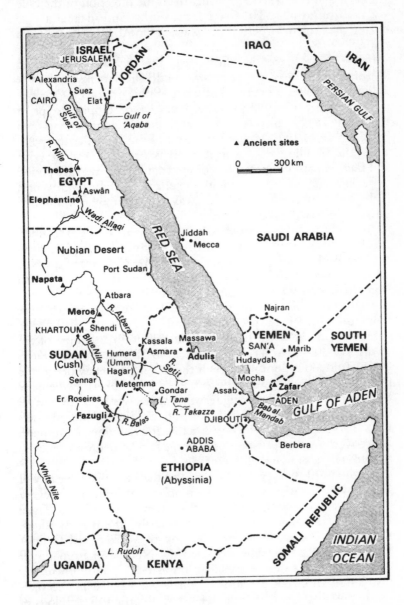

Ethiopia and its neighbours

would have been used by immigrants from Yemen, strongly suggests that it reached Abyssinia from the direction of the Nile and not from Arabia. The Greek language had spread far and wide during the Ptolemaic period and was used in Abyssinia as a lingua franca.

In the Bible Meroë is called Cush, the ancient Egyptian and Meroitic name for the country, while the Greeks named it Ethiopia and later it became known as Nubia or Sudan. Occupying the territory on the southern border of Upper Egypt, it represented an extension of Egyptian culture, though with its own language and script. Towards the end of the eighth century BC, when the Middle East was in turmoil as a result of the Assyrian and Babylonian conquests, Meroë overran Egypt, then in a period of decline, and provided her with the pharaohs of the twenty-fifth (Ethiopian) dynasty, who held sway for more than a hundred years.

Around this time, anxious to reinforce their southern frontier, the Egyptians established a garrison manned by foreign mercenaries on Elephantine island, near the First Cataract of the Nile where Aswan stands today. The garrison included a Jewish element about whom a good deal is known thanks to the collection of Aramaic papyri of the fifth century BC which were found there early in the present century.

Herodotus reported that in the sixth century BC some of the soldiers of the garrison revolted and moved across the border into the Meroitic kingdom. Although there is no direct evidence it is possible that some Jews went too. This seems likely as there are biblical references which suggest that there were already Jewish communities in Cush, or Ethiopia, at the time of the prophets Isaiah and Zephaniah, which was before the Babylonian captivity. Moreover, it was a prosperous country and 'at that time enjoyed the reputation of a kind of El Dorado'.[1]

By the third century BC the kings of the Ptolemaic dynasty of Egypt were greatly extending their sphere of influence in every direction and encouraging the development of commerce. Trade in the Red Sea, which was a royal monopoly,[2] flourished. Adulis, the port of Axum, 'took on the look of a provincial Graeco-Egyptian city'.[3] Caravans followed the Nile basin from Egypt through Meroë to the Abyssinian highlands. A monument and inscription in Greek at Adulis, which was copied in the sixth century AD by Cosmas Indicopleustes, recorded the exploits of

[1] Gardiner, *Egypt of the Pharaohs*, p. 357.
[2] Pankhurst, p. 12.
[3] Doresse, p. 28.

Ptolemy III, Euergetes I (247–222 BC), the son of Philadelphus in whose reign the Bible had been translated into Greek. During the reigns of these kings the port served both the coastal people and the hinterland and was used for the shipment of elephants to Egypt, where they were trained for military purposes. By one means or another the message of the Septuagint could have reached Axum either by way of Meroë and the Nile Valley or by the Red Sea through the port of Adulis.

In due course Meroë declined and by the fourth century AD the Axumite kingdom was prepared to take its place. The Jewish religion was already established there when King Ezana, one of Axum's greatest rulers, descended on his northern neighbour and absorbed his territory into his domains. As a result of this conquest the country which had been called Ethiopia became merged with Abyssinia and the name of the land known as Cush moved southwards from Meroë to Axum. It was Ezana who, towards the end of his reign, brought his country into Christendom.

The uncertainty as to the origin of the Falashas greatly impeded the long struggle for their recognition as part of the community of Israel. It was a frustrating experience. Nearly a hundred years elapsed after Bruce's stay in Gondar before the first Jewish emissary visited Ethiopia. The task was assigned by the recently founded philanthropic organisation, the Alliance Israélite Universelle of Paris, to Joseph Halévy, who was then making a name for himself as a Semitic and Ethiopian scholar. He went to Abyssinia at a bad moment, in 1867, when the country was in turmoil and the erratic behaviour of Emperor Theodore had provoked the British Government into mounting a military expedition to rescue his European captives.

Halévy, who had studied his subject profoundly, visited the people in their villages and was convinced that the Falashas were Jews and that it was the duty of their more fortunate brethren to come to their help. Years later, disappointed by the results he had achieved, he wrote a deeply moving description of the heroism of the Falashas in the sixteenth century when they defended their independence and resisted forcible conversion to Christianity, recalling the cry of the defenders of Masada: death rather than dishonour.

On the eve of the Franco–Prussian War the leaders of French Jewry were not in a mood to assume fresh commitments outside their normal sphere of operation, nor prepared to give Halévy their full backing. For the next forty years, interest in the Falashas dwindled until the Alliance decided to send another representative. This time they chose a Turkish rabbi, Haim Nahum, who, after visiting Abyssinia, reported – no doubt to the satisfaction of the heads of the Alliance – that there were far fewer Falashas than Halévy had estimated and that any programme of educational assistance, such as the Alliance sponsored in other countries, was fraught with almost insurmountable difficulties. Better to leave them alone.

Halévy's efforts, however, had not been entirely in vain. At the beginning of this century a new champion arose in the person of Jacques Faitlovitch, one of Halévy's pupils. In 1904 he made the first of several more or less prolonged visits to Abyssinia and from then until his death in Israel in 1955 he worked indefatigably on behalf of the Ethiopian Jews.

With the establishment of the State of Israel in 1948 and the 'ingathering of the exiles' the Falashas were entitled to hope that an end to their troubles was in sight. But this was not to be. Neither Israel nor world Jewry were yet prepared for their reception while they themselves were too weak and fragmented to force their claim. They were denied recognition as a portion of the Diaspora which had to be redeemed while, on his side, the Ethiopian emperor was in no mind to be deprived of a valuable section of his people who gave no trouble.

By slow degrees pressure on the rabbinical and lay authorities built up but it was not until early 1973 that the breakthrough came with the announcement by Ovadia Yossef, the Sephardi Chief Rabbi of Israel, that the Falashas belonged to the tribe of Dan and must be given the same right to return to Israel as other Jews. Two years later the Knesset, the Israeli parliament, followed suit by acknowledging that they had the right of immigration under the Law of Return.

But the change of attitude had come tragically late. During Haile Selassie's reign and until the Yom Kippur war of 1973, when diplomatic relations were sundered, Israel was on excellent terms with Ethiopia. By the time the Knesset adopted its new policy Ethiopia was in the throes of revolution and was fighting wars on two fronts, in Eritrea and against the Somalis. Though diplomatic relations were not resumed and any suggestions of mass emigration were discouraged, means were found to transport between two and three hundred, mostly young people, by air to Israel. But even this limited opportunity to meet the Falashas' age-old yearning to go to the Holy Land was short-lived and, in view of the problems facing the present regime, it seems unlikely to recur unless there is a drastic change in the situation. Emigration is opposed partly because it is contrary to traditional policy and partly because, indirectly, it brings support for Israel. As a member of the Organisation of African Unity, with close links with the Arab countries, Ethiopia treads warily so as not to antagonise her Muslim neighbours and, as a marxist state, committed to friendship with the Soviet Union and her satellites, from whom she receives considerable assistance, she is obliged to support the communist attitude towards Israel and Zionism. Outside assistance for the Falashas is, therefore, limited to an integrated rural development project devised and managed by the World ORT Union (Organisation for Rehabilitation through Training) with the support of technical assistance funds from several Western nations.

2

Legend and History

NO exploration of Ethiopia's history and the part that the Falashas have played in it can afford to overlook the biblical story of King Solomon and the visit paid to him by the Queen of Sheba. The tale and its ramifications have become an integral part of the nation's traditions and heritage. Whereas in Europe and in the Islamic world the story has taken on the role of a popular legend, which has inspired many works of art, music and literature, in Ethiopia it is a fundamental tenet of the national consciousness, common to Jews and Christians alike, though, it should be added, with the growing influence of Western thought, many people today are taking a more sceptical view of the tradition.

It is generally acknowledged by scholars that the account given in the Bible[1] has a basis in fact and is not simply a romantic legend. That it has, in the course of time, been embroidered with all kinds of myths need not detract from the historic truth which is at the core. In this respect it can be compared with the English legend of King Arthur, which, while heavily overladen with mythology, is based on an historic personage.

The Solomon-Sheba narrative, which occupies only thirteen verses, may be briefly summarised. After recounting the power, the wealth and the wisdom of King Solomon, the Bible says that 'when the Queen of Sheba heard of the fame of Solomon concerning the name of the Lord she came to prove him with hard questions'. She travelled with a great caravan of camels bringing rich presents of 'spices and very much gold and precious stones'. She was greatly impressed by what she saw at the court of the king and confessed that before her journey she had been sceptical of the stories which she had heard, but seeing is believing and she told

[1] 1 Kings 10:1–13 and 2 Chronicles 9:1–12.

the king that 'thy wisdom and prosperity exceedeth the fame which I heard'. What was even more significant was the deep sympathy she felt for the king's religion, which had inspired so much goodness and wisdom and created a happy atmosphere. 'Blessed be the Lord thy God which delighteth in thee, to set thee on the throne of Israel: because the Lord loved Israel for ever, therefore made he thee king, to do judgement and justice.' In return for her gifts the king gave the queen, besides the royal bounty, 'all her desire, whatsoever she asked.... So she turned and went to her own country, she and her servants.' Two verses are inserted in the narrative which hark back to the previous chapter about Hiram's navy which brought gold and precious stones from Ophir and almug trees (which have yet to be identified), but there is no mention of the birth of Menelik.

The brief report of what must have been an important meeting leaves many questions unanswered and so it is not surprising that in the course of time it became embellished with a vast accumulation of legends. A comparison could be drawn with the story of Queen Esther, whose activities at the Court of King Ahasuerus (who is often identified with Xerxes) were recorded some three centuries after the events described.[1] There is, however, a significant difference for the story of Esther looks today more like a piece of fiction, a kind of historical romance with a moral attached. The Queen of Sheba's visit to the King of Israel has a greater ring of historical truth and the fact that it has continued to the present day to inspire confidence and national pride among the people of Ethiopia places it in an entirely different category. While there is no question about Solomon's existence in the tenth century BC, no archaeological evidence has so far been presented to prove the generally accepted view that there is 'no reason to doubt the historical reality of the Queen of Sheba'.[2]

Who, then, was this elusive lady who captivated King Solomon, whom the royal house of Ethiopia proclaimed as their ancestress and whom the Falashas see as the cause of their presence in Ethiopia? It is strange that the Bible omits to tell us the queen's name or the location of the land of Sheba (or Saba).[3] Possibly these details were not regarded by the scribes as important and, as regards the location, it could no doubt be assumed that the people for whom the story was written knew (or thought they knew) near enough whence the queen came. We are told that she arrived in Jerusalem by camel, or at least in a caravan of camels, but that is

[1] Peake's *Commentary on the Bible*, 331i.
[2] Ullendorff, *Ethiopia and the Bible*, p. 134.
[3] The Hebrew form is Sheba while in the Greek Septuagint it becomes Saba.

hardly surprising as Jerusalem is far from the sea and the camel was by Solomon's time a domesticated beast of burden. We may guess from the gifts she brought with her – gold, spices and precious stones – that she came from the south. Indeed, in the New Testament[1] she is simply called Queen of the South, as though that was her usual appellation. While it is not disputed that she came from somewhere south of Palestine there are two principal opposing views regarding the exact location of her country.

Most biblical scholars and orientalists identify Sheba with the Sabaeans, a Semitic people who established a considerable civilisation in southern Arabia which flourished from about the eighth century BC until it was replaced by the Himyarites early in the Christian era. This identification, for which there is no archaeological or epigraphic evidence, rests on the similarity of the names and the general description in the Bible of the queen and her caravan. However, neither the gold nor the precious stones were products of southern Arabia, and the great quantity of spices which she brought could have come equally from Arabia or Africa provided that the term connotes myrrh and frankincense, since these aromatic gums are sometimes called spices in the Bible. If spices is used in the ordinary sense to mean seasonings for food it is likely that they came either from the Horn of Africa, which produced cinnamon, or from India or Ceylon, which, from time immemorial, had been exporters of pepper, cinnamon and other condiments. The numerous references both in this context and elsewhere in the Bible to gold from Ophir naturally excite speculation as to where Ophir was but scholars have not yet reached a conclusion and its location is disputed. Various places have been suggested as far apart as the African coast opposite Madagascar (Sofala), the western shore of the Red Sea at its southern end (the ancient Punt), the Arabian shore of the Persian Gulf[2] or even India, according to the Jewish historian Flavius Josephus.[3] The reference to Ophir in the Sheba story, however, is only by way of an insertion intended, it may be, to illustrate Solomon's power and wealth. The Bible does not say that the queen's gold came from Ophir, and it might have been the product either of the gold-mines worked by the pharaohs in the region of Wadi Allaqi, not far south of modern Aswan, in Nubia, or have come from the upper reaches of the Blue Nile, at Fazugli, perhaps the gold land of Havilah.

In medieval times in Europe the Queen of Sheba was usually

[1] Matthew 12:42 and Luke 11:31.
[2] Peake, 295d.
[3] *Antiquities of the Jews*, Book 8, ch. 6.

considered to have been an African and was sometimes depicted as black, or, as at Canterbury and Chartres Cathedrals, accompanied by negro servants. Many renaissance painters were inspired by the story and gave ample scope to their imagination against lavish, romanticised backgrounds while the African setting was gradually abandoned.

Jewish tradition, which does not seem to be greatly enamoured of the whole story and has been inclined to identify the queen with Lilith, the queen of the demons and the great temptress, leans towards the African place of birth. For the Ethiopians, of course, her African homeland is undisputed. This was also the view of Josephus, who, writing in the first century AD, recounted the Sheba story essentially as it is told in the Bible. He described the queen twice as Queen of Egypt and Ethiopia and once as Queen of Ethiopia, but never called her Queen of Sheba. This name is also absent from the New Testament, where she is called Queen of the South. In the *Kebra Nagast*, the classic Ethiopian saga, she enjoys both the title Queen of Sheba and Queen of the South as well as the names Candace and Makeda.

If neither Josephus nor the Gospels call her by her biblical name it is possible that it could have been introduced under the influence of the genealogical lists of the descendants of Noah included in the Book of Genesis. There we learn, in chapter 10, that the sons of Ham are Cush (Ethiopia) and Mizraim (Egypt), Phut (Upper Egypt) and Canaan, and the sons of Cush are Seba, Havilah, Sabtah, Raamah, and Sabtecha; and the sons of Raamah are Sheba and Dedan (probably northern Hejaz). Sheba thus becomes a grandson of Cush. Some of these names are duplicated in describing the descendants of Shem, including both Sheba and Havilah (the gold land beyond Abyssinia mentioned in Genesis 2:11) who were sons of Joktan (Qataban) together with, among others, Ophir. Thus Sheba is represented on both sides of the Red Sea and is associated with Cush, 'a vague term connoting the entire Nile Valley, south of Egypt, including Nubia and Abyssinia'.[1]

The association of Sheba (or Saba) with Cush in the genealogy of Noah could explain how the two became linked in Jewish tradition. This might also be the reason for Josephus's statement that 'Saba was a royal city of Ethiopia which Cambyses afterwards named Meroë after the name of his own sister'.[2] Josephus would have known of the capital of Cush (or Ethiopia) in his time as Meroë but somehow it had to be explained how the Queen of Sheba got the name by which she was called in the Bible narrative.

[1] *Ethiopia and the Bible*, p. 5.
[2] *Antiquities of the Jews*, Book 2, ch. 10.

It is possible that it was a common belief among Jews that the name of the city was changed by the Persian king, Cambyses, when he invaded Ethiopia in the sixth century and that Josephus was merely echoing a popular tradition. There appears to be no historical evidence to support this tradition and, indeed, its accuracy is doubtful because the Ethiopian capital had previously been at Napata until it was moved to a new site further up the Nile at Meroë about the time of Cambyses' invasion, which was some 400 years after the queen was supposed to have lived. The point, however, is that in the popular mind the chief city of Ethiopia was known as Sheba or Saba at the time of King Solomon while the capital of the Sabaean kingdom in south-west Arabia, called Marib, situated about seventy miles east of Sanaa, did not reach a high point of its civilisation until about the fifth century BC. The Sabaeans founded colonies on the west side of the Red Sea and this emigration across the water could perhaps account for the presence of the name of Sheba in the genealogies of both Ham and Shem. It is also worth noting the similarity between the name of Assab (or Sabae) on the Red Sea coast and Saba, to which Bruce had called attention. He detected, too, a relationship between this place-name and the Ethiopic *Azeb*, meaning south. At any rate, a Jewish tradition had apparently become established by the first century AD, when Josephus was writing, that the Queen of the South originated from Ethiopia and that her capital was called Saba until it was later renamed Meroë.

Josephus's reference to Saba appears in the context of his engaging story of Moses' expedition against the Ethiopians in his *Antiquities of the Jews*. It has no counterpart in the Bible and tells how, at Pharaoh's urgent request, and with his daughter's agreement, Moses was commissioned to lead an Egyptian army against the Ethiopians who were invading the country. With the aid of ibis birds, which the Egyptians carried in baskets and released to attack flying snakes,[1] Moses defeated the enemy and found himself in front of Saba, the royal city of Ethiopia. Owing to its natural advantages and the strength of its fortifications at the confluence of three rivers, the city proved impregnable. However, the Ethiopian king's daughter, Tharbis, seeing Moses from the city walls, instantly fell in love with him and promised to surrender the city if he would marry her. The bargain was struck and Moses, in the role of an Egyptian general, returned victorious to Egypt.[2]

[1]Herodotus also, in chapter XIII of A. J. Evans's edition, refers to the Egyptians' use of ibises for warding off flying snakes.
[2]A discussion of this episode is to be found in Dr Tessa Rajak's essay in the *Journal of Jewish Studies*, volume 19, no. 2, of 1978.

The legend, according to some scholars, could have been created in order to find an explanation for the passage in Numbers 12:1 which describes how in the wilderness of Sinai, after the people had consumed a surfeit of quails, 'Miriam and Aaron spake against Moses because of the Cushite woman whom he had married, for he had married a Cushite woman'. Whether this explanation is justified or not, the story has geographical merit for it provides a recognisable description of the site of Meroë – a place of great importance in antiquity – which stood south of the modern town of Atbara, not far from the confluence of the Nile and Atbara rivers in what is now called Northern Sudan or Nubia.

The ambiguity of the name Ethiopia can easily give rise to confusion as its location in ancient times was different from what is understood by Ethiopia today. The ancient Greeks invented the name, meaning the land of the burnt faces, and for long it embraced almost anywhere south and south-west of Egypt, far into central Africa and beyond. In the Septuagint the Hebrew word Cush (which was taken from ancient Egyptian) has been translated into Greek as Ethiopia, which corresponded with the ancient Meroitic kingdom. The modern state of Ethiopia which, until comparatively recently, was known abroad as Abyssinia is, for the sake of clarity, sometimes better referred to by that name.

The modern state has a perfectly good claim to its name for, as Professor Arkell has remarked,[1] 'the king of Meroë was called "king of the Ethiopians" in contemporary Greek in the third century AD and since the kingdom was later at least partly merged in the Axumite kingdom the name "Ethiopia" is correctly continued in Abyssinia today'. This overlap between the borders of ancient Ethiopia, its successor Axum and the present state has left a lingering irredentist demand for the revision of frontiers which still crops up from time to time.

When Burckhardt, the Swiss explorer, visited Shendy, 100 miles north of Khartoum, in 1814, he found 'the Ethiopians were still laying claim to it. They threatened to come down the Blue Nile once again and seize it'[2] following, perhaps, the example of King Ezana a millennium and a half earlier. Again, when the present western boundary of Abyssinia was defined by the Anglo-Abyssinian Treaty of 15 May 1902, Emperor Menelik II was reluctant to accept the suggested border with the Sudan. Eleven years earlier he had addressed a letter to the European powers in which he informed them of the boundaries of his

[1] *The History of the Sudan to 1821*, p. 113.
[2] A. Moorhead, *The Blue Nile*, p. 159.

empire as he understood them and which were considerably more extensive than the subsequent treaty acknowledged. The Emperor's letter expresses the ancient tradition that Ethiopia's frontier had previously extended into Sudan and thus embraced much of the territory of ancient Meroë. 'In defining today the present borders of my empire', he wrote, 'I shall attempt, if God grants me life and strength, to re-establish the old frontiers of Ethiopia as far as Khartoum and Lake Nyanza, including the country of the Gallas.'[1]

The renown of ancient Egyptian civilisation has to such an extent eclipsed the achievements of Napata and Meroë that the Meroitic or Nubian civilisation, which flourished from approximately the eighth century BC to the fourth century AD, remains practically unknown except to the experts. Its people were of Hamito-Semitic stock. Its culture was based on ancient Egyptian traditions and religion. The state was theocratic and ruled through the king by the priests of Amen. Its language, although written in hieroglyphics, was different from Egyptian. Numerous surviving inscriptions have been deciphered but the language has not yet been interpreted. A serious void exists, therefore, in our knowledge of Nubian history. The names of many of the rulers are known and there are many references to them in Egyptian, Greek and Latin literature. The Meroites were the Egyptians' southern neighbours whose common frontier was drawn at approximately the First Cataract on the Nile, where Aswan stands today. They occupied an important strategic position for they were the guardians of the great life-giving river on which the civilisation and existence of Egypt has always depended. Relations between the two countries, if not always friendly, were close and communications and trade were highly developed. The Nile Valley was one of the main routes by which the produce of Africa – ivory, ebony, incense, spices, skins, slaves and gold – were imported. The Meroites' southern border certainly extended as far as Sennar and possibly to the great western escarpment of the Abyssinian highlands where the Atbara and Blue Nile break through the mountains into the plains which, together with the White Nile, form the Nile basin. The ancient civilisation was developed well before the arrival of the markedly negroid Nuba tribes who migrated to the Nile basin about 2,000 years ago when the Meroitic kingdom was already showing signs of decline.

Although the Meroites never rivalled their great northern

[1] Abyssinia Handbook No. 97, prepared under the direction of the Foreign Office, 1919.

neighbour in wealth and power they were sometimes a menace. At the time of the twenty-third dynasty, about the middle of the eighth century BC, Egypt was passing through a period of recession and was vulnerable to attack from the south. Border disputes broke into open conflict (like the troubles mentioned by Josephus) and in 730 BC Egypt succumbed to an invasion under King Piankhi which established Meroitic rule over the whole of the country for a little over 100 years and has come to be known as the period of the twenty-fifth (Ethiopian) dynasty. The twenty-fourth dynasty consisted of two kings, Tefnakht and Boccoris, who were virtually vassals of the Ethiopians. Boccoris is said to have been burnt alive by Piankhi's nephew and successor Shabaka. The two states were united under an Ethiopian monarch, whose capital at that time was at Napata. For a short while Ethiopia became a world power. Josephus's reference to a 'queen of Egypt and Ethiopia' is, therefore, by no means fanciful, more especially as the records show that women played a very important role in the government of the country.

The period of Ethiopian supremacy coincided with the rise of a new and formidable power in the shape of the militant Assyrian Empire sweeping across the desert from the east. The dangers which this development created for the small states of the ancient Near East were reflected in the accounts contained in the Bible. The second Book of Kings and Isaiah illustrate very clearly the predicament of the Kingdom of Judah under King Hezekiah (*c.* 715–687), caught between the opposing powers of east and west. The kingdom of Israel had already been defeated by Sargon II in 722 and its people deported to Assyria when Hezekiah was attacked by Sennacherib, Sargon's successor, who had defeated the Egyptians at Eltekeh.

Hezekiah had been inclined to seek Egyptian support against the Assyrian invasion and in 701, with the encouragement of the Egyptians, he had joined a revolt of the Philistine cities. The Egyptian leader was Tirhaka, the son of Piankhi, who was to become the fourth Pharaoh of the Ethiopian dynasty, and is designated in the Bible variously as King of Egypt and King of Ethiopia. It was Tirhaka (689–664) who earned the scorn of Sennacherib's Rabshakeh, or chief of staff, when he warned Hezekiah that he was no more than a 'bruised reed... whereon if a man lean it will go into his hand, and pierce it'.[1] Despite his boasting, Sennacherib's assault against Jerusalem failed thanks to what the Bible called divine intervention in the form of plague

[1] 2 Kings 18:21; Isaiah 36:6.

which decimated his army, and the Assyrians were forced to return to Nineveh, where Sennacherib was murdered by his sons.

Tirhaka continued to resist the Assyrians but he was defeated by Sennacherib's successor, Esarhaddon, in 670. The Assyrian pressure was maintained and nine years later Tandamane, Tirhaka's nephew and the last king of the Ethiopian dynasty, was overwhelmed by Assurbanipal, whose armies penetrated as far south as Thebes and Karnak, where the main Egyptian treasure was ransacked and carried away to Nineveh.

The Kingdom of Judah had stood alone for 136 years after Israel had fallen and the ten tribes had been taken captive. The Babylonian Empire replaced the Assyrians as the dominant power and in 586 Nebuchadnezzar succeeded where Sennacherib failed and the inhabitants of Judah were driven into exile to lament by the waters of Babylon. But they did not all go. Some Jews preferred to follow the prophet Jeremiah and fled to Egypt where a community already existed.

The domination of the Middle East by the Assyrians and the Babylonians lasted for just over 300 years from the battle of Qarqar on the Orontes in 853, in which King Ahab of Israel fought in alliance with the Syrians,[1] until the invaders in turn were forced to abandon their conquests. The growing pressure from further east of the Medes and Persians under Cyrus the Great forced the submission of Mesopotamia and secured the release of the Jewish captives. It was left to Cambyses, Cyrus's son and successor, to continue the advance and, having conquered Egypt, he turned his attention to Meroë, which he threatened but failed to subdue.

The Persian dynasty ruled Egypt for close on 200 years until it, in turn, was overthrown by Alexander the Great in 332. Meanwhile, the Meroites had concentrated on their own homeland and developed their way of life under the influence of Egyptian civilisation. They had moved their capital from Napata to Meroë, which occupied an important strategic position on the Nile at the intersection of a number of caravan routes, and, thanks to a plentiful supply of raw materials and wood fuel, they established a thriving iron-smelting industry. From this so-called 'Birmingham of Northern Sudan' the knowledge of iron-working spread south and west throughout black Africa.[2] Though some doubt has been cast by W. Y. Adams, in his book on Nubia, on the importance of iron-working at Meroë, he has mentioned the significance of handmade pottery as a domestic craft and of cotton-weaving for

[1]Peake, 90a; 1 Kings 20.
[2]Arkell, p. 147.

making white garments with blue or green embroidery (much as are to be seen in Abyssinia today), and of basket-making and leatherwork. Could it be that the Falashas' well-known skill in all these crafts derives from this ancient tradition?

Kingdoms and empires rise and fall and by the end of the first century AD Meroë, though still an important state, had passed its peak. Both internal and external pressures were growing. A change in the climate, says Arkell, was resulting in a slow desiccation of the land, reducing the supply of agricultural products and of wood-fuel for the iron industry. From outside, there was a movement of Nuba tribes pressing in from the west while a new power was arising in the south-east diverting the profitable commerce which followed the Nile Valley to a seaborne route based on the Greek, or Ptolemaic, trading station at Adulis on the Red Sea, near the modern port of Massawa. In addition, the expanding Roman Empire was casting covetous eyes on the lucrative incense trade, one of the main sources of wealth in the Horn of Africa and south-west Arabia, handling great quantities of those fragrant resins used for burning on the altars of the Roman Empire and for embalming the Egyptian dead. The gums were produced – as they still are – in Somaliland (the ancient Punt) and in the Yemen and Hadhramaut as well as in Eritrea and Tigrai and in Sudan.

The almost total disappearance of the Meroitic civilisation is a strange phenomenon. Adams has pointed out that by the fourth century AD the great city of Meroë

seems to have been largely abandoned and its name forgotten. No memory of it survived in local tradition, and the 'City of the Ethiopians' was lost to the world's knowledge until the revival of classical learning made it known once again through the pages of Herodotus and Strabo. Even then it was often dismissed as fable: not until the end of the 18th century was the legend of Meroë invested with any substance. In 1772 the quixotic explorer James Bruce came upon the 'heaps of broken pedestals and pieces of obelisks' near the modern village of Bagrawiya, and wrote in his journal that 'it is impossible to avoid risking a guess that this is the ancient city of Meroë'.[1] The subsequent discovery of the remains at Napata, while verifying beyond question the existence of an ancient Nubian civilization, left some doubt as to which of its main centres was the 'capital' known to Herodotus. The matter was not finally settled until

[1] *Travels*, vol. 4, pp. 538–9.

1910, when excavations by the University of Liverpool Expedition (directed by Garstang) encountered the name Meroë in numerous inscriptions in the southern city.[1]

The new civilisation which filled the void left by Meroë was based on the city of Axum in the highlands of Abyssinia, 80 miles south of modern Asmara. Historical material is scanty, but it is clear that as Meroë declined in importance Axum grew in strength and influence. Like Meroë, Axum was less isolated from the mainstream of civilisation than is often thought and than Abyssinia subsequently became. The Horn of Africa was at the crossroads of traffic between the Mediterranean world and the Indian Ocean. Under the rule of the Hellenised Ptolemaic dynasty in Egypt the culture of the Mediterranean penetrated far to the south by land and sea. By the middle of the third century BC Ptolemy III Euergetes (247–221) had extended his influence as far as Axumite territory. The Jewish religion, which at this period was becoming well known in the Greek- and Latin-speaking world, was caught up in this process and 'it seems reasonable to suppose that Jews had penetrated as far as Upper Egypt, Nubia and possibly beyond' in pre-Christian times.[2]

It is against the background of the history of the ancient Near East that the story of both Ethiopian Judaism and Christianity has to be considered. And in that context the Solomon–Sheba legend occupies a unique place for it is basic to the history of the royal house around which the structure of the state developed in a manner which was remarkable even by feudal standards. No other royal dynasty has seriously claimed descent from the ancient kings of Israel nor, by inference, to a blood relationship with the founder of Christianity.

King Solomon reigned from about BC 961 to 922, or perhaps ten years earlier, while the first Book of Kings, which records the events of his reign, was probably edited shortly before the Babylonian exile. This leaves between the events themselves and their commitment to writing a gap of some three hundred years, which would allow ample scope for the development of tradition and legend. Moreover, the writings would doubtless reflect 'the later age in which they were composed as much as they mirror the time in which the principal subject lived'.[3]

While Solomon was an historical figure, the same cannot be said

[1]Adams, *Nubia*, p. 295.
[2]*Ethiopia and the Bible*, p. 16.
[3]*Solomon and Sheba*, ed. J. B. Pritchard, p. 31.

of the Queen of Sheba. There is little doubt that there is a kernel of truth in the story of her journey but it is not impossible that its date has been adjusted to coincide with Solomon's reign and thus to add yet more glory and importance to it. This is not an uncommon phenomenon. For instance, Professor J. B. Segal cites the example of a legend which grew up around the first king to be converted to Christianity.[1] His name was Abgar and about the year 200 he ruled the kingdom of Edessa, the modern Urfa, in Asia Minor. In the process of story-telling and, perhaps, to lend weight to the account of the conversion, the event was attributed to the reign of an earlier Abgar, roughly contemporary with Jesus, and after a short while letters were circulating which were said to have passed between the two. Another example, taken from Ethiopian history, of what A. H. M. Jones calls 'a very common tendency of popular history to attach famous events to famous names'[2] occurs in the traditional account of the conversion of Abyssinia to Christianity, as we shall see in the next chapter.

About two hundred years after Solomon, the Egyptians, under their Ethiopian, or Nubian, pharaohs, were attempting to build a defensive alliance to ward off the threat from Assyria with the help of small states such as Israel and Judah. It was a feature of Nubian society at that time that while it 'was by no means matriarchal, there can be no doubt that queens enjoyed an unusually high place both as consorts and as dowagers ... and it is evident that they often acted as counsellors, and sometimes as regents, for their sons'.[3] Tirhaka, who had been contemptuously called a broken reed by the Assyrian rabshakeh, records in one of his inscriptions that he summoned his mother all the way from Napata to be present at his coronation in Egypt.[4]

Can we not suppose – though admittedly it is pure conjecture – that after his coronation ceremonies were over the newly crowned pharaoh might have asked his mother to lead a delegation to King Hezekiah to invite him to join the alliance? Moreover, by the time that the queen mother had reached Thebes from Napata for the coronation she was half-way to Jerusalem and, perhaps, the most arduous part of the journey was accomplished. Her gifts of gold, spices and precious stones, all of which were available in Nubia and Upper Egypt, would come in useful in building a treaty of

[1] *Edessa*, p. 64.
[2] *A History of Ethiopia*, p. 29.
[3] W. Y. Adams, *Nubia*, p. 260.
[4] It is thought that the reference in 2 Kings 19:9 to Tirhaka as a king is probably an error as he had not by then ascended the throne but was commanding the army (ibid., p. 709).

friendship. Such an explanation is more convincing than the notion of a great queen undertaking a long and dangerous journey to ask a distant monarch a few riddles. Nor, with the lapse of time between the event and its recording, is it difficult to see how the visit might have come to be associated with the charismatic King Solomon rather than a less glamorous if no less worthy successor.

In contrast to the suggestion of a political motive for the Queen of Sheba's journey, some writers have suggested – on the assumption that she was an Arabian and not an African ruler – that the visit was prompted by economic considerations, due to the increasing maritime trade in the Red Sea in competition with the overland route from the Yemen. The traditional Red Sea traffic, however, was not only coastal but was more far-ranging and largely concerned with countries bordering the Indian Ocean. It was older than the reign of King Solomon. On the other hand, Sabaean prosperity in south Arabia, which depended largely on the overland incense routes, was developed at a much later period. Nor was Solomon the only Israelite ruler who was interested in the Red Sea trade and the port facilities in the Gulf of Aqaba. For example, 100 years after Solomon King Uzziah (Azariah) 'built Eloth and restored it to Judah',[1] while Jehoshaphat, an earlier king, 'made ships of Tharshish to go to Ophir for gold', though admittedly they failed to make the voyage.[2] These monarchs recognised, like the modern rulers of Israel, the commercial and strategic value of access to the Red Sea. At times – as in the case of Solomon – they developed, in alliance with the Phoenicians, a flourishing entrepot trade by exploiting the Sinai land bridge between the Red Sea and the Mediterranean as well as, perhaps, operating the nearby copper mines at Timna.

Egyptian inscriptions and reliefs, especially those at Queen Hatshepsut's temple at Deir el Bahri with their detailed and beautiful illustrations of the maritime expedition to Punt (Somalia), also emphasise the significance of the Red Sea trade route. The temple was built about 1480 BC, five hundred years before Solomon. If the suggestion promoted by Immanuel Velikowsky, in his *Ages in Chaos*, were accepted, that this eighteenth-dynasty Egyptian queen should be identified with the Queen of Sheba, it would require a complete rewriting of the usual conventions of Egyptian chronology.

The concept that the Queen of Sheba came from Ethiopia is basic to the country's tradition and is repeatedly affirmed in the

[1] 2 Chronicles 26:2.
[2] 1 Kings 22:48.

Kebra Nagast, or Glory of Kings, which expounds three principal ideas. First, that the queen journeyed to the Holy Land and returned to her country convinced of the truth of the Jewish religion, which she adopted. Second, that Menelik, the child of her liaison with the King of Israel, visited his father in Jerusalem when he was grown up and, escorted by a select band of young Israelites, brought back to his homeland the original Ark of the Covenant containing the tablets of the Law. Third, that Ethiopia 'was specially chosen by God to be the new home of the spiritual and heavenly Zion, of which his chosen people, the Jews, had become unworthy'.[1] This is the core of the tradition on which the Christian state of Ethiopia was built, as ancient Rome was built on the legends of Romulus and Remus.

Whether the queen's journey took place in the tenth century or the eighth is less important than the event itself, though the story becomes vastly more colourful by placing it in Solomon's reign rather than in Hezekiah's. Moreover, seen through the eyes of an Ethiopian – Christian or Jew – the notion that the Queen of Sheba was a Sabaean, who returned to Arabia after visiting Solomon, would destroy the whole foundation on which his history was built and would deprive the *Kebra Nagast* of its authority. The national saga proclaims that it was Ethiopia which became the new Zion, the resting-place of the Ark of the Covenant and the seat of the direct descendant of Solomon. It was not simply from vanity that the emperors took the title 'Conquering Lion of the Tribe of Judah, Elect of God'. It meant what it said.

In the process of time, the story of the queen's visit was inevitably enriched with a wealth of legend and mythology. Throughout the ages it has made such a strong popular appeal that it is found, adapted to the requirements of its environment, in Ethiopian, Jewish, Muslim and Christian traditions. The case for an Ethiopian – that is a Meroitic or Cushite – origin accords with Jewish and Ethiopian traditions, though not with Islamic writings and later European works. In the eighteenth century the English scholar William Whiston, who translated Josephus's *Antiquities of the Jews* (1737), added this comment to the story of Solomon:

That this queen of Sheba was a queen of Sabaea in South Arabia and not of Egypt and Ethiopia ... is, I suppose, now generally agreed. And since Sabaea is well known to be a country near the sea in the south of Arabia Felix, which lay south from Judea also;

[1] Budge, *The Queen of Sheba and her only son Menyelek*, p. xxxiv.

and since our Saviour calls this queen, 'the queen of the south' and says 'she came from the utmost parts of the earth', which descriptions agree better to this Arabia than to Egypt and Ethiopia, there is little occasion for doubting in this matter.[1]

Wallis Budge, who translated the *Kebra Nagast* into English in 1922, also thought it was doubtful whether the queen was an Ethiopian and far more probable that her home was in south-west Arabia, but, he added, 'her ancestors may have been merely settlers in Arabia, and some of them of Ethiopian origin'.[2]

It is thought that the *Kebra Nagast* was not transcribed from an oral source until the sixth century AD, when it was probably written in Coptic. It was translated into Arabic in the fourteenth century and soon afterwards into Ethiopic by a scholar named Isaac. In the process of establishing what has come to be regarded as the authorised version there was ample scope for introducing transformations and additions to suit the wishes of the royal dynasty and the church authorities. Although the saga does not hesitate to castigate 'the wickedness of the iniquitous Jews' and to describe them as 'the enemies of God',[3] it makes it abundantly clear that the Queen of Sheba was converted to the Mosaic faith. She said to Solomon, we are told:

> ... from this moment I will not worship the sun but will worship the Creator of the sun, the God of Israel. And that Tabernacle of the God of Israel shall be unto me my Lady, and unto my seed after me, and unto all my kingdoms that are under my dominion. And because of this I have found favour before thee, and before the God of Israel my Creator, who hath brought me unto thee, and hath made me to hear thy voice, and hath shown me thy face, and hath made me to understand thy commandment.[4]

Such a declaration of faith by the queen who is regarded as the foundress of the nation surely helps to explain how the precepts of the Old Testament have come to occupy such a dominant position in Ethiopian life and culture.

The Solomon–Sheba story is a favourite subject of Ethiopian art, reproduced in great variety in innumerable paintings which place great importance on the circumstances of the birth of

[1]*Antiquities of the Jews*, bk 8, ch. 6.
[2]Budge, op. cit., p. xxxv.
[3]ibid., p. 225.
[4]ibid., p. 29

Menelik I. While the queen was staying in Solomon's palace, runs the legend, the king, fascinated by her beauty and her intellect, made advances which she resisted. Eventually, the king made a promise that he would not touch her provided that she agreed not to take anything from his palace. One night he ordered his cooks to serve an exceptionally highly spiced meal. After everyone had retired to sleep the queen was desperate for a drink and poured herself a cupful of water from a pitcher which had been temptingly left in her room. The wily king, watching from behind a curtain, saw her take a drink – and thus remove something from the palace – and immediately challenged her to fulfil her part of the bargain. She conceded defeat and nine months later, after she had returned to Ethiopia, she bore a child whom she called Menelik, meaning the son of the wise man.[1]

When the boy grew up, we are told, he expressed a desire to visit his father. His mother encouraged him and presented him with a ring she had received from Solomon with which he could identify himself. The king welcomed his son most warmly and showed him every kindness and affection. In due course, when the time came for Menelik to leave his father provided an escort drawn from the sons of the country's nobility to accompany him to Ethiopia. The young men, however, decided that, in addition to the parting gifts they had already received, they would take with them the Ark of the Covenant containing the tablets of the Law which reposed in the Temple. Surreptitiously, this most holy object of veneration was removed at night and by the time the theft had been discovered the party was well on its way and its recapture impossible. When the escort arrived at the queen's court, the Ark, which was treated with the utmost reverence, was deposited in the capital, Axum, and eventually, after the country had adopted Christianity, it found its place in the Cathedral, where it is believed to remain until this day. Though Ethiopian history is vague about what happened in the centuries between Solomon and the Christian era the moral of the story is clear: Axum, which probably did not exist as a city in Solomon's day, had become the new Zion. On Menelik's return to Ethiopia the queen abdicated in his favour, the Ethiopians adopted the Mosaic religion and Menelik became the first king of the Solomonic line and an adherent of the new faith. The youthful escort, followers of the God of Israel, formed the nucleus of a Jewish community which remained loyal to Judaism.

[1] According to Budge, op. cit., p. lxxi, the name comes from the Amharic *Bayna Lehkem = Ibn al-Hakim* (in Arabic) = son of the wise man.

In Jewish folklore, stories about the Queen of Sheba do not appear until the later Midrashim, or biblical explanations. The most important source, says Ullendorff,[1] is the *Targum Sheni*, or interpretation to the Book of Esther, whose date is somewhere between 500 and 1000 AD. This story tells how King Solomon, who held command over birds and beasts, was informed by a hoopoe, one of the most attractive of subtropical birds, that it had found a country in the east full of gold and silver and watered from the garden of Eden; its ruler was the Queen of Sheba. The king instructed the hoopoe to deliver a message to the queen inviting her to visit him. When she complied she found the king sitting on a throne apparently surrounded by water, which in reality was glass. She lifted her skirt to approach the throne and in doing so exposed her hairy legs – some versions say they were the legs of a goat. Solomon remarked: 'Thy beauty is the beauty of women, but thy hair is the hair of man; while hair is an ornament to a man, it is a disfigurement to a woman.'[2] She then proceeded to ask the riddles with which she intended to test his wisdom but there is no mention of carnal relations.

Though we may doubt whether the Queen of Sheba came from Arabia or lived in Axum or visited King Solomon, it is possible that she belonged to the royal family of Meroë. It is interesting to observe that in the *Kebra Nagast* she is often called Candace, which was a Meroitic, not an Abyssinian, royal title. Similarly, we may question whether the Jewish religion could have reached Axum by the tenth century BC, while recognising that it could have penetrated as far as Napata, the first Meroitic capital, before the fall of Jerusalem in 586 BC.

Evidence on which to base a firm conclusion about Jewish penetration is scarce but, fortunately, the Bible comes to our assistance. There are three references which throw some light on the subject and all belong to the same period when the Middle East was in ferment and the great powers of the day were struggling for supremacy. In Palestine, Solomon's successors had partitioned the Kingdom into Judah and Israel. The latter had been conquered and its people taken into captivity by the Assyrians. The Jewish diaspora had begun and the Prophets were already calling for a return of the exiles to the homeland.

Zephaniah was among the first to take up the cause. He is described as 'the son of Cushi',[3] which would seem to indicate that he himself had some family connection with Ethiopia. He refers

[1] *Ethiopia and the Bible*, p. 138.
[2] Ginzberg, *Legends of the Bible* (1956), p. 560.
[3] Zephaniah 1:1.

to a diaspora in Cush: 'From beyond the rivers of Cush my
suppliants, my dispersed community shall bring my offering.'¹ If
Cush is understood to be Meroë the reference to the rivers is apt,
since much of the country was virtually enclosed by the great
waters of the Nile and the Atbara, thus almost forming an inland
island, or *Gezireh*, like the similar area between the Blue and White
Niles. Zephaniah was a contemporary of Josiah (*c*. 640–609 BC),
the King of Judah who unwisely fought against the Egyptian
pharaoh, Necho, and was killed at Megiddo (2 Kings 23:29). And
it was Necho who, as related by Herodotus, built a canal which
connected the Nile with the Red Sea, though in fact there had been
a canal even before his time. Necho also gave great encouragement
to navigation and it was during his reign that his ships, manned by
Phoenician sailors setting out from the Red Sea, achieved the
remarkable feat of circumnavigating Africa.

Not less relevant is the oft-quoted eleventh chapter of the Book
of Isaiah in which the Prophet forecast the day (verse 6) when

. . . the wolf also shall dwell with the lamb and the leopard shall
lie down with the kid and the calf and the young lion and the
fatling together and a little child shall lead them . . . And it shall
come to pass in that day that the Lord shall set his hand again the
second time to recover the remnant of his people which shall be
left from Assyria and from Egypt and from Pathros [Upper
Egypt] and from Cush [Ethiopia] and from Elam [east of
Babylonia] and from Shinnar [Babylonia] and from Hamath
[central Syria] and from the islands of the sea [the Mediter-
ranean]. And he shall . . . assemble the outcasts of Israel and
gather together the dispersed of Judah from the four corners
of the earth.²

Clearly, the diaspora had already reached much of the known
world, including the country known in Greek as Ethiopia.

The Prophet Jeremiah,³ too, refers to 'all the Jews which dwelt
in the land of Egypt . . . and in the country of Pathros', where,
on its southern frontier, at Elephantine, near the modern Aswan,
a military outpost manned by foreign mercenaries, including
Jews, had been established to defend 'the gateway of Africa'
especially against marauding Ethiopians. Jeremiah could have
had this distant community in mind when he mentioned the Jews
of Pathros.

¹ibid., 3:10.
²Verses 11, 12 and Peake 431g.
³44:1.

Our knowledge of this settlement derives from the papyri and ostraca written in Aramaic which were found in its ruins at the beginning of the present century. They were composed in the fifth century BC when the community was already well established and have been compared in importance with the Dead Sea Scrolls, written 400 years later, discovered at Qumran. The documents throw a vivid light on the everyday life of a Jewish community living in the Diaspora a long way from Jerusalem. They depict the domestic scene, including legal contracts and religious observances, and describe a temple of the same dimensions and plan as the Solomonic Temple in Jerusalem, which was erected for the worship of the one God and the practice of Judaism. The papyri can only give a partial picture of life in the garrison town but they demonstrate, among other things, that 'Passover, like the Sabbath, was taken for granted as a regular feature of religious life'.[1] A letter dealing with the observance of Passover can be accurately dated to 419 BC, 'the fifth year of Darius [II]'. There is nothing about the Sabbath in the papyri but, referring to the more personal letters inscribed on ostraca, or potsherds, Porten makes the homely comment that it 'appears to have been honoured more in the breach than in the observance'.[2]

At Elephantine the Jews had built their own temple and practiced sacrificial rites in accordance with biblical teaching. Porten has therefore concluded that the community was founded before the promulgation of Deuteronomy in 621, during the reign of King Josiah,[3] which means that it predates the Babylonian Exile and the limitation of the sacrificial cult to Jerusalem.[4] This would seem to show that it was already in existence at the time when Zephaniah was speaking about a dispersed community even further south 'beyond the rivers of Cush'. Moreover, documentary evidence proves that the temple had been built prior to the Persian conquest of Egypt in 525, for in one of the papyri it is written that 'our forefathers built this Temple in the fortress of Elephantine back in the days of the kingdom of Egypt and when Cambyses came to Egypt he found it built'.[5] Porten has suggested that the community was established about 650 BC. The erection of a temple (as distinct from a synagogue) and the practice of animal sacrifices was looked at askance after the Exile by the priestly

---

[1] Bezalel Porten, *Archives from Elephantine*, p. 131.
[2] ibid., p. ix; cf. Ullendorff, *Ethiopia and the Bible*, p. 16: 'There is no mention of the Sabbath in the Elephantine papyri.'
[3] Peake, 231c.
[4] Porten, p. 13 (cf. Deut. 12).
[5] ibid., p. 291.

authorities in Jerusalem,[1] who considered that they had a monopoly in these matters.

The papyri – which date from the post-Exilic period – show that
intermarriage was not unusual and, according to Porten,

> ... took place in the families of the lay leadership and Temple
> officialdom. Having long since adopted Aramaic – the *lingua
> franca* of the Persian Empire – as their spoken language and the
> language of their private letters and notes, the Elephantine Jews
> were apparently not overly concerned that their children could
> not speak the language of Judah. Untroubled by the fear of a
> second expulsion from the promised land – a fear which plagued
> some of the pious of Judah – and united around their own
> Temple, the Elephantine Jews apparently felt capable of absorb-
> ing a small number of pagans into their community.[2]

Intermarriage between Jews and Gentiles was not infrequent in
pre-Exilic times but it became a controversial issue after the return
from Babylon. In post-Talmudic times it was rigorously forbidden by the rabbinic authorities unless the non-Jewish partner
was converted strictly in accordance with the laws of the
Halachah.[3]

> There must have been some ceremony by which a newcomer
> indicated abandonment of his polytheistic practices and adop-
> tion of Judaism. The pagans who intermarried in Judah
> apparently became Jews. Those who wanted to join Zerubbabel
> in the building of the Temple claimed 'We worship (seek) your
> God as you do' (Ezra 4,2) ... Two distinctive signs of the
> covenant between God and Israel were circumcision and the
> Sabbath and it is likely that circumcision and Sabbath obser-
> vance were required of male proselytes. The fact that Egyptians
> practiced circumcision and that some of them refrained from
> eating pork (Herodotus II,47) may have served to facilitate
> proselytization. One marrying into the Jewish community
> might adopt a Hebrew name, not as a ritual of conversion, but as
> a matter of onomastic assimilation ... Many who intermarried
> did not change their names; however, they may have had two
> names as Jews had elsewhere in the diaspora.[4]

[1]ibid., p. 133.
[2]ibid., p. 350.
[3]cf. Peake, 332f: 'mixed marriages were never so strongly objected to by the
Jews as they were by their political and religious leaders'.
[4]Porten, p. 251.

All this is remarkably reminiscent of the life of the Falashas today. True, they have no temple but they have retained aspects of temple worship such as animal sacrifice, purification with the ashes of a red heifer and prostration before the Ark and in prayer.[1] They do not share the rabbinic opposition to intermarriage, which they practise freely provided the partner adopts the Jewish religion by a simple, though meaningful conversion ceremony,[2] and they take both biblical and Ethiopian names. Like the ancient Egyptians, the Copts (who are Christians) as well as the Muslims practise circumcision and abhor pork, which makes proselytisation easier. A number of Jewish-Aramaic words have entered the Ge'ez (ancient Ethiopic) language which 'belong to the pre-Christian Jewish leaven in Ethiopia'.[3] If that leaven entered Ethiopia from the Nile valley, and not from Arabia, we must look to the Elephantine community as the source of that linguistic infiltration.

In these circumstances, it is surprising that Professor Ullendorff, quoting with approval the views of Conti Rossini, concluded that 'such aspects of Elephantine religious life as emerge from the papyri are in sharp contrast to the entire cast of religious expression among the Falashas in particular and the Judaizing trends of the Abyssinian Church in general. This estimate remains true even when the fullest allowances are made for the inevitable deficiencies in our knowledge of the Elephantine community.'[4]

Herodotus has described[5] how, in the reign of Pharaoh Psammetichus III, who was subsequently dethroned by the Persian conqueror Cambyses, a garrison at Elephantine, not having been relieved for three years, revolted and migrated to Ethiopia. As the documents show that the Jewish community was already in existence by then, and that it formed part of the garrison, it is quite possible – if not probable – (*pace* Ullendorff) that this group of emigrants contained some Jews.

There are no records to show how long the Elephantine Jewish community lasted nor whether it survived the passing of Persian rule and the turbulent period which preceded Alexander the Great's conquest in 332 BC. The last Egyptian pharaoh before the coming of the Greeks, Nekhtharehbe, fled to Ethiopia about 340

[1]Leslau, *Coutumes et Croyances des Falashas* (Paris 1957), pp. 68, 72 and 73.
[2]ibid., p. 73.
[3]*Ethiopia and the Bible*, p. 124.
[4]*Ethiopia and the Bible*, pp. 16–17. This view is supported by Maxime Rodinson in 'Sur la Question des Influences Juives en Ethiopie' (*JSS* vol. 9, no. 1, 1964, p. 16) but is opposed by 'the deservedly great authority' of Ignazio Guidi in *Storia della letteratura etiopica*, p. 95.
[5]Book II, 30.

and the Elephantine Jews, like earlier discontented soldiery, may have followed his example and, perhaps, linked up with whatever co-religionists were already established there.

The papyri report a contemporary incident which occurred about a hundred years after Cambyses and which illustrates the good relations which existed at that period with the Persians whose generally sympathetic attitude had already been demonstrated by Cyrus in allowing the Jews to return to Judah from captivity in Babylon. In the year 410 the Elephantine Temple was destroyed by a band of Egyptians led by the priests of the temple of the god Khnum on the opposite side of the street. The attack seems to have been the culmination of a long-standing state of friction between the two religious houses which may have been exacerbated by the offence caused to the Egyptians' ram god by the Jews' custom of sacrificing lambs at Passover. In any event, the Jews petitioned the Persians and after much delay the Satrap of Samaria, called Sanballat, who is mentioned in the Book of Nehemiah,[1] gave orders that the Egyptians were to rebuild the temple at their own cost and that the culprits were to be severely punished. The religious authorities in Jerusalem, however, took the opportunity to inform the leaders of the Elephantine community that in future, though they might offer up meal offering and incense in the temple, they were not to make animal sacrifices. It is not clear why this restriction was imposed but three possible explanations have been suggested by Porten: 'the omission was a concession to Egyptian susceptibilities (no more sacrifice of the ram), to Persian susceptibilities (no more profaning of fire), a compromise between the latitudinarian Samaritans and the restrictive Judahites'.[2] Whatever the explanation, the report throws a most interesting light on Jewish communal life in a distant corner of the Diaspora nearly five hundred years before the conquest of Jerusalem by Titus.

When Strabo, the Greek historian and geographer who lived in the first century BC, was writing about Ethiopia he mentioned a colony of Egyptians living on an island far up the Nile who had gone to Meroë 'as exiles from Psammeticus and are called Sembritae, as being foreigners',[3] and were governed by a queen. These sound very much like the former members of the Elephantine garrison mentioned by Herodotus and, if so, it is remarkable that after five hundred years they should still have retained their separate identity as well as their sobriquet. Indeed, one may

[1] 2: 10.
[2] op. cit., p. 293.
[3] *The Geography of Strabo*, 16, 4, 8; see also Afterword, p. 177.

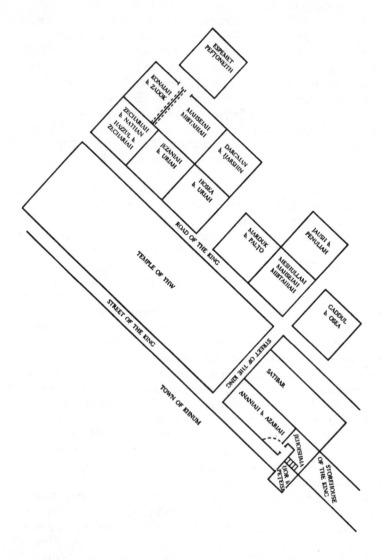

Plan showing the position of the Jewish Temple at Elephantine and the surrounding buildings. The Temple's orientation was towards Jerusalem and its dimensions approximated those of the Solomonic Temple.

from B. Porten, *Archives from Elephantine*, by courtesy of University of California Press

wonder whether, following the southward trend of civilisation along the Blue Nile, some of them may have moved on, perhaps as far as Sennar and later found their name translated into Ge'ez as Falasha, also meaning a stranger, not in a derogatory but in a literal sense as an exile from the Holy Land.

It would have been impossible for the descendants of the small Elephantine community, far removed from its roots in Jerusalem, to have survived if it had not admitted proselytes who became fully-fledged Jews by religion in accordance with the precepts of the Torah. James Parkes has pointed out that 'in the historical narrative of the Old Testament there is little reference to the conversion of non-Israelites. On the other hand, the successive editions of the legal codes recognised that a "stranger" could be joined to the community of Israel; birth was not the only means of entry.'[1] He goes on to explain that the 'exclusive connection between the God of Israel, the Children of Israel, and the soil of Israel, was broken by two developments. The first was the universalism of the great prophets and their vision of the time when many nations would gather together for worship in Jerusalem; and the second was the dispersion of a large section of the Children of Israel themselves into foreign lands. Both developments encouraged a missionary attitude to the foreign environment of Judaism. The natural theatre for such activities was the diaspora.'

Before the arrival of militant and aggressive religions, Jews were inclined to be missionaries, eager to spread a knowledge of the Torah and to enlist recruits to the Jewish way of life. It was the rise and domination first of Christianity and then of Islam which effectively put an end to this activity and turned the Jewish people, in self-defence, into an inward-looking community.

Proselytism in the Roman period, according to Salo Baron, 'must have been a tremendous force in Jewish life. Although there were no professional missionaries, uninterrupted religious propaganda seems to have gone on throughout the dispersion'[2] – a dispersion that began long before the fall of Jerusalem. How else, except as a result of conversion on a massive scale, is it possible to explain the size of the Diaspora at this time when it far outnumbered the Jewish population of Palestine? It is estimated that there were 8 million Jews in the world in the first century while the population of Palestine was approximately 2½ million including some half million Samaritans, Greeks and Nabateans.[3]

[1] *The Foundations of Judaism and Christianity*, p. 109.
[2] S. W. Baron, *A Social and Religious History of the Jews*, vol. 1, p. 172.
[3] ibid., p. 168.

In the Mediterranean countries east of Italy, excluding Palestine, where their settlement was most dense, the Jewish population represented as much as one-fifth of the total number of inhabitants.

The world situation, as Baron has indicated, was propitious for the spread of new ideas and 'Judaism found a great opportunity. It appealed strongly to generations in which the craving for the supernatural was coupled with a wish for a rational understanding of life, and dominated by a desire for moral rules which, while simple and easily grasped, were firmly rooted in the realm of the infinite. What Judaism brought to a religiously minded Hellenist was in some ways less, in others more than mere philosophy.'[1] It caught on apace though one major obstacle, the necessity for circumcision, deterred many Greeks and Romans because of the 'open derision of the protagonists at every subsequent gymnastic performance by them in the stadium'. This, however, was no hindrance to Egyptians, Meroites or Phoenicians, who had practised the rite for ages, nor for the Syrian women, who 'seem to have adopted Judaism in large numbers, as frequently happens in all religious conversions'.[2]

Both Judaism and the Jewish people expanded by the absorption of large numbers of people who could not be described as racially Jews but who, 'through a conscious process of assimilation', says Baron, were expected to divest themselves of all former ethnic characteristics and gradually to become ethnic Jews.[3] In this way the Jewish religion was spread, chiefly by a process of cultural diffusion, while migration, either from one country of the Diaspora to another or from Palestine as a result of the Roman conquest, also played a role.

At the same time Hellenistic culture was spreading far and wide. It is probable that the southern limit of its penetration into the heart of Africa, passing through Meroë in the Nile basin, was drawn at Axum in the Abyssinian highlands. Here Greek became the language of the court and here, suggests Baron, 'Judaism must have been firmly established during the Second Commonwealth, or else the Falasha Jews could not have remained until to-day ignorant of the festivals of Hanukkah and Purim.'[4] This is in contrast, it may be added, to the rabbinical Judaism of the

[1]ibid., p. 173.
[2]ibid., p. 177.
[3]ibid., p. 181.
[4]ibid., p. 169. This proposition requires modification in view of Leslau's assertion that the Feast of Esther (Purim) is celebrated by the Falashas (see below, p. 69). The festival of Hanukkah (or Chanukah), on the other hand, was instituted in Talmudic times and passed the Falashas by.

Yemenites on the other side of the Red Sea. Although, in Ptolemaic times, a trade route to Axum was established by way of the port of Adulis, there is no reason why communication from Egypt should not also have followed the traditional route along the Nile, taking advantage of the facilities provided by the Meroitic kingdom. Perhaps it is not without significance that practically every one of the innumerable Ethiopian pictures illustrating the story of Solomon and Sheba shows the queen travelling by reed boat on the Nile past the pyramids and following the route taken until recent times by Christian pilgrims going to Jerusalem. If, as seems likely, Jews moved southwards from Egypt in search of trade or to escape persecution they may well have settled for a time in Meroë, which could offer plenty of opportunities.

The Old Testament is not in a position to throw light on Jewish history after the fourth century BC but a well-known story in the Acts of the Apostles is revealing. It is related that St Philip, one of the seven Hellenist evangelists, was on his way from Jerusalem to Gaza when he met 'a man from Ethiopia, an eunuch of great authority under Candace, Queen of the Ethiopians, who had the charge of all her treasure and had come to Jerusalem for to worship'.[1] When Philip saw him he was sitting in his chariot puzzling over a text in the book of Isaiah. The evangelist offered to explain the passage and then proceeded to tell him of the new teachings which were circulating in Jerusalem. The upshot of their conversation was that, on seeing a nearby stream, the eunuch invited Philip to baptise him and then they parted and went their separate ways.

There can, of course, be no doubt (provided that the story is not purely legendary) that the eunuch came from the Meroitic kingdom though it may be thought that, in obedience to the biblical injunction about mutilation, he would be debarred from participating in the religious rites in the Temple, for which he had come to Jerusalem. The term 'eunuch' was, however, sometimes used in a wider sense to mean a high court official.[2] It has also been suggested that he might have belonged to the class of 'God-fearers, Gentile adherents of Judaism who did not or could not become actual proselytes'.[3] The name 'Candace', moreover, does not represent a specific queen but, like the Egyptian word 'pharaoh', was a generic term used in the Meroitic kingdom as a title for queen or queen mother and, according to Ullendorff, 'is almost

[1] Acts 8:27.
[2] See Peake, 170e.
[3] Peake, 782k.

certainly the Meroitic Katake',[1] which was later possibly cor-
rupted into Makeda, one of the names by which the Queen of
Sheba is called in the *Kebra Nagast*. The ruler in this story was
tentatively identified by Arkell as Queen Amanitere, who reigned
approximately from 15 BC to AD 15.

At the moment when he met St Philip the eunuch was studying
Chapter 53, verses 7–8, of the Book of Isaiah in the Greek
Septuagint version:[2] 'He was led as a sheep to the slaughter; and as
a lamb before his shearer is dumb, so he openeth not his mouth.' It
is clear that while he had left his home an adherent of Judaism he
returned as a Christian convert. It is unlikely that he lived in
religious isolation or that he was not part of a larger Jewish
community. Like the settlements around the Mediterranean,
which receive much attention in the New Testament, one may
suppose that this one also would have been composed largely of
proselytes who would have been more familiar with the Bible in
its Greek translation than with the Hebrew original. As for the
eunuch's mission, is it not possible that he was engaged on a
diplomatic errand to discuss with the Jews of Palestine the
possibility of concerted action against the common Roman foe
and had seized the opportunity to strengthen his religious
affiliation? News of the Zealot party in Palestine, which represented a resistance movement against Roman rule, could have
reached as far as Meroë which itself was under pressure from the
aggressive Roman armies which, in 23 BC, had sacked the former
capital of Napata.[3]

Some writers have conjectured that references to the Trogodytes and a people called the Coloboi (meaning mutilated), living
in the Red Sea coastal region and mentioned in the writings of the
historians Diodorus Siculus[4] and Strabo,[5] in the first century BC,
refer to Jews because they were circumcised 'like the Egyptians'.
Apart from this their customs appear to have nothing in common
with Jewish rites, though Strabo has a curious reference to another
coastal people whom he calls 'Creophagi [meat-eaters] of whom
the males have their sexual glands mutilated and the women are
excised in the Jewish fashion',[6] though the latter is decidedly not a
traditional Jewish practice.

On the eastern side of the Red Sea a series of states had

[1]*Ethiopia and the Bible*, pp. 142f.
[2]Hastings's *Dictionary of the Bible*, i, 790.
[3]Adams, p. 340.
[4]Book III, 32. The spelling of Trogodytes is that deliberately adopted by the translator, C. H. Oldfather.
[5]Book XVI, 4, 5.
[6]ibid., 4, 9.

established themselves in what is today the Yemen, some in succession to others, some contemporaneously. The first people to make their mark seem to have been the Minaeans, with their capital at Ma'in, whose king lists probably go back to the thirteenth century BC,[1] followed by the Sabaeans who, in the eighth century BC, coming from the north of the Arabian peninsula, settled around their capital at Marib to the east of present-day Sanaa. The Sabaeans are mentioned in the Book of Job (1:15) in the context of nomads who add to his afflictions, and it was from their country that the Queen of Sheba has been supposed to have originated – notwithstanding the chronological disparity, since Solomon lived several centuries earlier than they attained any significance. Another country in this area, the independent kingdom of Qataban (Joktan of the genealogy of Noah mentioned in Genesis), was roughly contemporary with Saba. Subsequently, at a period approaching the Christian era, arose the kingdom of the Himyarites.

The Sabaeans have left behind a rich legacy of archaeological and palaeographic material and doubtless much still remains to be excavated. They established colonies on the western side of the Red Sea and, from about 450 to nearly 300 BC, when the settlements came to an end, Sabaean culture had a marked influence on Axumite civilisation, but the notion, propagated by Conti Rossini and others, that Abyssinian history virtually began with these south Arabian colonies is now being strongly challenged. So, too, is the theory that the ancient Ethiopic language, Ge'ez, owes its origin to the Sabaean tongue and that the migration of a so-called Habashi tribe from Arabia formed the nucleus of the Abyssinian people. A. K. Irvine has pointed out that there is no evidence either for the existence of such a tribe in Arabia or 'for all that has been attributed to it'.[2]

The states of south-west Arabia owed their prosperity chiefly to two factors. They occupied the fertile highlands watered by the monsoon rains and they lay athwart the land routes which carried the highly profitable trade in frankincense from the Hadhramaut to all parts of the Roman world. Thus the land not only acquired the name of Arabia Felix but also attracted the envious attention of the Roman authorities. In 24 BC, a year before the sack of Napata, Emperor Augustus dispatched an expedition from Egypt under Aelius Gallus to conquer the land of the Sabaeans.

[1] F. Stark, *The Southern Gates of Arabia*, p. 6.
[2] *J.S.S.* vol. 10, pp. 178–96. cf. also R. Schneider in *Documents Histoire Civilisation Éthiopienne*, Rcd 230, CNRS, VII, 1976, and Donald L. Levine, *Greater Ethiopia*, p. 199.

However, it was ill prepared and failed in its objective.

Josephus recounts[1] that King Herod supplied 500 chosen men from his bodyguard – whom Strabo described as Jews[2] – to join this expedition to the Red Sea, where they rendered great service. It is possible that some of the soldiers remained behind after the force was withdrawn and that they formed the nucleus of a Jewish community, though the main immigration of Jews into western Arabia and the Yemen probably took place a hundred years later after the destruction of the Second Temple.[3] Alternatively, some scholars believe that Jews may have arrived 200 years before Herod at the time of the anti-Jewish persecutions in Egypt under the brutish Ptolemy IV Philopator. A tradition among the Jews of Yemen even claims that they are descendants of those who accompanied the Queen of Sheba on her return from her visit to King Solomon,[4] which is an interesting example of an Abyssinian legend crossing the Red Sea and being adapted to local conditions. It is doubtful whether there was any significant Jewish presence in this area before the first century AD though, as Professor Ullendorff has remarked, 'while none of the Biblical references reveals any intimate and detailed knowledge of Arabia, and South Arabia in particular, they nevertheless give an indication of Jewish contact with that country'.[5] On the other hand, once Jews arrived in the Yemen they remained in close contact with their co-religionists in Palestine and no doubt their numbers greatly increased since, S. D. Goitein says, they 'proselytized vigorously in their country of adoption'[6] – until, that is, the arrival of Islam put a stop to such practices by making apostasy a capital offence. One feels tempted to inquire how Professor Goitein reconciles this statement with his subsequent remark, in the same essay, that 'the Yemenites may be called the most Jewish of all Jews, so that it is rather unlikely that all or even most of them should be the offspring of Himyarites, for Judaism used to be essentially the religion of a people, not one adopted by conversion'.

No doubt scholars will for long be discussing which influences were paramount in shaping the forerunner of the modern Abyssinian state. Hitherto, it has been considered that south Arabian culture was dominant. The contrary view, strongly held by Bruce in the face of general opposition, that civilisation had

[1] *Antiquities of the Jews*, 15, ch. 9.
[2] Book XVI, ch. 4, p. 23.
[3] *Enc. Jud.*, vol. 16.
[4] S. Landshut, *Jewish Communities in the Muslim Countries of the Middle East*, p. 73.
[5] *Ethiopia and the Bible*, p. 17.
[6] In A. J. Arberry (ed.), *Religion in the Middle East*, vol. 1, p. 227.

travelled from west to east across the southern Red Sea rather than vice versa, was among the many factors, including his advocacy of an Ethiopian origin for the Queen of Sheba, which antagonised his contemporaries.

Now a reassessment is taking place and many former assumptions are being called in question. At the time when the Axumite state was being created there was no lack of communication between the two coasts of the southern Red Sea. The peoples of each side learned something from the other; cultural influences flowed freely. The close relationship between the ancient south Arabian language and Ethiopic had led Ullendorff to declare that 'it has long been almost axiomatic that the South Arabian immigrants imported into Africa a Semitic language ... which ... evolved into what we now call Ge'ez ... although there have at times been divergent views as to whether one or several of the South Arabian dialects were brought westwards across the Red Sea'.[1] In course of time Ge'ez became a 'dead' language, like Latin, and was used for literary and liturgical purposes, but it produced six 'living' languages of which the principal ones are Amharic, which for centuries had been the language of the Amhara Court and of the majority of the population of the central tableland, Tigrinya, and Tigre.

Today the claims of Africa to be considered as the original home of this linguistic group are attracting more attention. A. K. Irvine has stressed 'that the proof of the relationship between Ge'ez and Sabaean has not yet been presented'[2] while Grover Hudson goes further and says that 'the modern geographical distribution of Hamito-Semitic languages suggests a north-east African origin for the family, and Ethiopia would be the natural focus of the extension of the Semitic branch from such a centre of origin'.[3] He also quotes A. Murtonen, who reached what many would regard as a revolutionary conclusion that 'the original home of the Semitic speaking nations was probably the Horn of Africa'.[4]

It is not only in the field of linguistics that theories are developing which suggest that civilisation flowed eastwards from the Horn of Africa to south Arabia. At different periods movements of course took place in each direction but since the African side of the Red Sea, represented by the Nile basin, had a much older history of civilisation than the eastern side, it would be

[1]Ullendorff, *The Ethiopians*, pp. 118–19.
[2]'Linguistic Evidence on Ancient Ethiopia: The Relationship of Early Ethiopian Semitic to Old South Arabian', *Abbay*, no. 9, p. 43.
[3]*Folia Orientalia*, vol. 18, p. 159 (1977).
[4]ibid., p. 139.

ñatural for cultural development to spread from the older to the newer centre.

Hudson writes:

Building and agricultural practices, cattle keeping, socio-political organisation and writing have been named as the superior cultural element introduced into Axumite Ethiopia by South Arabians. Arguments have arisen that all of these except writing may now be considered native to Ethiopia or to North East Africa. As for writing, it is notable that the early inscriptions of South Arabia, of possibly the 8th but perhaps as late as the 5th century BC, are not significantly earlier, if at all, than the earliest Ethiopian inscriptions.[1]

The agricultural argument has been pursued by Christopher Ehret, who writes that:

the idea that agriculture in Ethiopia and the Horn is relatively recent and owes to Arabian influences can no longer be entertained in any form. That the plough, and the near eastern cereal cultivation associated with it, antedate the Sabaean intrusion can be demonstrated from comparative artefactual reconstruction; it is a necessary assumption from linguistic and other testimony as well. The inception of the use of the plough and of wheat and barley may date even several millennia before the South Arabian episode. Moreover, it can be argued on botanical grounds, cultivation of wheat and barley was itself preceded in the Horn by a still earlier indigenous cereal agriculture in which the staples would have been teff and/or eleusine (finger millet).[2]

Neville Chittick, the archaeologist, has written that 'grains of finger millet (*eleusine corocana*) were found in a stratum [near Axum] which is most likely to date from the third or fourth millennium BC. The grain thus seems to be the earliest African cultivated cereal yet identified.'[3]

Once again, Bruce displayed remarkable perspicacity when he described the movement of agricultural development from west to east and observed that the resin-producing trees which furnish myrrh and frankincense and are native to the Abyssinian and Somali coastal areas were introduced into Arabia in antiquity.

[1]ibid., p. 151.
[2]*On the Antiquity of Agriculture in Ethiopia* (1978).
[3]'Notes on the Archaeology of Northern Ethiopia', *Abbay*, no. 9, p. 15.

The frankincense trees (varieties of the *Burseraceae* family) have become fully naturalised in the Hadhramaut but myrrh (*Balsamodendronmyrrha*), as Bruce observed and Freya Stark[1] confirmed, has not succeeded there. The balsam tree (*Commiphora opobalsamum*), too, whose resin is used to make balm and was very highly prized as a medicament in ancient times, originated in Abyssinia and, says Bruce, was transplanted into Arabia and thence to Palestine, where it came to be known as Balm of Gilead. This was one of the products which was being carried from Gilead (east of the Jordan) to Egypt by the Ishmaelite camel caravan which purchased Joseph from his brothers after he had been thrown into a pit, as recounted in Genesis 37:25. Josephus mentioned a popular belief that the plant had been brought to Israel by the Queen of Sheba as a gift for Solomon,[2] while Strabo describes a park for growing balsam at Jericho.[3] Another Arabian agricultural import from Abyssinia was the coffee plant, which is a native of the province of Kaffa, from which some say it derives its name[4] and which came into European languages through the Arabic *Kahwah*. Until the end of the seventeenth century Yemen was the sole supplier of coffee on the world market, exporting it through the Red Sea port of Mocha, whose name came to be associated with the product itself. Yet another native Abyssinian plant which has become naturalised in the Yemen is the 'baneful little Qat tree'[5] (*Catha edulis*) whose leaves are chewed in vast quantities, especially in south-west Arabia, as a drug.

The generally held opinion that the ancient Abyssinian building technique, as expressed in the magnificent monuments of Axum of the fourth century AD, was introduced from southern Arabia is also undergoing a radical revision. Here again, modern scholarship had been anticipated to some degree by Bruce, who detected Egyptian influence at work, though admittedly he was far out in attributing the giant stelae to Ptolemy Euergetes, who ruled from 247 to 221 BC. Bruce may have been misled by the Greek inscription which both he and the French traveller Charles Poncet reported that they had seen at Axum, and which read 'Ptolemaioy Euergetou Basileos'.[6] There can be no doubt that Ptolemaic-Egyptian influences made themselves strongly felt in the Axumite kingdom and we know that both Ptolemies II and III organised

[1]*The Southern Gates of Arabia* (1936), p. 298. See also N. Groom, *Frankincense and Myrrh* (1981).
[2]*Antiquities of the Jews*, book VIII, ch. 6.
[3]XVI. 2. 41.
[4]F. R. Cana in *Enc. Brit.*, 11th edn. vol. 1.
[5]H. Scott, *In the High Yemen*, p. 95.
[6]*Travels*, vol. 3, p. 132.

expeditions to capture live elephants in the coastal regions.[1]
Nevertheless, the evidence of this inscription was surely insuffi-
cient to have led Bruce to assert that Ptolemy III Euergetes
conquered Axum and the neighbouring kingdom and 'resided
some time there'.[2]

Though the false stone windows in the peristyle hall of the
Sabaean temple at Marib in the Yemen, dating from the fifth
century BC, are strongly reminiscent of the false windows in the
great 'obelisk' of Axum, ancient Abyssinian architecture also
seems to owe much, as both Arkell[3] and Schoff[4] have suggested,
to the mixed influence of Egypt and India. Grover Hudson has
pointed out that archeological research 'for the past ten to fifteen
years has tended to emphasise the uniqueness of the Axumite
culture and to minimise ancient South Arabian influences'.[5]
Similarly, the great reservoir at Axum naturally recalls the ancient
water tanks at Aden or the ruined dam at Marib but, as Arkell has
explained, such reservoirs also exist in the 'island' of Meroë, where
they may have been constructed under influences coming into the
country via Axum from India, where such constructions 'have
long been an important method of storing rainwater'.[6]

Axum gained in strength as Meroë declined until it was ready to
step into the power vacuum which had been left. Records of this
period of Abyssinia's history are meagre but there is sufficient
evidence to show that its people were constantly in touch with the
centres of civilisation and were not isolated from the great
religious ferment which was manifesting itself throughout the
Roman Empire. Axum could not have attained its influential
position in the world if it had not had a firm base on which to
build. By the third century AD it was in control of the Red Sea area,
Western Arabia and Nubia[7] and had a reputation for running a
particularly impressive state. By the latter part of that century, it
had become so important that 'Mani (the founder of Manichae-
ism) wrote that Aksum ranked third among the great powers of
the world. In Byzantium the Aksumite ruler was referred to with
the rarely used honorific title *basileus*. To many Byzantine
emperors Ethiopia appeared a most desirable ally.'[8] The zenith of
Axumite power is generally placed in the fourth century under its

[1]E. Bevan, *A History of Egypt under the Ptolemaic Dynasty*, pp. 175–6.
[2]*Travels*, vol. 2, p. 484.
[3]A. J. Arkell, *A History of the Sudan*, p. 166.
[4]*The Periplus of the Erythraean Sea*, ed. W. H. Schoff (1912).
[5]'Geolinguistic Evidence for Ethiopian Semitic Pre-history, *Abbay*, no. 9, p. 80.
[6]Arkell, p. 166.
[7]J. Doresse, *Ethiopia*, p. 29.
[8]D. Levine, *Greater Ethiopia*, p. 7.

great king, Ezana, who, possibly irked by border raids from the west, found a pretext to overrun and sack what remained of the Kingdom of Meroë and absorbed it into his dominions. The transfer of Ethiopian power from Meroë to Axum was complete.

3

Judaism, Christianity and Islam

MOST countries have their own history or legend to explain how their religion reached them. The Ethiopians base their tradition on the story of Frumentius and Aedesius, two Christian boys from Tyre whose ship had either been wrecked or had fallen into the hands of ruffians at a port on the Red Sea coast. All the crew were lost and the two boys were taken as prisoners to the court of the Axumite King Ella Amida. They were well treated and Aedesius, the younger boy, was made cupbearer to the King while the elder and brighter of the two became his treasurer and secretary. When the king died, in the second quarter of the fourth century, his queen entrusted one of the two Syrians with the regency of the country until her infant son, Ezana, should come of age. Frumentius was diligent in spreading a knowledge of Christianity and establishing churches wherever he could. When the young prince was old enough to take over the government of the country, Aedesius returned to his native Tyre while Frumentius went to Egypt to report on his missionary activities to the great Athanasius, the Patriarch of Alexandria. He urged the Patriarch to send a representative to Axum to consolidate the work and in reply Athanasius consecrated him bishop and ordered him to return to Axum to continue his mission.

Meanwhile Ezana consolidated his position and established his sovereignty on both sides of the Red Sea but showed no great haste to embrace Christianity. His early coins bear the pagan symbol of the crescent and the disc which is also found on Sabaean monuments and was almost universal in the ancient Near East, including Egypt, while his early inscriptions extol the war god Mahrem. It was only towards the end of his reign, just before the middle of the fourth century, that his coins carried the Christian emblem of the cross. Possibly his decision to adopt Christianity as the religion of his realm was influenced by the example of Constantine the Great, who, only two decades earlier in 324, made Christianity the official faith of the Roman Empire.

It is usually considered that the earliest proof of the Ethiopian conversion to Christianity is the dedicatory formula contained in Ezana's last triumphal inscription, in which he boasts of his conquest of Meroë. Instead of giving thanks to a pagan god Ezana praises 'the power of the Lord of Heaven who is in Heaven and on Earth victorious over that which exists'. He gives credit for his victory to 'the power of the Lord of All' and, as 'the Lord of Heaven ... is now victorious for me and has subjugated my enemies for me in justice and in right [I will rule] doing no injustice to the people'.[1]

Nowhere in the inscription, written in archaic Ge'ez and discovered at Axum, is there any reference to Christianity but the terms 'Lord of Heaven' and 'Lord of All' and the call for justice have a distinctly Hebraic ring. A similar formula was used in a bilingual Himyaritic-Hebrew inscription of about the same period found in 1969 in south Arabia near the ancient Sabaean capital of Zafar. It describes the dedication of a Jewish place of worship and includes the words: '... through the power and grace of his Lord, who has created his soul, the Lord of the living and the dead, the Lord of Heaven and Earth, who has created everything'.[2] Both inscriptions are reminiscent of the 103rd Psalm (verse 19) 'The Lord hath established his throne in the heavens; and his kingdom ruleth over all'; and of the prophet Nehemiah, who 'fasted and prayed before the God of Heaven'.[3] Rather than expressing a specifically Christian sentiment this inscription of Ezana's appears to mark a monotheistic position which is neither pagan nor Christian. It seems to reflect the influence of Judaism at a time, possibly just prior to the king's adoption of Christianity, when the Jewish religion had attained a position of some importance on both sides of the Red Sea.[4]

The story of the conversion of Ethiopia by Frumentius recorded in a contemporary document left by Rufinus, the friend of St Jerome, seems authentic enough but, in the course of time, it

[1]From E. Littmann, *Deutsche Axum Expedition*, no. 11, transl. D. Appleyard.
[2]S. D. Goitein, 'The Jews under Islam', in *The Jewish World*, p. 179, and G. Garbini in *Annali di Inst. Orientale di Napoli*, NS20, 1970, pp. 153–66.
[3]Nehemiah 1:4.
[4]Anfray, Caquot and Nantin described, in the *Journal Des Savants* (1970, pp. 260–73), a recently discovered Greek inscription of Ezana which is clearly Christian and Trinitarian. In comparing this with the Ge'ez inscription (*Deutsche Axum Expedition*, no. 11) the authors suggested that the latter may indicate a step by the king in the direction of Christianity.

became embellished by the addition of more fanciful tales which, like the Solomon–Sheba legends, were gradually incorporated into the national mythology. According to one tradition, the country had been converted by the Ethiopian eunuch mentioned in the Acts of the Apostles – notwithstanding that his country was Meroë, not Axum, and that the event had occurred over 300 years before King Ezana's reign. In this version, the significance of Frumentius's achievement was reduced to confirming what had been accomplished by his supposed predecessors and of establishing the Church's priesthood.

Another legend provides a further example of how, in popular history, famous events occurring at one period can become attached to the names of famous people living in another period, often centuries apart. It also illustrates the alleged triumph of Christianity over Judaism. The legend maintains that twin brothers, Atsbeha and Abraha, were the first Christian kings of Ethiopia. This version is based on the true story of the successful campaign waged in the sixth century by the Axumite King Ella Asbeha, also known as Kaleb, against the Jewish King Dhu Nuwas of Himyar, the successor state to the kingdom of Saba in south-west Arabia. After his victory Ella Asbeha appointed Abraham, a Christian, formerly the slave of a Roman resident of Adulis, as his tributary ruler of Himyar. He was a staunch champion of Christianity and among other attainments was responsible for building a great cathedral in Sanaa, his capital. These events took place nearly 200 years after Frumentius, but legend has bent history so far that Ella Asbeha and Abraha have come to be regarded as the twin saint-kings who introduced Christianity into Abyssinia.[1]

While there is sufficient evidence to show when Christianity was adopted, it is much more difficult to give a date for the introduction of Judaism since there is a total absence of any documentary record. Scholars agree that the Jewish religion had a considerable following in the Axumite state before the time of King Ezana and as it is probable that there was a Jewish presence in the neighbouring kingdom of Meroë with which Axum was in communication Jewish influences could have followed the well-worn routes across the border by way of the Blue Nile and Atbara rivers, while similar, though somewhat different, influences could also have penetrated from south Arabia and subsequently disappeared.

Whatever may have been the date and the point of entry of the

[1] A. H. M. Jones and Elizabeth Monroe, *A History of Ethiopia* (1978 edn), p. 31.

Jewish faith, the religion caught on among that section of the Axumite population which belonged to the Agau tribes. These people represented the Ethiopian 'substrate population par excellence',[1] who had settled in the northern part of the highlands before the arrival of the Semitised Amharas and Tigreans. The Agau, today living principally in the area around Lake Tana and the Semien mountains with an offshoot in the neighbourhood of Keren in Eritrea, speak a Cushitic language which differs from the Semitic languages derived from Ge'ez. Until relatively recently the Falashas still spoke a form of the Agau language known as Kwarinyia, so-called from the area west of Lake Tana where some of them lived. When Bruce returned to England from Gondar he brought with him somewhat defective extracts from the Song of Songs and a vocabulary written in what he called 'Falashan', which he published in his *Travels*. The Falasha dialect is now almost extinct and the traveller will be hard put to find more than a few words spoken by the oldest members of the community. The dominance of Amharic, the official Ethiopian language, has driven many minor languages out of existence as formerly Anglo-Saxon imposed itself on the Celtic tongues in the British Isles. According to Leslau, writing in 1951, 'Agau is still used in many prayers and benedictions, though in general the priests utter these words without understanding them'.[2]

There are two alternative traditional theories to account for the origin of the Agau themselves. On the one hand, Ethiopian tradition maintains that 'the Agau tribe came into the country together with the army of Menelik I',[3] in other words that they are the descendants of the legendary Hebrew bodyguard provided by King Solomon as an escort for his son, which would not explain their speaking a Cushitic language. On the other hand, Halévy reported that the Agau considered that their ancestors had come from Sennar, on the Blue Nile,[4] at approximately the southern boundary of the old Meroitic kingdom, and not above 250 miles from Lake Tana as the crow flies, which is no great distance in terms of the movement of people and ideas. It is open to speculation whether the Sembritae, whom Strabo described as descendants of Egyptian exiles from Psammetichus, could have implanted a form of Judaism on the Agau tribesmen. But the Agau area of settlement certainly lay on the route from the Blue Nile to Lake Tana and not in the north of the country on the Red Sea

[1]Ullendorff, *The Ethiopians*, p. 39.
[2]*Falasha Anthology*, p. xxi.
[3]Ullendorff, *The Ethiopians*, p. 132.
[4]*Excursion chez les Falachas en Abyssinie*, p. 9.

facing Arabia. Halévy himself leaned towards the theory that
Judaism was introduced into Ethiopia by Himyaritic prisoners
who were brought to the country by King Kaleb (Ella Asbeha)
after his victory over Dhu Nuwas. This, however, is scarcely
tenable, since the Ethiopian conquest of the Yemen took place
some 200 years after the Axumite kingdom had been converted to
Christianity and long after the introduction of Judaism. Indeed, it
is conceivable that copies of the Greek Septuagint could have
reached Axum with the early Ptolemaic travellers long before we
know of any Jewish settlements in south Arabia.

Just as the assumption that civilisation moved from Arabia into
Abyssinia is coming under increasing scrutiny, so too it becomes
necessary to re-examine the theories of the Arabian origin of
Judaism in the Horn of Africa. While the legends associated with
the Queen of Sheba cannot commend themselves as history, the
hard core of the story leaves little doubt that she existed and
suggests that she was more likely to have been an African than an
Arabian ruler. The story of Menelik's Hebrew escort, while
devoid of historical or biblical evidence, serves to illustrate the
close connection between the Old Testament and the everyday life
of the country and it explains, for those who have no means to test
historical accuracy, the presence of an ancient Jewish population in
a predominantly Christian state.

The late President of Israel, Itzhak Ben-Zvi, took the view that
had the Falashas 'been descendants of Yemen Jews it is conceivable
that they would have carried an original Jewish-Hebrew tradition
that came direct from Palestine and would not have depended on
the Greek text of the Septuagint',[1] which, moreover, was
ostracised by the Jewish religious leadership in conformity with its
opposition to Hellenism.[2] The presence of not more than a
smattering of Aramaic words in the Ge'ez Bible lends weight
to this argument. The Jews of Himyar were closer to their
Palestinian origins and remained in touch with Judea even after its
conquest by the Romans. The sheer primitiveness of Ethiopian
Judaism, retaining certain elements of temple worship which were
considered obsolete even in the early Axumite period, ignorant
both of Hebrew and Talmud, would seem to indicate that the
community received very little religious nourishment from the
other side of the Red Sea.

While Professor Ullendorff is insistent that 'the frequently
canvassed origin of the Falashas from the Jewish garrison at

[1] *The Exiled and the Redeemed*, p. 297.
[2] J. Parkes, *A History of the Jewish People*, p. 30.

Elephantine or the conjecture that Jewish influences in Abyssinia had penetrated by way of Egypt are devoid of any reliable historical basis',[1] it is nevertheless difficult to accept his opinion that it is 'probable that some Jewish elements at least were included in the South Arabian waves of migration across the Red Sea into Abyssinia'.[2] Though an interchange of peoples across the Red Sea no doubt occurred in both directions, any possible 'waves of migration' must have taken place far earlier, between the fifth and second centuries BC, before Jewish elements had become established in the Yemen.

Commercial contacts also existed between the ports of Arabia and of Axum as we can see from the description of trade and navigation in the anonymous *Periplus of the Erithraean Sea* of the second century AD. North of Himyar, in the Hejaz, the Jewish religion spread rapidly and 'whole tribes seem to have gone over to Judaism and accepted monotheism before the rise of Muhammad' and, by the seventh century, they had acquired a wide range of 'knowledge of the Old Testament and of midrashic or homiletic narratives'.[3] What has been said of the Hejaz was no doubt equally true of neighbouring Yemen, where 'Judaism struck deep roots throughout the length and breadth of the Himyar kingdom'[4] and converted several of the rulers to its faith from about the end of the third century AD onwards.

It would thus appear that while Judaism spread at roughly the same period in Abyssinia and Arabia it arrived and developed independently in each area. The rise of Christianity in Axum in the fourth century faced an already existing Judaism with an active opposition 200 years before the advent of Islam created a similar but more serious threat for the Jews in Arabia. In the Hejaz the Jewish community came to an ignominious end but in the Yemen, though suffering persecution, the community continued vigorously until the establishment of the State of Israel in 1948, when it migrated virtually *en bloc*. In Arabia, the Jews were well versed in both biblical and post-biblical literature and they knew Hebrew. The Jews of the Axumite kingdom, on the other hand, seem to have had no knowledge of Hebrew beyond a few words and no experience of Judaism outside of the Bible. The Jews of Arabia remained in contact with Palestine, as witness the journey of Rabbi Akiva, one of the leaders of the Jewish revolt against Rome, to the south of the peninsula about the year

[1]Ullendorff, *Ethiopia and the Bible*, p. 16.
[2]ibid., p. 18.
[3]A. Guillaume in *The Legacy of Israel*, p. 133.
[4]Ben Zvi, *The Exiled and the Redeemed*, p. 294.

AD 130,[1] while the Abyssinian Jews seem to have become isolated at a very early date and were left to fend for themselves.

Even at this stage there may have been a theological schism which divided the two communities for there does not appear to be any evidence to show that the Arabian Jewish communities influenced their Ethiopian co-religionists in any way. Nor is there any record of influence being exerted in the reverse direction. By the time that the Christian king of Axum, Kaleb (Ella Asbeha), mounted his campaign against the Jewish king Dhu Nuwas in the Yemen, about AD 523, the Jewish population of Abyssinia was in no position to aid their co-religionists. The expedition was undertaken at the request of the Byzantine Emperor, Justin I, to whom the Christians of Himyar had appealed for help against their Jewish rulers, alleging that they were being persecuted, though, according to Professor Bernard Lewis,[2] the attack was really a reprisal for the repression of their Jewish subjects by the rulers of Byzantium. Kaleb responded to the appeal and the embarkation of the expeditionary force at Adulis was witnessed by the Alexandrian merchant Cosmas Indicopleustes, who left a description of the scene in his book *The Christian Topography*.[3] Kaleb's victorious campaign marked the end of the independent Jewish kingdom in the Yemen and the establishment of a Christian state in its place. There is nothing to show that Jewish prisoners transported to Axum brought any influence to bear on the indigenous Agau Jewish population, though a Falasha tradition has it that they established the gold- and silver-smithing trades for which Axum became famous. The residue of the Jewish population of the Yemen which did not convert to Christianity or, later, to Islam, retained its identity for fourteen centuries in the face of great hardships until the moment arrived in 1948 when all but a small remnant were air-lifted to the Promised Land, under a scheme known as 'Operation Magic Carpet'.

Christianity had a short span in the Yemen. Not more than fifty years after the Axumite occupation the country was conquered by the Zoroastrian Persians and the Ethiopians withdrew. But even this situation was not to last long for soon the armies of the Prophet were sweeping all before them across the whole Arabian peninsula and imposing the rule of Islam.

A new predicament now faced the Christian enclave in Ethiopia. Muhammad's conquest of Mecca in 630 which heralded

[1]*Ethiopia and the Bible*, p. 17.
[2]*The Arabs in History*, p. 24.
[3]Pankhurst, *Economic History of Ethiopia*, p. 44.

the spread of the new, militant religion along the east coast of the Red Sea was followed in the next twelve years by the conquest of Syria, Iraq and Egypt. The threat to Axum's independence was a very real one. Though Ethiopia may have escaped an Arab onslaught thanks to the forbidding aspect of its mountainous terrain, some credit may also be given to a long-established Islamic tradition. In return for the hospitality which the Axumite King Armah had shown to a group of Muslim refugees fleeing from persecution in Mecca (before its conquest by Muhammad), the prophet had commanded his followers to leave the Abyssinians in peace, thereby exempting them from the horrors of the *Jihad* or Holy War.[1] This order, however, did not prevent the Arabs from occupying various places on the African coast, including the Dahlak archipelago which guarded the entrance to the harbour of Adulis which was destroyed about this time. 'Arab control of the ports necessarily had serious consequences for the Axumites. Their empire's hitherto flourishing foreign trade shrank to modest dimensions, while cultural intercourse with the non-Arab peoples of the Middle East became increasingly difficult.'[2]

With the exception of Nubia, which had been Christianised in the sixth century, the Axumites now found themselves surrounded by Muslim and pagan peoples and practically cut off from the rest of the world. The Nubian Christian kingdoms established their capitals at Dongola and Soba on the Nile and resisted Muslim domination for close on a thousand years. Meanwhile, a mixed Arab and Negro people, known as the Funj, formed a powerful Islamic nation centred at Sennar who gradually created an effective barrier between the Christians of Abyssinia and those of Nubia, whom they eventually overran in the sixteenth century.

With the rise of Islam Ethiopia was thrown back on its own resources, obliged perforce to become self-reliant and inward-looking. Christians and Jews alike were cut off from the mainstream of their religious inspiration by their enveloping, mainly hostile neighbours. The Christians retained tenuous links with the church in Alexandria, which continued until 1955 to be responsible for the appointment of the Abuna, or Patriarch, of the Ethiopian Copts. The Ethiopian Church also retained, after the time of Saladin in the twelfth century, a link with Jerusalem through its own small representation at the Church of the Holy Sepulchre and the few pilgrims who made the hazardous journey to the Holy Land.

[1] ibid., p. 54.
[2] ibid., p. 57.

For the Ethiopian Jews the situation was worse. They had no links with Jewish communities in other parts of the world and there was no Jewish ecclesiastical or secular power which could enter a plea on their behalf. An iron curtain separated them from their co-religionists abroad. Gibbon's thousand years of hibernation – roughly from the rise of Islam to the coming of the Portuguese in the sixteenth century, which was nearer 900 years – might have been more suitably applied to the Jews and in fact extended for them up to the beginning of the nineteenth century. The miracle is that they retained their identity through all that long, dark winter, a bleak epoch redeemed only by the conviction that they were the standard-bearers of the word of God and that one day they would be reunited with Jerusalem, the source of their inspiration.

As the Dark Ages closed in on the mountain fastnesses of Ethiopia, the once-powerful Axumite empire fell into decline; no strong ruler appeared on the scene and the state disintegrated. Historical records of the period are scanty and much of the available information relies on Muslim writers whose expanding civilisation was competing for dominance with the Christian powers. The hegemony of Axumite rule, controlled by an aristocracy which had adopted both a Semitic language, Ge'ez, and a Semitic religion, Christianity, was coming to an end. Individual tribes set up their kings and rulers. From the north, Islamised Beja tribes, who have been described as 'the people with the closest affinity to the ancient Egyptians',[1] invaded the country in the eighth century and established themselves along the Red Sea coast. The indigenous Agau tribes, too, set up their own independent rulers. Some of them were Christian, some retained their pagan religion, some followed the Jewish religion and some, like the Kemant who still persist in small numbers, developed a combination of all three.

The Jewish Agau, the Falashas, speaking a Cushitic tongue, settled in the area around Lake Tana and in the high Semien mountains where they created their own kingdom. Here, in isolation from the outside world, they developed their own form of Judaism, obeying as faithfully as they knew how the laws and precepts of the Pentateuch. Unaware of the Mishnah and Talmud, which had scarcely been compiled before they were cut off from the outside world, the Falashas knew nothing of the rabbinical fence erected to protect the Jewish religion and people from contamination by gentile philosophy and customs. They did not

[1]Ullendorff, *The Ethiopians*, p. 40.

observe the prohibition on marriage with non-Jews, for the Torah, the Law, contains no such restriction, though the Book of Jubilees is very severe on the subject. Indeed, the Old Testament contains many examples of national leaders who contracted such unions, including such eminent figures as Abraham, Jacob and Moses or kings like David and Solomon. Among the Falashas the story of Ruth has been one of the best loved in the Bible for, like her Jewish husband Boaz, they were prepared to welcome the stranger who accepted their religion: 'thy people shall be my people, and thy God my God.'[1] Ruth was additionally popular because, as the ancestress of Solomon, she occupied an important place in both Jewish and Ethiopian tradition.

Intermarriage between Falashas and their neighbours has, indeed, been one of the main stumbling-blocks obstructing their recognition by the orthodox Jewish community. It was not until 1973 when Ovadia Yosef, the Sephardi Chief Rabbi of Israel, declared that the Falashas belong to the tribe of Dan that official recognition was given to their status as Jews. Once the religious authorities had relented the government of Israel had no logical reason for withholding recognition since racial distinction plays no part in Israel's constitution.

The strictness with which the Falashas have been accustomed to observe the tenets of their faith would surprise the most orthodox western Jew. While they adhere tenaciously to the precepts of the five books of Moses they also recognise the whole of the rest of the Old Testament and acknowledge a number of Apocryphal and pseudepigraphic books such as Tobit, Judith, the Wisdom of Solomon, the Wisdom of Ben Sira (Ecclesiasticus), the two books of Maccabees, the Book of Baruch and the books of Enoch and Jubilees. The latter book, dating from the mid-second century BC, of which the most complete version is the Ethiopic text translated from Greek, has exerted a particularly strong influence on the Falashas. Its impact on their religion deserves closer attention than it has hitherto received for much of their ritual and their calendar are based upon it.[2] The influence exerted by the Book of Jubilees bears some resemblance to the position it occupied among the Essenian sect of Qumran. Both communities followed this book in adopting a solar calendar in opposition to the traditional lunar calendar used by the Jewish hierarchy at Jerusalem.

Contact with western Jews and the increasing impact of

[1]Ruth 1:16.
[2]*Enc. Jud.*, vol. 10, col. 325.

Western thought and customs have inevitably eroded much of the rigidity with which the traditional beliefs and customs have been maintained but among the priests and in the numerous villages scattered in remote districts the ancient religion is still practised with the old zeal.

An admirable summary of the Falasha form of Judaism by M. Wurmbrand is to be found in Volume 6 of the *Encyclopaedia Judaica* on which the following remarks are largely based. The central feature of their religion, common to Jews everywhere, is the belief in the one and only God, the God of Israel, who has chosen His people and who will send the Messiah to redeem them and return them to the Holy Land. As in the days of the Temple, the Falashas do not have rabbis – who are essentially teachers – but priests (*Cahenat*) who conduct religious ceremonies and claim descent from Aaron. In practice, every Falasha who is of good character and from a respected family can assume the priestly functions if he is well versed in the prayers and the Bible. In every region the priests elect a high priest from their midst who becomes the spiritual leader of the community and is empowered to ordain candidates into the priesthood. In all religious affairs the priest is assisted by the *dabtara* or cantor. The Falashas also have monks and nuns who live in abstinence and consecrate the whole of their lives to the service of the Creator. Some of them live together in monasteries, while others live in seclusion in the deserts or in the vicinity of the villages. The simple folk have the greatest respect for these monks.

The centre of religious life is the *mesgid*[1] or synagogue which is found in every village. It is in most cases a round *tukul*, or wood and thatched hut, but there also are some square stone structures. If the synagogue is large enough it is usually divided into two rooms, one of which is known as 'the holy of holies'. In the courtyard of the synagogue there is a stone altar for the offering of the paschal sacrifice. It appears that formerly sacrifices were also offered on the new moons and on other occasions. In the *mesgid* seven prayer services are held daily (cf. Ps. 119, verse 164), but most Falashas content themselves with the participation in the morning and evening prayers, which are said in Ge'ez. Among the observant – and one must recognise that strictness is no longer universal – on the Sabbath and Festivals most of the day is spent in prayer at the *mesgid*. The sanctity of the Sabbath is rigorously observed. Work ceases on Friday at midday when all purify themselves by immersion and the wearing of their Sabbath clothes. The lighting

[1]According to Leslau (*Coutumes et Croyances des Falachas*, p. 64) the word *mesgid* comes from the similar Arabic word meaning mosque but is originally derived from Aramaic.

of candles or the kindling of fire, the drawing of water, going beyond the limits of the village and (as in the Book of Jubilees[1]) sexual intercourse are forbidden on the Sabbath. From Ethiopian sources it also appears that in ancient times the Falashas observed the Sabbath rest even when at war and only fought when attacked. In the *mesgid* a section of the Torah, which is in the form of a book not of a scroll, is read in Ge'ez and it is then explained in Amharic. Every seventh Sabbath, from the first Sabbath of the month of Nisan onwards, is known as *Lengeta Sanbat* (also as *yasnabat sanbat*, the Sabbath of Sabbaths) and is celebrated with additional ceremony.

The Falashas determine their festivals by means of a lunar calendar adapted to the solar year which consists of 12 months of 29 and 30 days alternately; every fourth year is a leap year. In accordance with the biblical injunction[2] the year begins with Nisan, not Tishri as in the western world. The Falashas celebrate the new moons and the Jewish festivals as prescribed in the Pentateuch.

On Passover they offer up the paschal sacrifice and eat unleavened bread for seven days. Pentecost is celebrated on the fiftieth day after the last day of Passover. The first of the month of Tishri, which is the religious New Year, is known as *Berhan Sarak* ('The Light Shone'). The sounding of the ram's horn is no longer customary. On Tishri 10 the Falashas observe the fast of the Day of Atonement (*Astasreyo*, 'The Pardon'), and from the 15th to the 20th of the month the festival of Tabernacles. They do not, however, build a *sukkah* (tabernacle) or have the *lulav* (palm branch) and *etrog* (citron). In addition, the Falashas have a number of special festivals and numerous fast days. The fast of the month of Av to commemorate the destruction of the Temple is observed from the first to the 17th of the month and the Fast of Esther is also kept. Halévy reported that in his time Purim (Feast of Esther) was not celebrated[3] though Leslau found that it was included in the calendar.[4] It is possible that the feast-day had fallen into disuse and was revived as a result of contact with European travellers like Faitlovitch.

Falashas pay meticulous attention to the laws of cleanliness and purity. Their wives stay in a special hut on the outskirts of the village during menstruation and they return to their homes only after having purified themselves by immersion. A special hut is

[1]50:8.
[2]Exodus 12:2.
[3]Halévy, *Travels in Abyssinia*, p. 61.
[4]Leslau, *Coutumes et Croyances des Falachas*, p. 88.

also prepared for women in confinement. The uncleanness lasts for forty days if a male child is born and eighty days if it is a female child (cf. Leviticus 12). Upon the conclusion of her time of uncleanness, the woman shaves her head, immerses herself, and washes her clothes before returning to her home, while the custom is to burn the confinement hut. A man undergoes purification after touching somebody or something impure by isolating himself from the community for one or more days and then washes his body and his clothes with ashes and water and sometimes shaves his head.[1]

The Falashas do not eat raw meat like other Ethiopians and they observe the Pentateuchal laws concerning the ritually clean and unclean animals and the purging of the sinew of the femoral vein. *Shechitah* (ritual slaughter) is carried out by a priest and the Falashas do not eat meat slaughtered by Christians. They wash their hands before partaking of food and recite blessings before and after.

Circumcision of boys, in accordance with the biblical prescription, takes place on the eighth day after birth. There is no fixed date for the excision of girls, which is a custom widely practised in Africa but is not prescribed by Jewish law and has presumably been adopted from the pagan past of the Agaus. There is little doubt that the practice will die out as Western influences gain ground. When an Israeli authoress not long ago asked a Falasha elder in a remote village whether he approved of the custom she was told: 'The clitoris is removed so as to paralyse the centre of feeling. Any woman who is not circumcised will run after men like a mare after a stallion and will become a prostitute.'[2]

The Falasha dietary laws do not include the prescription forbidding mixing meat and milk as this is a Talmudic interpretation of the biblical prohibition against seething a kid in its mother's milk[3] which had not reached the Falashas before the period of their isolation. The practice of purification by sprinkling the ashes of a red heifer, 'the water of separation', as ordained in Numbers 19, is still maintained. The ashes are kept in an earthenware jar, sometimes to be seen hanging on the inner wall of the synagogue.

Among the relatively few Christian characteristics which have been adopted by the Falashas perhaps the most significant is the institution of a monastic system for monks and nuns which, according to Falasha tradition, was introduced in the fifteenth

[1]ibid., p. 72.
[2]Yael Kahana, *Among long-lost Brothers* (Hebrew), (Jerusalem, 1978).
[3]Exodus 23:19 and 34:26; Deuteronomy 14:21.

century by Abba Sabra and the son of an Ethiopian king, Zar'a Ya'qob, whom he had converted to Judaism.[1]

If the Falashas have acquired a small number of practices from their Christian and other neighbours – as Jews have elsewhere in the world – Ethiopian Christianity has borrowed enormously from Judaism. Whether these traits are due to Falasha influence in pre-Christian times or were introduced as a result of the Ethiopians' profound veneration for the Old Testament is difficult to say. The fact is that Ethiopian monophysite Christianity shows a far greater acceptance of Jewish customs than any other major branch of the Christian religion. Possibly the isolation of the country during its formative years from European Christianity, whether eastern or western, immunised it from outside influences just as the isolation of the Falashas prevented their development beyond strict biblical Judaism. In addition, the importance of the Solomon–Sheba legends has imbued the Ethiopian people generally with an unusually strong attachment to the Old Testament. The persistence of so many Jewish practices is all the more remarkable considering that ever since the first Portuguese penetration of the country at the end of the fifteenth century both Roman Catholics and Protestants have done their best to persuade the Ethiopians to abandon them.

Besides circumcision on the eighth day after birth (which is also practised but at a more mature age by the Egyptian Copts) the Ethiopian Christians observe the Mosaic distinction between clean and unclean meat, rejecting the flesh of beasts that do not chew the cud and cleave the hoof or have been torn or strangled. They also 'regard those who have had sexual intercourse as impure for the following day, refusing them access to their churches, and furthermore they observe the Sabbath as well as Sunday, celebrating the liturgy on both days alike and exempting both days from fasts'.[2] Some of the Jewish customs are 'obviously conscious adaptations of the Mosaic law to Christian practice. Infants are, for instance, baptized on the fortieth day if males or the eightieth if females, the Christian rite of baptism being governed by the Mosaic regulations on presentation at the Temple.'[3] The purification ordinances of the Old Testament have in this way been adapted to the story of Mary's presentation of Jesus in the Temple, which marked the termin-

[1] Leslau, *Falasha Anthology*, p. xxv. A form of monasticism had also been practised in Palestine by the Essenes and the community at Qumran. See also Preface p. xv.
[2] Jones and Monroe, *A History of Ethiopia*, p. 39.
[3] ibid., p. 40.

ation of her forty days' purification as recorded in Luke 2:22–4.[1] The Christians, however, do not share the Falasha custom of isolating their women in menstrual and confinement huts.

The influence of Jewish observances on the Ethiopian church is most apparent in the unique position occupied by the *Tabot*[2] or Ark of the Covenant. The original Ark containing the tablets of the Ten Commandments which, tradition maintains, was stolen from Jerusalem is supposed to reside in the cathedral at Axum. Reproductions are kept in every church and are the object of the greatest veneration. Churches, like synagogues, if they are large enough contain a section known as the Holy of Holies. For the Christians this is the place of the *Tabot*, for the Jews it is the abode of the Torah and in both cases it may only be entered by the priests. The relationship to the original Temple worship is striking and has led Rathjens to remark that 'the Old Testament traits in the character of the Abyssinian church are the remains of a Jewish cult practised by a part of the Abyssinian people before the introduction of Christianity'.[3] At the festival of Epiphany, in particular, when the *Tabot* is carried in procession to the accompaniment of singing and dancing, one is forcibly reminded of the biblical passage when 'David and all the house of Israel brought up the Ark of the Lord with shouting and with the sound of the trumpet'.[4]

A great deal of the Falasha form of Judaism has been taken direct from the ancient ceremonies of the Temple. They reminded some of the early travellers, such as Bruce and Beke, of the customs of the Samaritans in Palestine who claim to be descendants of the remnant of the lost Ten Tribes of Israel. There are certainly resemblances between the Falasha form of worship and the Samaritan ritual though there are also wide divergencies. Both conserve, but for different historical reasons, many aspects of pre-dispersion Judaism. Like the Samaritans, the Falashas offer animal sacrifices – or they did until recently, as reported by Leslau in 1947. Ben Zvi states that the Samaritans take great care in the observance of the levitical rules appertaining to cleanness and uncleanness and are very strict about the prescribed treatment of women during menstruation and in separating them from the rest of the household.[5] On fundamental issues, however, there are

[1] cf. Leviticus 12.
[2] According to Ullendorff the word is derived from the Jewish Aramaic *tebuta* (*Ethiopia and the Bible*, p. 82).
[3] *Die Juden in Abessinien*, p. 45.
[4] 2 Samuel 6:15.
[5] *The Exiled and the Redeemed*, p. 128.

major differences between the two sects. The Samaritans firmly reject the Oral Law and rabbinic teaching whereas the Falashas are eager to be instructed in it. Unlike the Falashas, the Samaritans accept only the five books of Moses but not the whole of the Old Testament. For the Samaritans Mount Gerizim, near Nablus, represents Zion, not Jerusalem, which, in common with all other Jews, the Falashas regard as the Holy City. Despite these heresies, the Government of Israel accorded the Samaritans full rights under the Law of Return soon after the establishment of the state. The Falashas, with their scrupulous attachment to the whole of the Old Testament, were obliged to wait nearly thirty years before they were granted equal treatment.

4

The Middle Ages

I N the Dark Age following the decay of the Axumite empire
and the rise of Islam in the seventh century scant news of
Ethiopia reached the outside world. Even more isolated than
the Christians were the remnant of Israel who, against tremendous
odds, were to retain their identity though completely cut off from
their co-religionists abroad. The nearest parallel to this remarkable
achievement is provided by the Jewish colony in China which
grew up at Kaifeng-Fu, an important city on the great silk route in
the province of Honan, at one time the imperial capital. The
colony existed for something like 1,800 years until it finally
expired early in the present century, a victim of gradual assimilation and neglect by world Jewry.

In the circumstances, it is not surprising that the Falashas
became more the subject of legend than of history. As Ethiopia
retired into its shell, surrounded by hostile neighbours, there was
little occasion for travellers to visit the country. In the Christian
world stories were told of the mysterious Prester John, a Christian
king who ruled a mighty empire in the unknown heart of Africa.
But it was not until the Age of Discovery, when the first
Portuguese adventurers set foot in Ethiopia in the fifteenth
century, that authentic reports were sent back to Europe, though
they had little to say about the Jewish population.

The earliest known Jewish report to have survived came from
the ninth-century traveller Eldad ha-Dani, who is considered by
some scholars to have been a native of Yemen and, as his name
indicates, associated himself with the tribe of Dan. He was
celebrated in his day as a traveller and philologist and died in 890
while on a visit to Cordoba. Many tales were woven about his
journeys and he wrote extensively about the lost ten tribes of
Israel. He claimed that one of them, Dan, had migrated to Cush
(Ethiopia) and, with the help of Naphthali, Asher and Gad, had

founded an independent Jewish Kingdom in what was appropriately known in the Bible as the gold land of Havilah beyond Abyssinia. This country, according to Genesis (2:11), was surrounded by the river Pishon while another river, Gihon, 'compasseth the whole land of Cush', and later came to be associated with the Nile. Eldad had a lively imagination for he recounts that the 'sons of Moses' who lived in Havilah were cut off from the world by 'Sambatyon, an impassable river of rolling stones and sand which stops only on the Sabbath when it is surrounded by fire and covered by a cloud. It is possible to see and speak with these sons of Moses but not to cross the river.'[1]

Eldad received support for his views from a famous contemporary rabbi, Zemah ben Hayyim, who was one of the Gaonim, or leaders, of the Sura academy in Babylonia, where the Talmud had been compiled over 300 years earlier.[2] There is nothing to show that Eldad had ever visited Ethiopia but his various tales evidently contained a modicum of truth and it has been suggested that his aim in telling them was to raise the morale of contemporary Jews by giving them news of tribes of Israel who lived in freedom, such as the Himyarites, the Falashas and the Khazars.[3]

Three hundred years after Eldad ha-Dani, Benjamin of Tudela, the Spanish Jewish merchant and traveller, reported that in the country on the opposite side of the Red Sea from Yemen 'there are Jews who are not subject to the rule of others, and they have towns and fortresses on the tops of the mountains'.[4] Benjamin, too, was recounting from hearsay but he did travel as far as Yemen and beyond and no doubt he was truthfully repeating what he had heard.

Another 300 years elapsed before the next known report. This came from Elia of Ferrara, a scholar who emigrated to Palestine in 1434 and related that in 1438 he had 'met a young Falasha in Jerusalem and was told how his co-religionists preserved their independence in a mountainous region from which they launched continual wars against the Christian emperors of Ethiopia'.[5] These reports are very meagre but they are evidence of a continuous thread of legend and history which stretches back a very long way.

Whatever may have been the basic cause of the hostility between

---

[1] *Enc. Jud.*, vol. 6, col. 576.
[2] *Enc. Brit.*, eleventh edn, vol. 9, p. 165.
[3] *Enc. Jud.*, loc. cit.
[4] R. L. Hess, 'An Outline of Falasha History', *Journal of Ethiopian Studies*, 6 (1967), p. 99.
[5] ibid.

the Jews and Christians mentioned by Elia, it is clear that the early church showed little sympathy for the religion from which it sprang although, in spite of profound differences, it yet had much in common. St Athanasius of Alexandria, the patron of Frumentius, the missionary who had converted King Ezana, set an example of intolerance by declaring that 'the Jews were no longer the people of God, but rulers of Sodom and Gomorrah. . . . What is left unfulfilled', he asked, 'that they should now be allowed to disbelieve with impunity?'[1] Other early church fathers went much further and their opinions could not but influence the young Ethiopian church. Marcel Simon has explained[2] how Christian anti-Semitism, which is theological not racist, expanded in the fourth century during the same period as the conversion of the Roman and Axumite empires. He quotes from the writings of St John Chrysostom to justify his contention that he was 'without question the master of anti-Jewish malediction'. This 'saint', who has the distinction of being called the golden-mouthed because of his eloquence as a preacher, was the first Christian leader to apply the word 'deicide' to the Jewish nation.[3] The following is one of his gems of invective contained in a sermon:

> . . . the synagogue is a criminal assembly of Jews . . . a place of meeting for the assassins of Christ . . . a house worse than a drinking shop . . . a den of thieves; a house of ill-fame, a dwelling of iniquity, the refuge of devils, a gulf and abyss of perdition . . . whatever name even more horrible could be found will never be worse than the synagogue deserves.[4]

Many other early church fathers, who had a profound influence on the development of Christian teaching, could be cited in a similar vein as, for instance, St Gregory of Nyssa, who composed this indictment of the Jews:

> Slayers of the Lord, murderers of the prophets, adversaries of God, haters of God, men who show contempt for the law, foes of grace, enemies of their father's faith, advocates of the devil, brood of vipers, slanderers, scoffers, men whose minds are in darkness, leaven of the Pharisees, assembly of demons, sinners, wicked men, stoners and haters of righteousness.[5]

[1]Malcolm Hay, *The Foot of Pride*, p. 25.
[2]Varus Israel: *Étude sur les relations entre Chrétiens et Juifs dans l'Empire Romain*, p. 246.
[3]Hay, op. cit., p. 30.
[4]ibid, p. 28.
[5]ibid, p. 26.

Of the famous St Simeon Stylites, who reputedly lived for thirty-six years on top of a fifty-foot pillar in Asia Minor in the fifth century, it was said by G. F. Abbott that he abandoned 'all worldly luxuries except Jew-hatred'.[1] If such were among the sentiments which animated early Christian teachers and influenced Ethiopian thinking through the liturgy and the *Kebra Nagast* it is small wonder that antipathy developed between Church and Synagogue in the realm of the Lion of Judah, the Negus Negusti or King of Kings.

Early written records of Ethiopia are so scarce that its history can only be reconstructed with the aid of the relatively few foreign contemporary documents available, by conjecture based on surviving legends, and from later histories compiled by Christian writers who do not attempt to conceal their prejudices. Although, by the time of Ezana in the fourth century, the Axumite civilisation had reached an advanced stage of development, there are very few written records before this time and none at all from Jewish sources. There are no references in contemporary writings to Jews dwelling in the Axumite empire as there are for south Arabian Jewry, and the Mishnah and Talmud, which might have been expected to mention such an outlying Jewish community, are silent on the subject. Nor do the Beit She'arim tombs in Israel, which shed some light on the Jews of Himyar, give us a clue. The Falashas themselves maintain that they used to possess records which described their early history but they have either been destroyed or hidden. They continue to hope that one day their archives – if indeed they exist – will be recovered.

There are no epigraphic records of a Jewish community living south of Aswan between the time of the Elephantine settlement and the quasi-mythological tale of Eldad ha-Dani – a gap of thirteen centuries. The explanation could be that we are not so much following a movement of people, such as the expulsions from Spain and their resettlement elsewhere, as a spread of ideas, like the dissemination of early Christianity or the diffusion of learning after the fall of Constantinople. Such unspectacular developments are sometimes recorded in contemporary documents which deteriorate or are destroyed. Thus, we should have known nothing of the Elephantine community if it had not been for the chance discovery of the Aramaic papyri; and the Dead Sea Scrolls lay hidden, unsuspected, for nearly two thousand years. Who knows what is yet to be found or, in the case of Meroë, still awaits interpretation?

[1] *Israel in Europe*, quoted by Hay, ibid.

78   *The Falashas*

The conflict between the migration and cultural diffusion theories of history was noted by Adams in his history of Nubia when he remarked that the 'migration theory is no more adequate as a general explanation than it is for the history of most other parts of the world. . . . It fitted so neatly', he said, 'with the racist outlook of the later nineteenth century that migration theory became one of the unacknowledged tenets of the first archaeologists and prehistorians, and its legacy is with us still.'[1] Jewish history, too, has been a victim of this theory owing to the long-standing confusion of race with religion. The Jews are a people distinguished by their religion and culture but cannot be considered a race in the anthropological sense. They belong to various ethnic groups and represent a rich mixture of different stocks. So long as the Jewish religion is prepared to accept proselytes – and in ancient times it welcomed them in great numbers – Jews cannot lay claim to racial purity, which, as a concept, finds no place in the Laws of Moses.

The adoption of Judaism by a section of the Agau population is an example of 'cultural diffusion or local evolution', which was gradual and not abrupt. The spread of ideas along the length of the Nile represented a migration not so much of people as of thought. Similarly, the conversion of Ethiopia to Christianity was a gradual process, possibly dictated by King Ezana's caution in order not to alienate his subjects. First, he seems to have abandoned his pagan beliefs in favour of a monotheistic faith, about which he may have learnt either from his contacts with south Arabia or from the Judaised Agau, and which he next rejected under the impact of Christian evangelisation. The king's conversion to the new religion may even have been an astute political move which he calculated would bring his country into the orbit of the mighty Byzantine Empire. This would have been a more attractive proposition than the adoption of Judaism, then in retreat before the onrush of the first of its daughter religions.

The spread of Christianity was followed after three centuries by the expansion of Islam – another example of cultural diffusion – when the Axumite kings found themselves increasingly preoccupied with the growing threat on their borders from the followers of Muhammad. Many of the Agau Jews withdrew to the high mountains of Semien where they established an autonomous kingdom around the Amba Ayhud, or Jews' Rock. This natural fortress, the scene of many a pitched battle, became the symbol of Jewish resistance: when it fell, many centuries later,

[1] *Nubia*, p. 666.

Falasha independence for all practical purposes came to an end. The Agau country extended in a wide circle around Lake Tana, from the Takazze river in the north to the Abbai or Blue Nile in the south, an area of some 400 square miles.[1] Not all the Agau became Jews and not all of the latter concentrated in the Semien mountains in the north of the area, many remaining in their original homeland in the Kwara country south and west of Lake Tana.

Under the pressure of Muslim Arabs from Egypt the nomadic Beja tribes of the Red Sea coast forced the Axumite rulers to withdraw from territory in the north and extend their control further south. The latter 'penetrated central Ethiopia in an effort to subjugate the pagan and Judaized Agau to convert them to Christianity'.[2] For a while they were successful but retribution was to come. In the 970s the Agau lashed back with a campaign in which Axum was sacked, her churches were burned and most of her royalty were killed. The Agau were led by a woman, variously known as Judith or Esther, whose husband was supposed to have been the governor of the district of Bugna in Lasta province. Scholars are divided as to whether she and her followers were Jews or pagans and there is also a fairly wide discrepancy in assessing the date of the revolt. The end of the tenth century seems to be the generally accepted period. As there are no contemporary records of the rebellion it is unlikely that we shall ever know for certain whether Judith was a Jewess though, if she is more than a legend, there seems no good reason why she should not have been. It remains a matter of opinion, depending on one's view of Ethiopian history. Bruce, in relating the story, which he learnt about during his travels, had no doubt that Judith was an historical character and he claimed that her motive was 'to attempt the subversion of the Christian religion and with it the succession in the line of Solomon'.[3] He suggested that, having seen how the Christian religion had been overthrown by Islam in Egypt, Judith and her party believed that 'a revolution in favour of Judaism was thought full as feasible in the country as it had been in Egypt'. Other authors are less precise, though one modern English scholar has boldly called her 'a bloodthirsty Falasha queen',[4] while Ullendorff, echoing Conti Rossini at the other end of the scale, says that the legend has been shown 'to possess no basis in historical fact'.[5] Perhaps it should be left as an open question for future historical research though the existence at that period of an

[1] Haberland, *Untersuchungen zum Aeothiopischen Königtum* (1965).
[2] Levine, *Greater Ethiopia*, p. 70.
[3] *Travels*, vol. 1, p. 526.
[4] D. Buxton, *Travels in Ethiopia*, p. 27.
[5] *Ethiopia and the Bible*, p. 25.

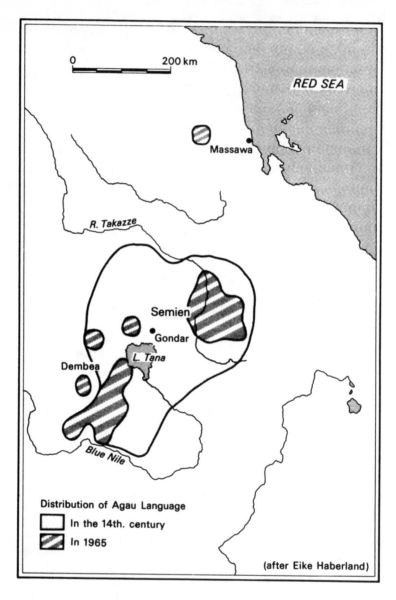

Distribution of Agau language

Agau Jewish principality in the Semien mountains is not disputed. Whether true or false, the story of the Jewish princess who overthrew the Christian monarchy and made herself Queen of Ethiopia for a span of forty years is widely believed and richly embroidered by tradition. The legend is reminiscent of the tale of the Berber Jewish queen, Dahyah al-Kahina, who fought against the Muslim invaders in the Atlas mountains in the eighth century and was killed in battle. One of the few documents of the period of Queen Judith is a letter written shortly after 979 by the Abyssinian king to his Christian contemporary, King George of Nubia, asking for assistance to counteract the persecution of Christians by a queen who had usurped his throne. At the end of Judith's reign the Solomonic line regained control for a short period but was replaced in the first half of the twelfth century by a new dynasty of ancient Agau origin known as the Zagwes, who provided eleven successive rulers, of whom, it is believed, the first five were Jewish or pagan and the remainder Christian.[1] Of the latter, the most famous was Lalibela during whose reign in the early thirteenth century the magnificent rock-hewn churches of Roha, in Lasta province, were built in a town which now bears his name.

These monuments are not only of great archaeological interest but also witness to the royal builder's deep attachment to biblical tradition. The churches themselves, says Doresse, 'in their originality of design and artistic achievement ... must be ranked amongst the finest architecture of the Christian world'.[2] By using place-names from the Holy Land, such as the River Jordan, an attempt seems to have been made to present the new capital city as a kind of new Jerusalem. The biblical precept against graven images is scrupulously observed in Ethiopia but in one of these rock-hewn churches an exception has been made, possibly unique in the country, where effigies of saints have been carved in relief.[3] The prohibition against making a representation of the human figure does not extend to paintings, which adorn Ethiopian churches in profusion. According to tradition Lalibela brought craftsmen from Jerusalem or Egypt to help construct the churches, the Muslim persecutions having driven out numbers of Egyptian Copts.[4]

The establishment of the Zagwe dynasty created its own legend in Falasha lore. Tradition has it that besides taking the Queen of Sheba into his bed King Solomon also worked his will on her

[1]Pankhurst, p. 61.
[2]*Ethiopia*, p. 113.
[3]Buxton, *Travels in Ethiopia*, p. 166.
[4]Doresse, *Ethiopia*, p. 95.

servant, who bore him a son called Zagwe. In due course Zagwe founded his own dynasty and his half-brother Menelik provided him with members of the bodyguard whom he had brought from Israel and they spread into the provinces of Wollo, Gojjam and Shoa, where they became the ancestors of the Falashas. This is a variation of the Ethiopian tradition that the Agau tribe came into the country with the army of Menelik I. There are differences of opinion among the Falashas as to the number of Zagwe rulers who were Jews but there appears to be agreement among them that Judith was a Falasha. While the Zagwe revolt against Axumite rule may be interpreted as 'a reaction of the (hamitic-speaking) Agau element against the dominant semitic aristocracy'[1] as well as a protest against the southward pressure of the Abyssinians, it was apparently not a religious movement since some of the greatest Christian works were undertaken during the period of their rule.

The Zagwe line came to an end after 135 years in 1270 when the ruling monarch, Naakuto Laab, was driven from his throne and murdered following a revolt fomented in the province of Shoa by a prince of the Amhara named Yekuno-Amlak, who claimed to belong to the legitimate Solomonic line. The old order was now resumed and with it opened a period of rapid development which was to continue for another 200 years.[2] From this point onwards historical records in the form of chronicles of the acts of the kings were kept, much like those of the Old Testament. In addition, the great epic work known as the *Kebra Nagast*, which had been in existence for centuries, was codified with the aim of proving the descent of the Solomonic line of kings, and it has remained in this form ever since as the official documentary evidence to support the Ethiopian succession.[3] The book's constitutional importance was very clearly demonstrated after General Napier's expedition to Abyssinia in 1867, when the British army brought back the emperor's own copy as booty. Theodore's successor, King John, was constrained to write to the British Government just before his coronation begging them to return the precious volume, 'for', he wrote, 'in my country my people will not obey my orders without it', and the Trustees of the British Museum, into whose care the book had been consigned, complied with the request.[4] The constitution of 1955, which confirmed Haile Selassie in his position as Emperor, also in-

[1] Jones and Monroe, *A History of Ethiopia*, p. 48.
[2] Doresse, *Ethiopia*, p. 115.
[3] ibid., p. 114; see also 'Ethiopia and the Bible', p. 75 n.
[4] Budge, *The Queen of Sheba and her only son Menyelek*, p. xxvii.

The Middle Ages 83

corporated the ancient tradition that the royal line 'descends without interruption from the dynasty of Menelik I, son of the Queen of Ethiopia, the Queen of Sheba, and King Solomon of Jerusalem'.

Now, with the return of the Solomonic line and the recording of historical events, we have documentary evidence from Ethiopian sources of the existence of a section of the population practising the Jewish religion. The isolation of the country, however, prevented anything approaching an accurate description of the country's history and people from reaching the outside world for another two hundred years. The breakthrough came as a result of the remarkable voyages of the Portuguese. Prince Henry the Navigator, in a crusading spirit, had dreamed in the first half of the fifteenth century of a military link between Christian Europe and the semi-fabulous Christian realm of Prester John. In 1487 King John II had dispatched a mission overland under Pedro de Covilham and Alfonse de Payva with the dual aim of making contact with the only Christian state in Africa and the more mercenary object of diverting the spice trade away from Venice to Portugal.[1] The following year Bartholomeu Diaz rounded the Cape of Good Hope, thus proving that the Indian Ocean was accessible from Europe by sea, and in 1498 Vasco da Gama sailed as far as India by the same route.

While these great voyages were taking place Portugal and Spain were engaged in their final struggle against the Moors in the Iberian peninsula. The climate of opinion was fanatically 'anti-infidel' and Jews were no less the object of hatred than Muslims. No doubt the emissaries to Abyssinia were not more tolerant than their fellow countrymen at home and they did not conceal their distaste for some of the Jewish practices which they found among Prester John's Christians. The effect of these journeys on the history of Ethiopia was profound for contact between Europe and Ethiopia was once again established, and the country had, at least temporarily, ended its isolation from the rest of the Christian world.

The historian of these early missions was Francisco Alvarez, the Catholic chaplain who accompanied the first Portuguese embassy, led by Rodrigo de Lima, which remained in the country for six years until 1526. His account of his journey into the interior excited a great deal of interest in Europe and was widely translated and republished. Perhaps it was wishful thinking which prompted him to declare that 'in no part of the kingdoms or lordships of the

[1] *The Ethiopians*, p. 3.

Prester John are there Jews'[1] and it was left to later Jesuit and other writers to correct his error. Stray references to Ethiopian Jews of this period were diligently assembled by the bibliophile Sidney Mendelssohn, whose little-known book, *The Jews of Africa*, was edited by Hyamson in 1920.[2] He mentioned that Jacques Basnage, the French Protestant preacher who wrote a history of the Jews in 1706, related that the Jesuit Bishop de Oviedo wrote in 1557 'that the Jews possessed great inaccessible mountains; and they had dispossessed the Christians of many lands which they were masters of, and that the kings of Ethiopia could not subdue them, because they have but small forces, and it is very difficult to penetrate into the fastnesses of their rocks'.[3] John Pory, the English translator of Leo Africanus's *History and Description of Africa*, early in the seventeenth century, reported that:

> at this day also the Abassins affirm that upon Nilus towards the west there inhabiteth a most populous nation of the Jewish stock under a mighte king. . . . And likewise on the north part of the kingdom of Goiame (Gojjam) and the southerly quarter of the kingdom of Gorhan there are certain mountains, peopled with Jews, who there maintain themselves free and absolute, through the inaccessible situations of the same.[4]

Balthazar Tellez, the Portuguese Jesuit missionary, in his *Travels of the Jesuits in Ethiopia*, reported that in the seventeenth century many Jews lived 'free from any subjection to the Empire ... between the Emperor's dominions and the Cafres dwelling near the river Nile',[5] which would correctly place them in the Agau territory of Agawmeder. Both Tellez and Basnage stated that Hebrew was being used by the Falashas in their synagogues, though confirmation for these statements is lacking and it is more likely that they mistook the Falasha dialect of Agau for Hebrew.

Among the seventeenth-century writers on Ethiopia was Job Ludolf, the German scholar who has been called 'the founder of Ethiopian studies in Europe'.[6] He knew about the existence of Jews in the country and was critical of his predecessors, the Jesuit priests, whom he chided because they 'never took care to enquire when, or upon what occasion, the Jews came first into Ethiopia.

[1] Beckingham and Huntingford (eds), *The Prester John of the Indies*, vol. 2, p. 512.
[2] See F. R. Bradlow in *Quarterly Bulletin of the South African Library*, vol. 22, no. 4 (1968).
[3] Mendelssohn, *The Jews of Africa*, p. 15.
[4] ibid., p. 17.
[5] ibid.
[6] Ullendorff, *The Ethiopians*, p. 9.

What sacred books they use, whether with points or without points.' Such information, he said, would be of great value to scholars.[1]

One other work of this period should be mentioned although it does not refer to the existence of a Jewish community. Father Jerome Lobo's *Voyage to Abyssinia* was published in Portugal about 1659 and a translation into English from the French version was made by Samuel Johnson as his first literary work. The book had so deeply impressed him that when he came to write his romantic story *Rasselas*, as a pot-boiler to pay for his mother's funeral expenses, he located the action in the mountains of Abyssinia. Because he had built up a quite unrealistic picture of Ethiopia he was offended by Bruce's description of Lobo as a liar. Johnson had met Bruce but had not formed a high opinion of him and inclined to think that the Scottish explorer was an impostor who, in any case, scarcely served to promote the popular eighteenth century picture of the noble savage.

By degrees Bruce's reputation has been rehabilitated and today it is recognised that, significant as was the journey, 'perhaps the most important result of his travels was the collection of Ethiopic manuscripts which he brought with him from Ethiopia. They opened up entirely new vistas for the study of Ethiopian languages and history and placed this branch of Oriental scholarship on a much more secure basis.'[2] Among those documents were many which contained valuable information about the history of the Falashas while Bruce's own observations cast a valuable light on the condition of the community at the time of his two-year stay in and around Gondar in 1769 and 1770.

Fifty years after the short account of Elia of Ferrara in the first half of the fifteenth century, another Italian, Rabbi Obadiah of Bertinora, a scholar and traveller, reported that he had seen two Falashas in captivity in Egypt. In the following century the Spanish-born Rabbi David ben Abi Zimrah of Cairo, known as the Radbaz (1479–1573), in reply to an inquiry as to the legitimacy of a Falasha slave woman's son by her Egyptian master, said that the Falashas were Karaites who could be accepted into the Jewish community (as distinct from Karaites living among Rabbinite Jews) if they were to learn Jewish laws and customs. He quoted from other sources to show that they belonged to the tribe of Dan but, according to Professor Chaim Rabin, 'he evidently did not believe it, though he conceded that they were at least potentially

[1]Mendelssohn, op. cit., p. 24.
[2]Ullendorff, *The Ethiopians*, p. 13.

Jews'.[1] He observed that if they did not follow the Oral Law it was
not because, like the Karaites, they rejected it, but because they had
no scholars to teach it. They should, therefore, be treated like
children who have been captured by gentiles.[2]

From this time until the nineteenth century there are no Jewish
records and Bruce's account of the part the Falashas played in
Ethiopian history, based on the royal chronicles and his own
observations, must suffice to fill the gap. James Bruce, the laird of
Kinnaird in Stirlingshire, was born in 1730. He was a huge man,
six foot four inches tall and athletic. He developed a character,
according to his first biographer, Alexander Murray, which
'became bold, hasty and impetuous, accompanied, however, with
a manly openness that shewed the usual concomitant, a warm and
generous heart'.[3] He was a good linguist, a keen student of history,
geography and natural history, and a skilful draughtsman. He
learnt Arabic and Ethiopic. It was his acquaintance with the
writings of Ludolf, his biographer suggested, that 'perhaps
determined him to explore the sources of the Nile'. This was his
aim when he set out for Abyssinia, where, after many adventures
including shipwreck in the Mediterranean, he landed at Massawa
on 19 September 1769. Overcoming great difficulties and risks he
made his way to the capital, Gondar, where he lived as a member
of the court of Emperor Takla Haymanot II. During all his travels
he displayed a degree of courage, tenacity and resourcefulness
which can stand comparison with that of almost any other
explorer. He made ample notes and accumulated a vast store of
documents, drawings and specimens of which a large number still
survive in national libraries and royal and private collections. He
returned to England in June 1774, having been abroad, mostly in
North and East Africa, continuously for twelve years. Murray
wrote:

> The public was impatient to hear his adventures; and every
> person of distinction or learning, who had any curiosity to
> know the wonders of foreign countries, sought his acquain-
> tance. He shewed his numerous and beautiful drawings, which
> obtained particular praise; and his collection of Ethiopic
> manuscripts, a sufficient proof, to such as could read them, of
> his travels in Abyssinia. Soon after his arrival in London he was
> introduced at court, and graciously received by his Majesty,
> who was pleased to honour with his royal approbation Mr.

[1] In a letter to the author.
[2] Enc. Jud. vol. 6 col. 1153.
[3] *Life and Writings of James Bruce* (1808), p. 8.

I(a) Granite Sphinx of Tirhaka, King of Egypt and Ethiopia (689–664 BC. 'This bruised reed . . . whereon if a man lean it will go into his hand, and pierce it' (*II Kings 18, 21*). 'A brutal realism . . . is here more apparent than in any other royal likeness of the period' (*Africa in Antiquity*, vol. II, p. 168).

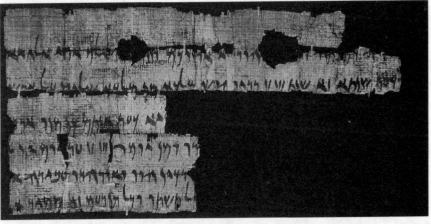

(b) Letter in Aramaic from the Elephantine archive containing instructions to the Jewish garrison for celebrating Passover (Staatliche Museen, Berlin).

II(a) The Queen of Sheba brings presents to King Solomon; a fresco by Raphael (1483–1520) in the Loggia of the Vatican.

(b) The Baptism of the Ethiopian Eunuch by Aelbert Cuyp (1620–1691).

III(a) James Bruce of Kinnaird (1730–1794) from the portrait by Martin in the possession of the Earl of Elgin.

(b) Filosseno Luzzatto (1829–1854) the eldest son of S. D. Luzzatto of Padua.

(c) Fasilidas' Castle at Gondar built in the seventeenth century with the help of Falasha craftsmen.

IV(a) The Rev. Henry Stern preaching to the Falashas at Shargee, from his *Wanderings Among the Falashas in Abyssinia* (London 1862).

(b) Emperor Theodore, by Baudran from Lejean's *Théodore II* (Paris 1865).

V(a) Rabbi Dr. Israel Hildesheimer of Eisenstadt (1820–1899).

(b) Joseph Halévy (1827–1917).

(c) Jacques Faitlovitch (1881–1955) with Getie Jeremias and Solomon Isaak, from *Quer durch Abessinien* (Berlin 1910).

VI(a) Jacques Faitlovitch and Tamrat Emanuel.

(b) The Falasha School in Addis Ababa, closed in 1936.

VII(a) Norman Bentwich with a group of Falashas at Tedda in 1961; Kahen Rafael Hadani is standing on Bentwich's left.

(b) Letter in Hebrew addressed to 'our brethren, sons of Abraham, Isaac and Jacob who dwell in Abyssinia' and signed in 1906 by forty-four leading Rabbis in various countries.

VIII(a) Ovadia Yossef, the Sephardi
Chief Rabbi of Israel in 1973.

(b) Yona Bogale (*third from right*) and his brother with Falasha
settlers at Abder Rafi in 1970.

IX(a) Falashas ploughing near Ambober in 1970.

(b) Falasha women selling pottery and mats in the market at Tedda in 1970.

X(a) Falasha dwellings near Ambober in 1970.

(b) Falasha elders with Mikhail Admass Eshkol (*right*) at Enda Bagona, Tigrai province.

XI(a) Stone-built synagogue at Enda Bagona.

(b) A conference of Falasha villagers at Benker with Simon Guedj of the World ORT Union and Dajani Aron, the agricultural adviser, in June, 1979.

XII(a) The new ORT school at Senker Tekkem under construction in June 1979.

(b) A rally of Ethiopian Jews in Jerusalem on 28 May 1995, addressed by Eliahu Bakshi Doron, the Sephardi Chief Rabbi.

Bruce's labours in the cause of discovery, and to accept those drawings of Baalbec, Palmyra and the African cities, which the traveller had promised to make for his collection.[1]

The excitement which had been generated by his first appearance in London's intellectual society was, however, short-lived. Personal animosities created by Bruce's somewhat arrogant manner combined with sheer incredulity at some of his stories caused widespread hostility and derision. Some doubted whether he had even been to Abyssinia, others compared him with Baron Munchausen, the alleged German author of tall stories, while his drawing of a harp copied exactly from an ancient Egyptian tomb seemed so improbable that it earned him the nickname of the Theban liar.[2] He met Samuel Johnson in 1775 at the home of his cousin William Gerard ('Single Speech') Hamilton but he did not impress either Johnson or his biographer Boswell and the former joined the ranks of the sceptics. Edward Gibbon, the historian, was also a friend of Hamilton's but while it is unlikely that he ever met Bruce it is reasonable to suppose that he would have heard about him from Hamilton, who may have helped to colour his view of Ethiopian history.

Dispirited and angry, Bruce left London for his native Scotland, where he settled down to a domestic life and the supervision of his much-neglected ancestral estate. It was not until eleven years after his return to Britain, and following the death of his second wife, that he began to work seriously on the material which he had brought back from Ethiopia. Five years later, in 1790, the account of his travels was published in London in five massive volumes. Lord Sheffield drew Gibbon's attention to the publication in a letter which displayed more than a superficial interest:

> Everybody is looking into Bruce's Travels. Part takes the attention but they are abominably abused. Banks[3] objects to the Botany, Reynell[4] to the Geography, Cambridge to the History, the Greeks to the Greek, etc., etc., yet the work is to be found on every table. Bruce printed the work, and sold 2,000 copies to Robertson for £6,000. He sells to the booksellers at 4 guineas, and they to their customers at 5 guineas.[5]

On the whole the book was given a good reception, was translated

[1] ibid., p. 115.
[2] Reid, *Traveller Extraordinary*, p. 295.
[3] Sir Joseph Banks (1744–1820).
[4] James Rennell (1742–1830) F.R.S.
[5] R. E. Prothero, *Private Letters of Edward Gibbon*, 21 September 1790.

into French and German and soon achieved three English editions. But it took time for Bruce's reputation to recover from its early setback while his standing was not enhanced by his ill-founded boast that in discovering, as he thought, the headwaters of the Blue Nile he had reached the source of the main river. He died, in 1794, as the result of an accident at his Scottish home and did not live to see the new and more scientific generation of explorers who found that 'far from being a romancer, he was a most reliable guide'.[1]

His work provided European readers with an authentic account of the role played by the Falashas in Abyssinian history after the Zagwe dynasty and a description of their situation at the time of his visit. The legendary tales of Jews living on mountain tops and engaging in battles with their Christian adversaries began to assume the appearance of reality.

Bruce took a considerable interest in the Falashas and, as he lived in Gondar and travelled far and wide in its neighbourhood, he had many opportunities for meeting them. 'I did not spare my utmost pains,' he wrote, 'in inquiring into the history of this curious people, and lived in friendship with several esteemed the most knowing and learned among them, and I am persuaded, as far as they knew, they told me the truth,' but, he added, 'it required great patience and prudence in making the interrogations, and separating truth from falsehood.'[2] He brought back with him a translation of the Song of Songs in the 'Falashan' dialect of Agau which, with specimens of other languages, he deposited at the Bodleian Library. The Song, he said, was popular with old priests of the Coptic church but was forbidden to the young ones, to the deacons, laymen and women. The Abyssinians believed that it was written by Solomon in praise of the daughter of Pharaoh whom he had taken as one of his wives.[3] This was also the view of Christian scholars in the fifth century and of Grotius in the seventeenth, who regarded the Canticles as 'conjugal prattle' between Solomon and the Egyptian princess.[4] It is not surprising, therefore, that the famous verse 'I am black, but comely, O ye daughters of Jerusalem, as the tents of Kedar, as the curtains of Solomon'[5] has sometimes been interpreted as referring to the Queen of Sheba.

During his inquiries into their history, Bruce found that the

[1]Moorehead, *The Blue Nile*, p. 43.
[2]*Travels*, vol. 1, p. 483.
[3]1 Kings 9:16.
[4]*Enc. Brit.*, 11th edn, vol. 5, p. 214.
[5]Song of Songs 1:5.

Falashas had no written records since, they said, they had all been lost or destroyed in the course of their various wars and especially when they opposed the invasion of the Muslims under Ahmad Grañ. He was puzzled by the Falashas' ignorance of Hebrew and was not altogether satisfied with their explanation that, having lost all their books, they had forgotten what they once knew. He found that in general they shared their Christian neighbours' beliefs in their early history as related in the *Kebra Nagast* with a few embellishments of their own. They had confused the Himyarite Jewish king, Dhu Nuwas, whom they called Phineas, with their own leader at the time of Ethiopia's conversion to Christianity and they claimed that their present 'king' was his lineal descendant and belonged to the royal house of Judah. 'The Abyssinians,' says Bruce, 'by way of reproach, have called this family Bet Israel, intimating that they were rebels' who had separated from the Solomonic line.[1] This version contrasts with the opinion that the Falashas themselves prefer to be called Bet (or Beta) Israel because they consider the name 'Falasha' has a pejorative meaning, though their use of the term 'Beta Israel' seems to be of recent origin. Today it is adopted by more educated Ethiopian Jews to signify their dislike for the name 'Falasha' and, at the same time, to express their feeling of unity with the State of Israel and Jews in the rest of the world.

The Falashas' skill as craftsmen had been observed by Bruce, who went so far as to remark that 'they carried the art of pottery ... to a degree of perfection scarcely to be imagined'.[2] He also spoke of the lavish decoration of an audience chamber in one of the palaces in Gondar, undertaken shortly before his visit by Greek craftsmen, whose roof 'in gaiety and taste, corresponded perfectly with the magnificent finishing of the room. It was the work of the Falasha, and consisted of painted cane, split and disposed in mosaic figures, which produces a gayer effect than it is possible to conceive.'[3]

During the two and a quarter years that he spent in Abyssinia Bruce had ample opportunity – besides journeying to the source of the Blue Nile, south of Lake Tana – to observe its people and to assess their virtues and vices. His stay coincided with an extremely disturbed period in the country's history when the power of the monarch was declining and that of the *rases* (or barons) was getting out of control. His many adventures are told in his book, 'with a verve and a sense of farce unsurpassed in the literature of

[1] *Travels*, vol. 1, p. 485.
[2] ibid.
[3] *Travels*, vol. 2, p. 634.

travel'.[1] He must have cut an astonishing figure in Gondar with his immense height, red hair and ruddy complexion in striking contrast to the people around him; a visitor from another world or an African version of Mark Twain's Yankee at the court of King Arthur. He harboured no illusions about the barbarity of his hosts, with whom he rode to war, whose ailments he treated and in whose feasts he participated. He described in some detail one such celebration where the participants devoured the living flesh of a cow or bull 'having satisfied the Mosaical law' by first spilling six or seven drops of blood on the floor. The wretched beast, skinned and eaten alive, was allowed to bleed to death while the revellers of both sexes, fortified by drink, 'are very much elevated; love lights all its fires, and everything is permitted with absolute freedom. There is no coyness, no delays, no need of appointments or retirement to gratify their wishes; there are no rooms but one in which they sacrifice both to Bacchus and to Venus.'[2] He wrote of the prevalence of superstition and mentioned that 'the Falasha are addicted to this in still a greater degree, if possible'. He also remarked that 'it is always believed by every individual Abyssinian that the number of hyenas the smell of carrion brings into the city of Gondar every night are the Falasha from the neighbouring mountains, transformed by inchantment'.[3]

On his journey by the traditional route from Axum to Gondar, soon after crossing the gorge of the Takazze river, which separates the province of Tigrai from the Semien mountains, Bruce found himself near the Jews' Rock, 'famous in the history of this country for the many revolts of the Jews against the Abyssinian kings'.[4] He described the almost impregnable formation of this natural fortress which had once been the residence of the Falasha kings but, when he passed by, was the seat of a rebellious Amhara governor of the province. He mentioned that the region 'is in great part possessed by Jews, and there Gideon and Judith, king and queen of that nation, and, as they say, of the house of Judah, maintain still their ancient sovereignty and religion from very early times'.[5] However, Hess thinks that Bruce may have allowed himself to romanticise since Falasha independence had virtually ceased a century and a half earlier. It is possible, nevertheless, that in Bruce's day the Falashas enjoyed some measure of autonomy for he tells us that since their defeat by the Amharas 'they have

[1] Beckingham, C. F. ed., *Travels to Discover the Source of the Nile by James Bruce*, p. 19.
[2] *Travels*, vol. 3, p. 305.
[3] *Travels*, vol. 2, p. 19.
[4] *Travels*, vol. 3, p. 189.
[5] ibid., p. 252.

adopted a more peaceable and dutiful behaviour, pay taxes, and are suffered to enjoy their own government'.[1] He presented a picture of the Jewish settlements in those high mountains which, but for the absence of the Agau language, has scarcely changed to this day:

> The language of Lamalmon [now known as the pass of Wolkefit] is Amharic; but there are many villages where the language of the Falashas is spoken. These are the ancient inhabitants of the mountains who still preserve the religion, language and manners of their ancestors, and live in villages by themselves. Their number is now considerably diminished, and this has proportionally lowered their power and spirit. They are now wholly addicted to agriculture, hewers of wood and carriers of water, and the only potters and masons in Abyssinia. In the former profession they excel greatly and, in general, live better than the other Abyssinians; which these, in revenge, attribute to a skill in magic, not to superior industry. Their villages are generally strongly situated out of the reach of marching armies, otherwise they would be constantly rifled, partly from hatred, and partly from hopes of finding money.[2]

As he neared the capital, Bruce again saw 'several small villages, inhabited by Falasha, masons and thatchers of houses, employed at Gondar'.[3]

In Bruce's time the size of the Agau population, like that of the Falashas, was diminishing under the impact of Amhara rule and its tendency to assimilate minorities. The two main areas of Agau and Falasha settlement were in the Semien mountains and in the region of Gondar and Lake Tana, which was also known as Lake Dembea. While he was in the latter area, heading, as he thought, for the source of the Nile, Bruce found that 'the language here is Falasha, though only used now by the Jews who go by that name: it was anciently the language of all the province of Dembea',[4] though 'it has now given place to Amharic'.[5] Again, as he travelled further south he reported that 'there are distant places towards the Jemma on the side of the Nile where they speak . . . Falasha'.[6] Here he is referring to the headwaters of the Blue Nile, the Little Abbai river, in which region remote Falasha villages are still to be found.

[1]*Travels*, vol. 1, p. 486.
[2]*Travels*, vol. 3, p. 190.
[3]ibid., p. 195.
[4]ibid., p. 535.
[5]*Travels*, vol. 4, p. 27.
[6]*Travels*, vol. 3, p. 559.

Distribution of Falasha population

It has always been difficult to ascertain the size of the Falasha population. The best estimate today gives a figure between 28,000 and 30,000. Faitlovitch, at the beginning of this century, thought it was about 50,000. In the middle of the last century Halévy estimated the number at between 150,000 and 200,000 or one tenth of the total population of Abyssinia. Bruce, however, was told that at the time of the defeat of King Gideon early in the seventeenth century the Falashas 'were supposed to amount to 100,000 effective men'.[1] If this figure is anything like correct and assuming one effective man per family of five people the Falasha population at that time would have amounted to about half a million souls. Bearing in mind the difficulties with which Amhara rulers had to contend in suppressing the Falasha kingdom, this figure does not seem exaggerated. The Jews were a force to be reckoned with. The continual decline in the Falashas' numbers after they lost their independence is a reflection of the hardships they have had to bear, the impact of wars and lawlessness, the poverty caused by their loss of lands, the tyranny of greedy feudal-type landlords and the pressure, reinforced by foreign missionaries, to be converted to Christianity and to assimilate into the dominant, Amhara community. The royal chronicles, and the *Kebra Nagast*, on which we have to rely for most of our information and which were Bruce's principal sources, are the product of Amhara civilisation. They were written in large measure to justify the claim of the Solomonic dynasty to the imperial throne and to ensure the supremacy of the Ethiopian Orthodox Church. The bias of the court historians is apparent in their references to Jews, Muslims and Roman Catholics or Franks and their prejudices inevitably colour their writing. Bruce himself was once accused by a high cleric, Abba Salama, of being a Frank who 'was accursed, and should be stoned as an enemy to the Virgin Mary'.[2] On another occasion, just before leaving the country, he was obliged to declare that he was not a Roman Catholic and he explained that a priest of his Protestant religion, 'preaching in any country subject to those Franks, would as certainly be brought to the gallows as if he had committed murder, and just as speedily as you would stone a Catholic priest preaching here in the midst of Gondar'.[3] It is as well to remember that parts of eighteenth-century Europe, especially the Iberian peninsula, were little more religiously tolerant than 'savage' Abyssinia and that heretics were still being burnt at the stake in Bruce's day.

[1] *Travels*, vol. 1, p. 486.
[2] *Travels*, vol. 4, p. 75.
[3] ibid., p. 265.

5

Resistance and Defeat

I N the written records of Ethiopia the first mention of the
Falashas appears in the chronicles of the reign of Amda Sion
(1314–44).[1] This king was the grandson of the founder of
the restored Solomonic dynasty, the real builder of the Ethiopian
state, who extended its borders through a number of military
campaigns. Among the areas where royal control was least secure
were the mountainous region north of Lake Tana and the plains to
the west of the lake, Agau country, where the Falasha settlements
were to be found. There was no direct administration of those
areas and in effect they were tributary states. The Ethiopian Jews
– depicted in the Chronicles as renegades, crucifiers, former
Christians who denied Christ[2] – enjoyed a great measure of
independence, which, however, was threatened from two directions. On one side, the expanding Amhara state was attempting to
absorb the outlying principalities and force their people to adopt
Christianity. On the other, there was a growing menace from the
militant Islamic tribes pressing in from the east and south. Faced
with this unenviable situation the Falashas in Amda Sion's reign
allied themselves with the Muslims. This policy proved to be
disastrous for, in the fighting which ensued, the Amharas were
victorious and the Falashas, in Bruce's account, left many slain
while the rest were forced 'to hide themselves in their inaccessible
mountains'.[3]

One hundred years later, having recovered their strength, the
Falashas broke into open rebellion. The cause of the revolt is not
clear and the Chronicles for this period are sadly deficient. At all
events, the Amhara king, Yeshaq (1412–29), replied to this

[1]R. L. Hess, *Proceedings of the Third International Conference of Ethiopian Studies,*
(Addis Ababa, 1969), vol. 1, p. 101.
[2]G. W. B. Huntingford, *The Glorious Victories of Amda Seyon,* p. 61.
[3]Bruce, *Travels,* vol. 2, p. 220.

challenge to his authority and the Falasha army was defeated at Kosage, north of Gondar. In memory of his victory, says Bruce, the king 'built a church on the place and called it Debra Isaac, which remains there to this day'.[1]

The tradition of this campaign lived on and Faitlovitch reported[2] that when he was passing through Begemeder in 1908 his guides pointed out a peak which was still called the Falashas' camp for it had been their headquarters in their fight against King Yeshaq. The Falashas maintained that the whole of Begemeder once belonged to them. These traditions support the view that their territory had once extended over a large part of the Agau-speaking country and as far south as the Bashilo tributary of the Blue Nile. This river, with its ravine nearly 4,000 feet deep, provided one of the most formidable obstacles to the opposing armies in the Abyssinian campaign of 1868 as they both converged on the fortress at Magdala. At one time it probably formed the boundary between the Amharas and the Falashas.

A desire was now emerging among the Amharas to establish links with Europe and in the reign of Zar'a Yaqob (1434–68) – in the view of some scholars the greatest ruler Ethiopia had seen since Ezana – a delegation was sent from the Abyssinian church in Jerusalem to the seventeenth church council in Florence. 'From this time', writes Bruce, 'there appear marks of a party formed in favour of the church of Rome.'[3] Ethiopia was beginning to break away from its long isolation. It was during this reign that one of the king's sons, Abba Saga, rebelled against his father, adopted the Jewish religion and, according to Faitlovitch,[4] took refuge in the Hoharwa mountains with a Falasha monk called Abba Sabra.[5] The two formed a close collaboration and together they developed the Falasha form of monasticism on lines similar to those of the Christians.

Whatever may be Zar'a Yaqob's claim to be considered a great ruler the chronicles of his reign depict him as a ferocious and cruel despot and a religious fanatic. He compelled pagans to abandon their customs and persecuted those who did not conform to the orthodox tenets. Members of a reformist sect known as the children of Estifa, or Stephanites, had their noses and tongues cut off and were then stoned to death. His chronicler called him 'the exterminator of the Jews'.[6] It may seem paradoxical that he should

[1] ibid., p. 66.
[2] *Quer durch Abessinien*, p. 112.
[3] Bruce, *Travels*, vol. 2, p. 69.
[4] Faitlovitch, *Quer durch Abessinien*, p. 89.
[5] According to Kaplan, op. cit., p. 69, Abba Sabra is "generally believed to have been a Christian".
[6] Louis Haber, 'The Chronicle of the Emperor Zara Yaqob (1434–68)', in *Ethiopia Observer*, vol. 5 (1961), no. 2, p. 167.

have prescribed that the Sabbath should be as holy as Sunday
without any distinction. He embodied his many injunctions in his
so-called holy books, which included *The Book of Light*, in which
Jews are accused of eating children.

It is possible that it was in reaction to his father's fanaticism that
Abba Saga adopted Judaism and that a number of tribes in the
Agau area, including the Falashas and those who had been forcibly
converted, rose in revolt. The Chronicle records that the rebels,
'having abandoned the faith of Christians, embraced the Jewish
religion, killed a great number of the inhabitants of the province of
Amhara and, when the king came to do battle with them, they
defeated his troops, drove them away and burned down all the
churches in their districts'.[1] The Christians' homes were pillaged
and the people deprived of everything, including the *Mateb* or
small blue cord worn around their necks as a sign of their religion.
The destruction covered a wide area and extended, we are told, to
all the people of Ethiopia.

It was during Zar'a Yaqob's reign that Elia of Ferrara[2] had met
the young Falasha in Jerusalem who had told him about the
continual wars which raged between his people and the Amhara
kings. Perhaps as a consequence of the newly established contact
with Rome a touch of intolerance had been wafted from Europe
which fanned the emperor's religious fervour.

His crusading enthusiasm was maintained by his son and
successor, Ba'eda Mariam (1468–78), who resumed the war
against the Falashas and for seven years fought them in the
provinces of Begemeder, Semien and Sellemt. Their resistance
was stubborn but eventually they were obliged to surrender and
the apostates forced to return to Christianity and to rebuild the
churches they had destroyed.[3] This campaign, long-drawn-out
though it was, marked one of the few military successes of Ba'eda
Mariam's reign and was made possible by a truce which the king
concluded with the Muslim Sultan of Adal on his eastern frontier.[4]
The Falashas now found themselves, *mutatis mutandis*, in the same
plight as the Jews of Khazaria described by Arthur Koestler in *The
Thirteenth Tribe* – squeezed between the conflicting ambitions of
the followers of the Cross and the Crescent and resented by both.
Many of them succumbed to conversion; others became crypto-
Jews like the Marranos of Spain.

Frequent fighting between Amharas and Muslims broke out

[1]ibid.
[2]See above, p. 75.
[3]Hess, op. cit., p. 103.
[4]Ullendorff, *The Ethiopians*, p. 70–1.

during the reign of Lebna Dengel (1508–40). At first the king successfully withstood the foreign incursions but the pressure was renewed under the leadership of Ahmad ibn Ibrahim, commonly called Grañ, 'the left-handed', who was a formidable military commander, for whom both Christians and Jews were equally objects of hatred. According to Bruce[1] the Falashas in the Semien mountains, having failed to obtain protection from the emperor, rebelled against him in 1537 and, under their King Gideon and Queen Judith, changed sides and joined the Muslim invaders. Hess surmises that this move was undertaken by the Falashas in order to re-establish their independence of the Amharas which had been eroded in the previous reigns.[2]

The Muslim conquest was marked by wholesale destruction, cruelty and ruination. 'Much of the literary and intellectual heritage of Abyssinia was irretrievably lost'[3] and it is probable that it is to this period in particular that we owe the destruction of many of the Falashas' records. The tornado stirred up by Grañ continued into the reign of Lebna Dengel's son Claudius (Galawdewos) (1540–59), which is notable for the decisive role played by the Ethiopians' new-found European allies. In reply to a call for help the Portuguese – who had retained a presence in the country since the end of the previous century – dispatched a force of 400 picked volunteers to Massawa under the command of Christopher da Gama, a son of the famous navigator. Firearms were now brought into use on both sides and, despite some setbacks, including the death of Christopher da Gama, the Ethiopians and their allies prevailed. Grañ had been able to secure some support from the Turks who were then establishing themselves in the Red Sea ports but, in 1543, he was utterly defeated and the Muslim occupation came to an end almost overnight.[4] Meanwhile, the Falasha stronghold, the Jews' Rock, having apparently been occupied by the Muslims, was returned to Falasha occupation under Ethiopian suzerainty.

With the defeat of Ahmad Grañ and notwithstanding a serious incursion by Galla tribes from the south and south-west, the Emperor Claudius was able to turn his attention to the encouragement of economic and cultural development. Signs of strain between the Roman Catholic visitors from Europe and the indigenous Coptic Christians were beginning to appear and it was during this reign that the 'Confession of Faith' was written as an

---

[1] *Travels*, vol. 2, p. 165.
[2] Hess, op. cit., p. 103.
[3] Ullendorff, *The Ethiopians*, p. 73.
[4] Pankhurst, *An Introduction to the Economic History of Ethiopia*, p. 78.

answer to the Jesuit mission led by Bishop de Oviedo. The document reaffirmed the Emperor's faith in the monophysite doctrine and defended those Abyssinian customs which contained Hebraic traits, such as the observance of Saturday in addition to Sunday, the dietary laws and the practice of circumcision. If the defeat of Grañ saved Ethiopia for Christendom, the robust defence put up by the monophysite church, both now and later, prevented the country from falling within the Roman Catholic sphere and thus becoming a Portuguese colony. Ethiopian independence rested on its ability to withstand both the onslaught of Islam and the threat of European temporal and spiritual expansion. While the Portuguese presence no doubt made some contribution by the influence it exerted on Ethiopian art and architecture, it also had the baleful effect of strengthening the Ethiopian church's antagonism to the Falashas and especially to their denial of the Christian messiah.

When Claudius was succeeded by his brother Menas (1559–63) he lost little time in reopening the campaign against the Falasha stronghold in Semien where their leader, 'Radaet the Jew', as Bruce called him, successfully warded off the attack.[1] But, in his short reign, the king had other preoccupations, including harrying the Jesuits, and it was left to his son and successor Sarsa Dengel (1563–95) to continue the war against the Falashas. The campaign lasted altogether for seventeen years, from 1577 to 1594, which is testimony enough to the tenacity and fighting spirit of the Jewish resistance. The epic story of this struggle for survival, as recounted in the Ethiopian royal chronicles, was translated into French and Hebrew by Joseph Halévy and published in Paris in 1907.

Sarsa Dengel mounted his campaign on the pretext that the Falashas, led by their king, Radai, had failed to pay their tribute. It is better, recorded the chronicle, that the emperor should fight against those who are guilty of the blood of our Lord Jesus Christ than to make war on the Gallas.[2] Halévy, a balanced and respected scholar, described the war as 'a veritable crusade, inspired by religious fanaticism . . . for the wolves who devour the sheep it is always the sheep who started it. The chronicler, imbued with religious prejudices, described the Falasha leaders as proud and insanely provocative; the historian will not allow himself to be thus misled.'[3] Sarsa Dengel's motive, like that of Ba'eda Maryam a hundred years earlier, was nothing less than the extermination of the Jewish religion and it is difficult to escape the

[1] *Travels*, vol. 2, p. 206.
[2] J. Halévy, *La Guerre de Sarsa-Dengel contre les Falachas*, p. 38.
[3] ibid., p. 77.

conclusion that the Portuguese had some influence, behind the scenes, in formulating the policy. The idea that the Falashas, armed only with spears and shields, would have provoked a war against superior forces equipped with firearms is highly improbable. 'Cet animal est méchant, lorsqu'on l'attaque il se défend.'

The Falashas in the rugged Semien mountains built their villages on the summit of rocky prominences, natural fortresses, called *ambas*. At the beginning of Sarsa Dengel's reign they lived in a kind of semi-independent principality divided into four provinces ruled by members of the same royal family and owing allegiance to the Negus Negasta or King of Kings of Ethiopia. Kalef (or Kaleb) and Radai were brothers while the other two chiefs were called Gweshan and Gideon, each with his capital on a different *amba* but owning land in the valleys below.

The relations between Jews, Christians and Muslims were, according to Halévy, friendly and would have remained so but for the religious fanaticism inculcated by the priests. At all events, the crusade was launched and Kaleb and Radai were the first to bear the brunt of the attack. Kaleb pursued a scorched earth tactic and won some battles but the discrepancy in arms was overwhelming and in 1581 his *amba* was taken and the inhabitants massacred on the orders of a priest named Abba Newai. Some women and girls were taken prisoner and the Christian chronicler recounts, with a note of admiration for their heroism, how they threw themselves over the precipice, dragging their captors, to whom they were bound by their wrists, after them, preferring to die rather than live in dishonour.

Radai, too, had some successes but eventually his fortress, Amba Worq, the gold mountain, was captured and he sued for peace. He was led by the priest, Abba Newai, into the king's presence, having covered his head, in biblical fashion, with ashes as a mark of mourning, while Sarsa Dengel took his wife, his children and his possessions as hostages. Radai was thrown into prison and the king celebrated communion on the *amba* as a sign of its purification. Many of Radai's people were able to escape but their leader suffered martyrdom. Yonael, the King's general, offered him his life if he would beg the Virgin Mary for mercy but, if not, 'the sword is before you'. Radai replied: 'Is not the mention of the name of Mary forbidden? Make haste! If I die it is better for me that I should depart from a world of lies to a world of justice, from the darkness to the light; kill me, swiftly!' To which Yonael answered: 'If you prefer death to life, die bravely and bow your head.' He bowed his head and Yonael struck him with his sword and with a single blow which severed his head and cut both his knees the blade came to rest in the ground. Those who witnessed the scene admired the strength of the sword and 'the courage of the Jew in death who declared the things of the earth are bad and the things of heaven are good'.[1]

Following the defeat of Kaleb and Radai the Ethiopian army required an interval for reorganisation and the absorption of contingents supplied by Muslim vassals. It was now the turn of Gweshan and Gideon to face the crusaders. Once again, an excuse for the attack was found by accusing Gweshan of planning a raid in Woggera province (between Semien and Gondar, where many Falashas live today), of burning a village and taking prisoners. Whether the charge was true or false (and given the discrepancy in their relative strengths it seems unlikely to be true) the pretext was sufficient to enable the king to besiege the Falasha stronghold. The defenders on their *amba* fought bravely and not without some success. They tried to block the advance by rolling rocks and boulders on to the enemy below but it was an uneven struggle with the Falashas outnumbered and lacking in firearms to match the invaders. Finally, their water supply was cut off and they were forced to surrender. Many were disarmed and ruthlessly massacred on the orders of the king's general. Gweshan and a few followers held out on their *amba*. But finally it was scaled at night and the town set on fire. Recognising that all was lost, Gweshan and his companions, together with Gideon's wives and sister, threw themselves over the precipice. Their bodies were decapitated and the heads presented to the king.

Gideon, too, recognising that further resistance was useless, chose suicide rather than captivity. In a remarkable passage, which suggests that he was conversant with the works of Josephus, the Falasha leader exhorted his picked soldiers to remember the words of their forefathers when Titus, the Roman general, wanted to take them prisoner saying: 'It is better to die honourably than to live in shame.'[2] Like the heroes of Masada in 73 AD or the martyrs of York[3] in 1190 they fell to and cut each others' throats with their swords and spears.

Thus the war in the Semien mountains came to an end and one more dramatic chapter was written in the history of the Jews, but one which, to this day, carries no memorial and whose heroes and martyrs remain unsung.

According to Bruce the Falashas lost 4,000 dead in their last battle when Gweshan died. From the mountain fortresses the

[1]ibid., p. 66.
[2]cf. Josephus, *The Wars of the Jews*, vol. 7, ch. 5.
[3]For an account of this episode see Abrahams, *The Legacy of Israel*, p. xix.

king turned his attention, at the beginning of 1594, to the Kwara region, west of Lake Tana, 'where the Jews had many strongholds, and he received everywhere their submission'.[1]

It might have been supposed that the calamities which befell the Falashas during the reign of Sarsa Dengel would have broken their spirit and forced them to abandon their faith. But no, the hard core of Agau Jews clung to their religion and have continued to do so to the present day, proclaiming by their tenacity their confidence in the God of Israel and in His commandments.

Twenty years after their defeat in the mountains the Falashas had sufficiently recovered to join in a rebellion against Emperor Susneyos, who had ascended the throne in 1607. This reign proved to be a period of great confusion. The early years were marked by numerous revolts in which the Agaus participated and were ruthlessly suppressed. This was followed by a bitter religious struggle which resulted from the adoption of Roman Catholicism by the emperor.

The Falashas were ruled by a new king Gideon when, in 1615, a pretender to the Ethiopian throne, named Amdo, appeared in the Sellemt region to the north of the Semien mountains. The local governor captured him and put him in prison. Gideon apparently considered this an excellent opportunity to acquire an ally. He sent out a raiding party at night which rescued Amdo and brought him back. Soon the standard of revolt was raised and Amdo, with Gideon's assistance, 'found himself at the head of an army, strong enough to leave the mountain, and try his fortune in the plain below, where he laid waste Shawada, Sellemt, and all the countries about Semien which persevered in their duty to the king'.[2]

The early successes were followed by others but soon the emperor brought up his main army, equipped with firearms. Gideon and Amdo were forced back into the mountains and one of their main strongholds, Messiraba, which 'had been fortified by art, furnished with plenty of provisions, and a number of good troops' was captured and 'the whole inhabitants, without distinction of age or sex, put to the sword, for such were the orders of the king'.[3] Further defeats followed, and the last stronghold, Seganat, resisted stoutly but it too 'was at last taken, Gideon himself escaping narrowly by the bravery of his principal general, who, fighting desperately, was slain by a musqueteer'.[4]

The situation had become hopeless and Gideon, fearing for the

[1] *Travels*, vol. 2, p. 231.
[2] ibid., p. 289.
[3] ibid., p. 290.
[4] ibid.

very survival of his people, sued for peace. The King agreed to pardon him in return for the surrender of Amdo. Gideon accepted and Amdo was convicted of rebellion and murder and crucified with great cruelty. The peace was short-lived. Treacherously and without warning the King ordered a general pogrom of all Falashas living between Lake Tana and the Semien mountains. Gideon was killed and, with his death, Falasha independence virtually came to an end. Bruce wrote that the official reason for the massacre was revenge for the Falashas' support of Amdo's rebellion but he saw the real cause in the hand of the new religion and the King's Jesuit advisers. He placed the date at 1616, though some writers, including Ben Zvi, favour 1624. Gideon, according to Bruce, was 'a man of great reputation, not only among his subjects but throughout all Abyssinia'.[1] He was reputed to have been immensely rich and his treasures to have been hidden in the mountains where, in Bruce's day and no doubt long after, they were sought in vain.

A few escaped the massacre in the company of Phineas, who succeeded Gideon as leader. Bruce wrote:

> ... the children of those that were slain were sold for slaves by the king; and all the Falasha in Dembea, in the low countries immediately in the king's power, were ordered upon pain of death to renounce their religion, and be baptised. To this they consented, seeing there was no remedy; and the king unwisely imagined that he had extinguished by one blow the religion which was that of his country long before Christianity, by the unwarrantable butchery of a number of people whom he had surprised living in security under the assurance of peace. Many of them were baptised accordingly, and they were all ordered to plow and harrow upon the sabbath day.[2]

Ever since the Portuguese first came to Abyssinia at the end of the fifteenth century the Roman Catholic Church had attempted to gain ascendancy in the country. The missionary spirit was strong among the Europeans and they were irked by the peculiar form of Christianity which they encountered, with its markedly Judaic characteristics. By the middle of the sixteenth century the Jesuit order had become interested in Ethiopia and decided to undertake the conversion of its people.[3] The Pope gave the project his blessing and in 1557 Bishop André de Oviedo's

[1]ibid., p. 292.
[2]ibid., p. 293.
[3]Pankhurst, op. cit., p. 81.

mission landed on the Red Sea coast a short while before Massawa was occupied by the Turks, with whom, astonishingly, the bishop soon made common cause. In 1603 a far abler missionary arrived in the person of the Spanish Jesuit Pero Pais, who rapidly gained influence at the Ethiopian court. When Susneyos had firmly established his authority, Pais 'began working systematically and adroitly by teaching Ethiopian children, by building churches, by dangling before the king the prospect of a military alliance with Spain, always on condition that he would submit himself and his country to the Church of Rome'.[1] By degrees Susneyos succumbed to the Jesuit propaganda and after Pais's death in 1622 he came under the influence of his less diplomatic but no less enthusiastic successor, Alphonso Mendes, who was also a Jesuit. The latter succeeded in persuading the emperor to make a public confession of his adherence to the Roman Church and he attempted to have the country converted by force. Mendes insisted that such Jewish practices as circumcision and the observance of Saturday as a day of rest should be prohibited. This also implied the renunciation of the traditional monophysite faith and the acceptance of the authority of the Pope. The Falashas were not the only victims of the Jesuits' mania. Heavy penalties were inflicted on those who refused to work on Saturday. Bruce records that one of the principal generals at the king's court was 'beaten with rods and degraded from his employment for observing the Jewish sabbath' while a certain monk had his tongue cut out for maintaining his faith in the monophysite doctrine of the oneness of the nature of Christ.[2]

The country became disaffected, revolts broke out and after severe fighting Susneyos finally decided to abandon the Jesuits and to abdicate in favour of his son Fasilidas (Basilides) (1632–67), who immediately banished the missionaries, first to Fremona in Tigrai and then from all Ethiopia. The ignominious failure of the Jesuit mission was ascribed by Bruce to the lack of enthusiasm for the adventure by the King of Spain and Portugal who, he thought, was more concerned with other foreign conquests, and failed to support the Jesuits with armed force, leaving Susneyos 'to the prayers of Urban VIII, the merit of Ignatius Loyola, and the labours of his furious and fanatic disciples'.[3] The expulsion of the Jesuits and the restoration of the monophysite faith protected the country from foreign intervention and avoided the worst excesses of the Inquisition, which, among other things,

[1]ibid., p. 82.
[2]Bruce, *Travels*, vol. 2, p. 339.
[3]ibid., p. 400.

would probably have spelt the annihilation of the Falashas.

Although Susneyos failed in his intention to destroy the Jews, they never fully recovered from the persecutions and forced conversions which they endured during his reign. Their autonomous state effectively came to an end, though in Bruce's day they may have been allowed a limited measure of self-government, and M. L. Marcus, possibly basing himself on Bruce, wrote in 1829 that the Falashas were still ruled by Jewish kings until 1800.[1] Nevertheless, to all intents and purposes their independence ended with the massacre of 1616.

The arrival of Fasilidas on the throne not only removed the threat of European colonisation but also brought some urgently needed governmental reforms, of which the most important took place in 1636, when the peripatetic form of government was replaced by a permanent capital at Gondar. Although the 'frankish' priests had been expelled and arrangements made with the Turks at Massawa and Suakim to prevent any possibility of their return, Fasilidas was wise enough to allow Portuguese laymen and the Indians they had brought with them to remain in the country. He exploited their skills by employing them in his ambitious construction programme, and it is to his reign that we owe the first of a series of splendid palaces, churches and bridges in and around Gondar which, though today partially in ruins, represent a unique feature of Ethiopian civilisation. The king also recognised the value of his Falasha subjects and, instead of persecuting them, he employed them as craftsmen on his buildings and encouraged them with the allotment of land to settle in the neighbourhood of his capital. The town grew both in size and in cultural importance, providing a centre in which music and poetry, literature, painting and calligraphy, in addition to architecture, flourished.[2]

The establishment of a central government at Gondar had the disadvantage that it led to the growth of regionalism, to the increase in the power of the feudal nobles and to an opportunity for the Galla tribes to overrun the frontiers and penetrate the social structure of the country. Fasilidas was succeeded by two rulers who maintained reasonably strong governments but thereafter the central authority declined, local chiefs increased their power, and intrigues undermined the stability of the court. This was the situation which Bruce found when he arrived at Gondar in February 1770, and it continued in much the same pattern until

---

[1]"Notice sur l'époque de l'établissement des Juifs dans l'Abyssinie', *Nouveau Journal Asiatique*, 1829.
[2]Pankhurst, op. cit., p. 86.

the middle of the following century when order was for a short time restored under the Emperor Theodore.

The publication in 1790 of Bruce's account of his travels, including his history of Ethiopia and his reference to the Jewish elements blended into the country's life and culture provoked much interest in Europe but made little impact in Jewish circles. Neither the story of the persecution and resistance under Sarsa Dengel and Susneyos nor the astonishing saga of Jewish survival in the depths of darkest Africa produced any positive reaction until, in the second quarter of the nineteenth century, in response to news which was beginning to circulate of Protestant missionary activity, a spasmodic interest was eventually aroused.

6

Missions and Missionaries

THIRTY years after Bruce had left the country his biographer, Alexander Murray, remarked: 'No European has traced his steps or penetrated into Abyssinia. Even the name of the present king is uncertain.' Ethiopia was in the midst of what has been called the 'Zemene mesafent', the Era of the Judges, when petty rulers fought among themselves, the Emperor's authority was constantly challenged and, as in Old Testament times, 'there was no king in Israel: every man did that which was right in his own eyes'.[1]

If the interior of the country remained largely *terra incognita* the Red Sea was rapidly assuming a new significance. With Napoleon casting longing eyes on the Levant and Egypt and threatening British interests in India, the military as well as the commercial importance of the area was attracting increasing attention. The cutting of the Suez Canal was still more than fifty years away but the land route between the Mediterranean and the Red Sea was – as it had been in antique times – busy with trade between Europe and the East. If Britain was to retain her leading position a fresh look had to be taken at the countries bordering the sea and the French would have to be forestalled. By the beginning of the nineteenth century, European explorers were once more attracted to the interior of the continent. Bruce's careful charts of the Red Sea were coming in useful and the British and French governments, in traditional rivalry, were each considering establishing relations with the rulers of Ethiopia. The first mission after Bruce's travels was undertaken by George Annesley, Viscount Valentia, who commanded a British ship in the Red Sea engaged in a hydro-graphic survey. He dispatched his secretary, Henry Salt, to explore the country in 1805 and, four years later, Salt was sent on an official

[1]Judges 21:25.

mission by the British Government to make contact with the King of Abyssinia. He published an account of his journeys in 1814 but his movements had been hampered by the unsettled state of the country and he failed to reach Gondar. He mentioned the Falashas in his book but added nothing significant to the existing knowledge of the subject.

The Church, too, began to show an interest and in 1826 Samuel Gobat, a French-speaking Swiss Protestant who had been trained at St Chrischona's mission in Basle, was sent to Abyssinia by the Church Missionary Society. With the spread of British influence and interests to the farthest corners of the world the Church of England was becoming conscious of the immense possibilities which presented themselves to propagate its own version of Christianity. The Church Missionary Society was founded in 1799 to be followed ten years later by the London Society for Promoting Christianity amongst the Jews, which has come to be known by the initials C.M.J.

Gobat encountered difficulties reaching Abyssinia and spent three years in Egypt awaiting permission to enter the country. Eventually he arrived in Tigrai province and proceeded from there to Gondar, where, according to Eric Payne,[1] 'a real interest was shown by both Amharas and Falashas'. He spent several years in the country and, in 1836, was replaced by Dr Isenberg and Dr Krapf, who worked in Tigrai, where the Jesuits had also set up a mission. The Jesuits, says Payne, persuaded the ruler of the province to banish the C.M.S. missionaries and, while Krapf moved to Shoa province and devoted himself to the Gallas, Isenberg returned to England to compose the first Amharic dictionary and grammar in English. Gobat, meanwhile, was transferred to Malta and in 1846 was appointed the second Anglican bishop in Jerusalem in succession to Michael Solomon Alexander, a converted German-born Jew who had previously been Professor of Hebrew and Rabbinical Literature at King's College, London University. Gobat had early evinced an interest in converting Jews and, at a meeting of the C.M.J. in 1838, he advocated starting missionary activity among the Falashas. Nothing was done at the time but when he was installed in Jerusalem he extended the missionary activities of his see through Egypt and the Sudan to the highlands of Ethiopia. By 1855 public security had been improved under the firm rule of the new emperor Theodore II and Bishop Gobat decided that the time was propitious for recommencing missionary activities

[1]*Ethiopian Jews*, p. 29.

while paying special attention to the Falasha population.

Leaders of the missionary movement in England had reached the conclusion that the followers of the ancient independent churches in the Middle East, such as the Armenians, Nestorians, Copts and Ethiopians, could serve as an intermediate stage in bringing Protestant Christianity to their Muslim neighbours. The first step, however, was to revivify the churches themselves by bringing them into closer relationship with the Church of England. Similarly, it was thought that converted oriental Jews had the qualities needed to make excellent missionaries and C.M.J. operations were extended in various countries of the Ottoman Empire. In the case of the Falashas, however, converts were to be used as a means to improve the moral and religious standards of the wayward Ethiopian Copts whose beliefs and behaviour deeply shocked the puritanical British missionaries. If the Falashas could also be employed to bring the Gospel to the Muslims, that would be an additional bonus.

Apart from the missionaries two of the early explorers of Abyssinia – one English and one French – also deserve mention since they both made contact with the Falashas and brought news of them to the notice of western Jewry. Charles Tilstone Beke (1800–74) was a geographer and biblical critic, born in Stepney, who travelled widely in Abyssinia during the years 1840–3 and was especially notable for his pioneering work in surveying the course of the Blue Nile. He had been so much impressed by the similarity between the religious tenets of the Samaritans and the Falashas, whom he called 'an Israelitish people of Abessinia', that he wrote to the editor of the *Jewish Chronicle* reproducing an extract from his contribution to the fourteenth volume of the *Journal* of the Royal Geographical Society. He described a visit he paid in March 1842 to an Agau-speaking Falasha village in Agawmeder district, south of Lake Tana. He found that the people were weavers, smiths and potters who strictly observed the laws of personal purification and concluded that 'there seems little doubt that the Falashas of Abessinia belong to the sect of the Samaritans. When and how their religion was introduced into that portion of Africa is a question which we do not at present possess the means of deciding.'[1] This letter possibly represents the earliest report of the existence of an Ethiopian community to appear in a Jewish newspaper. A year later Beke again wrote to the *Jewish Chronicle* giving a summary of the history of the Falashas, based on Bruce's work, and adding that 'here and there, over almost the

[1] *Jewish Chronicle*, 5 February 1847.

entire country, are found the scattered remnants of a once numerous Israelitish people, who still retain the religion of their ancestors, though in an extremely debased form'.[1] Beke attained considerable recognition as an explorer and scholar and had aspired to become Her Majesty's Consul in Abyssinia following the murder of Walter Plowden in 1860. But he was not the Foreign Office's favourite candidate and, at the time of the imprisonment of the British captives in 1866, Beke was uncharitably portrayed in the House of Commons by Henry Layard as a 'fussy, busy, mischievous, intriguing, meddling, troublesome person'.[2]

This harsh description was no doubt shared by Antoine Thomson d'Abbadie, a French explorer, born in Dublin, who travelled extensively in Abyssinia about the same time as Beke. Together with his younger brother Arnoud, Antoine contributed much to the knowledge of the geography, archaeology and linguistics of the country but he also became involved in political intrigues and in furthering the interests of France and the Roman Catholic missionaries. He was strongly criticised by Beke especially for his assertion that the Blue Nile, and not the White Nile, was the main river, an assertion which prompted the Englishman to return the gold medal which he had been awarded by the Geographical Society of France.

The d'Abbadie brothers spent eleven years in Abyssinia and returned to France in 1848 to prepare their vast accumulation of material for publication. In 1849 Antoine was in London and on 16 November an interview with him appeared in the *Jewish Chronicle*. D'Abbadie reported that the Falashas held 'celibacy in high honour', which was no doubt a reference to their acceptance of a form of monasticism, and also that 'they consider suicide from religious motives as highly meritorious'. He had met a young Falasha who expressed a strong desire to visit Europe 'in order to acquire the correct notions on Judaism' which, on his return, he would convey to his brethren. He made d'Abbadie promise that he would try to interest European Jews in his request. He also reported that there was a Jewish kingdom existing in the south of the country.

Four years earlier, d'Abbadie had published his 'Notice sur les Falashas' in the *Journal des Débats*, which had been reprinted in the *Bulletin* of the French Geographical Society, and had come to the attention of a brilliant young Jewish scholar. Filosseno Luzzatto (1829–54) of Padua, the eldest son of the Hebrew scholar S. D.

[1]ibid., 31 March 1848.
[2]Bates, *The Abyssinian Difficulty*, p. 70; Hansard, 26 November 1867 (245).

Luzzatto, had been inspired, when only thirteen, by Bruce's *Travels* to find out all he could about the Falashas. At sixteen he read d'Abbadie's article and was so deeply moved by it that he immediately wrote to the explorer, who was then in Abyssinia, asking for further information. Communication with the interior of Ethiopia was difficult and young Luzzatto had to wait exactly two years before he received a reply. In his interview in the *Jewish Chronicle* d'Abbadie had mentioned this exchange of correspondence and had regretted that he was not better informed on Jewish subjects.

D'Abbadie gave the Falashas a solemn undertaking to bring their wretched condition to the attention of the Jews of Europe and, with Luzzatto's help, he was as good as his word. The young scholar worked enthusiastically on the material which was placed at his disposal and in 1851 he had the satisfaction of seeing the first of many long instalments of his work published in the *Archives Israélites* of Paris[1] which continued to print his contributions until his premature death on 25 January 1854. In a short obituary the editor noted that Luzzatto wrote the last instalment in great pain and that he was working on his favourite subject until the last days of his life. He died in Padua from a disease of the brain which according to Mario Stock, the historian of the Jewish community of Trieste, a local tradition ascribes to syphilis contracted during a long stay in Paris. His tombstone disappeared during the Second World War when the old Jewish cemetery was damaged by Allied bombing but a record of the inscription in Hebrew and Italian has been preserved in the community archives. Would the Falashas' fate, one wonders, have been different if he had lived? In England, too, d'Abbadie and Luzzatto received some support. The *Jewish Chronicle*, more of a newspaper and less of a magazine than the *Archives Israélites*, in 1851 published nine weekly instalments of translations extracted from the French articles as well as a report of Filosseno's death.[2]

Luzzatto, perhaps a little unjustly, criticised Bruce for not paying more attention to the Falasha religion. He stressed the importance of a knowledge of the Falashas for the study of the history of the Jewish religion and hoped that, with the help of inquiries made by d'Abbadie on the spot, he might be able to fill the gaps left by Bruce. He had compiled a long list of questions for the French explorer to ask Abba Ishaq, 'the most wise spiritual leader of the Falashas', who lived at the monastery at Hoharwa,

---

[1] The *Archives Israélites de France*, a quarterly journal, was founded in 1840 and closed with its issue of 21 November 1935.
[2] *J.C.*, 17 March 1854.

north-west of Gondar. First of all he wanted to know how the Falashas came to be in Abyssinia. He received the following answer:

> We came with Solomon. Zogo, the son of the Queen of Sheba's servant, is the father of the Zagwes. We came after Jeremiah. We came under Solomon; we came by Sennar and from there to Axum. Undoubtedly, we came under Solomon.

It is noteworthy that this reply was made before Western contacts had begun to influence the thinking of the Falasha leaders. It represents, therefore, the pure Falasha tradition which can still be found in the outlying villages. Although it may be difficult to reconcile Abba Ishaq's statement that 'we came after Jeremiah' with his insistence that 'we came under Solomon', it is significant that there is no suggestion of an Arabian point of origin and that entry to Ethiopia was believed to have been made from Sennar on the Blue Nile. Luzzatto himself rejected the historicity of the Solomon–Sheba story of the Falashas' origin but considered that the post-Jeremiah tradition was entirely valid. He reached the conclusion that the Falashas were Hellenised Jews who travelled from Egypt to Abyssinia by way of Meroë about the middle of the third century BC at the time of Ptolemy III, Euergetes I (246–221), when ptolemaic power was at its zenith. The proof, he said, was to be found in the Falasha religion. The Elephantine papyri had not been discovered in his day but he cited the pre-rabbinate religious practices of the Jews at their second-century BC temple at Leontopolis, near modern Cairo, where, as at Elephantine, they also offered sacrifices, in support of his contention. Although he accepted what is now called the migration theory of history, Luzzatto came closer to solving the problem of the origin of the Falashas than many subsequent scholars – mesmerised, it seems, by the attraction of the Arabian school of thought.

Besides receiving answers to a number of questions about their religious practices – which have been largely confirmed by writers such as Leslau – Luzzatto was also informed categorically that the Falashas had no books in Hebrew, which he was also told by a Jewish doctor from Aleppo who had visited Ethiopia and whom he interviewed on his return. Luzzatto was deeply conscious of the Falashas' yearning to make contact with western Jews – 'We beg you to send us someone,' they demanded – and he was anxious to secure publicity for these brave and deserving people. It was their strict observance of the Law, the Falashas said, which prevented them from travelling by sea 'to find distant brothers; for how can we observe the Sabbath?' Alternatively, a journey by the land route across the Muslim-occupied desert, which would have permitted them to observe the day of rest, would have been a hazardous undertaking for an 'infidel'. The Torah's injunction on the subject of travel, 'abide ye every man in his place, let no man go out of his place on the seventh day',[1] was reinforced by the *Book of Jubilees*, which, among other things, forbade travel by ship on the sea on the Sabbath under pain of death.[2] It was not until Talmudic times that a way round this regulation was devised.

Abba Ishaq reported that he regarded the name 'Falasha' as an insult and that he and his people called themselves by the Agau name '*Kayla*', which, he said, meant 'who has not crossed the sea';[3] but, he added, the Jews of Kwara, to the south-west of Gondar, seemed content to accept the designation 'Falasha', from which it seems that the insult was not very grave and doubtless depended upon how the term was used. Over two thousand Falashas, Ishaq informed Luzzatto, had emigrated from the Semien mountains to the Azabo Galla country further east. Their descendants were still living there in his day and could be the forebears of the present communities in Lasta and Maichew. He also reported that there were Falashas living in the Gurage-speaking area in Shoa province, south of modern Addis Ababa, though, despite unconfirmed reports, there is no conclusive evidence of the existence of this community at the present day. Luzzatto expressed some surprise that Ishaq made no mention of Falashas living in Tigrai province though d'Abbadie had found a group of 140 Tigrinya speakers. This separation of the Jews of Tigrai from their co-religionists to the south of the river Takazze persists to the present day and, though it may be partially explained by linguistic differences, it deserves closer study since practically all attention so far has been focused on the Amharic speakers.

About the same time as Filosseno Luzzatto's untimely death in 1854 two events occurred which were destined to produce a significant impact on the history of Ethiopia and on the situation of the Falashas. A new Emperor ascended the throne and the Anglican mission to the Jews resumed its operations with increased vigour.

The unruly era of the *rases*, when petty chieftains fought one

---

[1]Exodus 16:29.
[2]50:12; see R. H. Charles, *The Book of Jubilees*, p. 260.
[3]Halévy interpreted this to mean 'one who does not cross a running stream on the Sabbath' (*J.C.* 27 August 1869). Dr Appleyard has advised me that this Agau word may be translated 'he (or they) did not cross'.

another to extend their territories and the writ of the Negus was only nominal, had provided an ideal setting for an ambitious, free-booting young warrior. Kassa, who later became Emperor of Ethiopia under the name of Theodore II, was born about 1818 in Kwara province, the son of a minor local chieftain who died when he was a child. His mother was of humble origin and the official histories have little to say about her. During his lifetime Kassa claimed to be of royal blood and a scion of the Solomonic line, but the claim has never been substantiated. Among the Falashas of Kwara, however, there is a different legend. They say that Kassa's father, Hailu Waleda Georgis, was a Falasha converted to Christianity who married a similar convert called Esther who, having lost her virginity before marriage, had been expelled from the tribe in accordance with custom and thus was thrown into the arms of a Christian husband. When she became pregnant she went to a Falasha monk to seek an interpretation of a dream which foretold that she would give birth to the sun. The monk told her this meant that her child would become an important person. When a boy was born she called him Kassa, meaning 'compensation', because she had been badly treated by her people and God had compensated her. After her husband's early death, Esther fell on hard times and was forced to earn a livelihood by selling flowers of the kosso tree, which, as Bruce had written, were used as a remedy for tapeworms, a very common malady.[1] The trade in kosso is much despised and in later years Theodore was taunted by his enemies on account of his mother's lowly occupation. The Falashas maintain that the emperor used to show them consideration and that on his campaigns he gave presents to the Falasha monks and invited their prayers.

On the death of his father Kassa was sent to a monastery near Lake Tana. He escaped from it when it was sacked by Galla rebels from Gondar and he found refuge with an elder half-brother, named Kinfu, who sent him to school at another monastery in Kwara province. This proved to be a formative period in the boy's life. He not only acquired a reputation for great bravery and skill in many activities but he was also a serious and able student. It was here that he learnt of an ancient prophecy that a saviour named Theodore would one day rule over Ethiopia. He kept this well in mind and dreamt of himself as the saviour who would not only restore order in Ethiopia itself but, as Consul Plowden wrote, would 'reclaim all the provinces lately conquered by Egypt along

[1] The use of this plant as a medicament is described by R. Pankhurst in 'Europe's discovery of the Ethiopian taenicide – *Kosso*', in *Medical History*, vol. 23, no. 3, July 1979.

his northern frontier; even to Khartoum, as his by right; nor does his military ardour hesitate to dream of the conquest of Egypt and a triumphant march to the Holy Sepulchre'.[1] After he had finished his schooling Kassa became an outlaw (*shifta*) and rapidly achieved a dominating position which eventually led to his gaining a decisive victory over his rivals and culminated in his coronation as Emperor in February 1855.

Bishop Gobat's plans to reopen Ethiopia for missionary activity bore fruit when, in the same year as the coronation, Dr Krapf, who had already had experience of the country, returned to resume his work and brought with him a young German called Martin Flad. Theodore and the Abuna, or Patriarch, gave them permission to undertake missionary activities provided that the missionaries were not ordained priests and that all converts, of whatever origin, were baptised into the Ethiopian Coptic Church. The emperor also insisted that his real need was for artisans who would help to raise the technical standards of his people and it was therefore agreed that any assistants required by the missionaries should be skilled craftsmen who could also preach the gospel. It became a matter of some discord at a later date which of these functions was the more important. The emperor clearly thought his country was in little need of foreign Christian preachers but was sorely lacking in the know-how which would enable him to achieve his ambitions and, especially, to provide him with guns and ammunition.

After three years in the field, Flad returned to Jerusalem to report to Gobat and soon returned to Ethiopia, supported by a young wife who was a qualified pharmacist and armed with thirty-three camel-loads of bibles in Amharic. Flad had given a favourable report to his bishop and indicated that he found a more encouraging response among the Falashas than among the Amharas. This news delighted the C.M.J., whose conversionist activities were gaining much popularity in mid-Victorian England and were attracting support from all classes of society, not least among a god-fearing section of the aristocracy. For thirty-seven years the C.M.J.'s affairs were presided over by that great missionary enthusiast and philanthropist the seventh Earl of Shaftesbury, to whose memory, ironically, the pagan statue of Eros was erected in Piccadilly Circus.

When the C.M.J. celebrated its fiftieth anniversary, in 1859, it decided to expand its activities and, according to Payne, in order 'to test whether it was the will of God for them to start a mission

[1]Bates, *The Abyssinian Difficulty*, p. 18.

amongst the Falashas ... they sent out the most courageous missionary on their staff, Henry Aaron Stern'.¹ The most courageous he may have been but he was also among the most maladroit and undiplomatic. He cannot escape a major share of the responsibility for the situation which led, by degrees, to the dispatching of the costly military expedition under General Sir Robert Napier which was later mounted in order to free him and others from imprisonment. This campaign left the country as unsettled as it was before it began and retarded all missionary activity for many years. Stern was a German Jew, born in 1820, who had been converted by the C.M.J. in London and, wishing to become a missionary, was sent to Jerusalem where, at the age of twenty-four, he was ordained by his fellow convert Bishop Alexander. He saw service in Mesopotamia, Persia and the Yemen, from where he had been obliged to flee to Aden in fear of his life. Whatever his shortcomings, Stern was zealous and ready to face whatever hardships came his way. He arrived in Ethiopia in March 1860 accompanied by another missionary called Bronkhorst.

In spite of the fact that he was an ordained clergyman, Stern was given permission by the emperor and the Abuna to work among the Falashas provided, once again, that all converts were baptised into the Ethiopian church. After a year visiting Falasha villages, with Flad acting as interpreter, Stern returned to England to report to the C.M.J. and to write his book *Wanderings among the Falashas in Abyssinia*, which, while casting much light on conditions in Ethiopia, was surprisingly thin on information regarding the Falashas. The book, first published in London in 1862, contained disparaging remarks about the emperor – including the story of his mother's lowly status – and was contemptuous in its comments on the Ethiopians and their church.

The Emperor Theodore, meanwhile, having established his supremacy in Ethiopia, aimed to extend his contacts beyond the frontiers of his realm. He saw himself as the great Christian ruler who would lead a new crusade against Islam. Who better to join forces with him than the great Christian Queen of England, the head of the most powerful nation in the world? In 1862 he addressed a letter to Queen Victoria in which he proposed that he should send an embassy to England and gave it to the new British Consul, Captain Cameron, the successor to Walter Plowden, who, he anticipated, would deliver it in person. However, Cameron used messengers instead and when, eventually, the letter

¹*Ethiopian Jews*, p. 36.

reached the Foreign Office in London nothing was done about it. The fact was that, at that time, Ethiopian and British interests were far from being in harmony. They differed fundamentally in regard to their attitude towards the Ottoman Empire in particular and to Muslims in general. Theodore's ambition for a crusade found no response in Britain, where a pro-Turkish stance had been adopted in creating the Anglo-French-Turkish alliance against Russia for the prosecution of the Crimean War of 1854–6. Besides, the growing importance both of the Indian possessions and the vital communications route through the Red Sea made the need for maintaining friendly relations with the Islamic world a pillar of British policy. The British Government's failure to reply to his letter, which seems to have been due rather to bureaucratic muddling than deliberate discourtesy, was no doubt a major factor in upsetting the emperor. But minor slights and criticisms easily offended this proud and hot-tempered autocrat. The French, to whom he also made approaches, fared no better and at one moment he exclaimed to Flad, 'I hate all you Europeans; you are all, at heart, my enemies.'[1]

Another cause of irritation was the news which had reached him that the British Consul in Jerusalem was no longer safeguarding the interests of the Ethiopian church in Jerusalem. The Turkish authorities had been allowed to expel the clergy from that part of the Church of the Holy Sepulchre which they had occupied for centuries and had forced them to move on to the roof.

And so the relations between Theodore and the Europeans deteriorated. The crisis came when Henry Stern, on a second tour of inspection, was returning, in October 1863, from Gondar to Massawa to embark for England. As he reached the plain of Woggera and finding to his surprise that the emperor was encamped there he decided that 'duty, as well as courtesy, forbade me to advance without saluting His Majesty'.[2] The audience which followed could scarcely have been more disagreeable. Stern and Captain Cameron, the British Consul, were already in Theodore's bad books. The emperor was in ill sorts and had been drinking with his soldiers. When he found that Stern was accompanied by two of Cameron's servants, who were escorting him to the coast, his suspicions were aroused. On a flimsy excuse he ordered the servants to be beaten to death. Forced to witness this atrocity, Stern made an involuntary gesture which the emperor interpreted as a mark of defiance and he immediately

[1]Bates, op. cit., p. 49.
[2]ibid., p. 47.

ordered him, too, to be beaten. He was not killed but was left unconscious and when he recovered he was chained hand and foot and taken to Gondar to be looked after by Flad.

The emperor then ordered Stern's possessions to be searched, with the result that he received confirmation of his suspicion that he, together with Rosenthal, another converted German-Jewish missionary whom Stern had recruited, had been writing disparagingly of him and his people. Theodore was furious and ordered the arrest first of the missionaries and a little later of Cameron. Thus began the long saga of the Abyssinian captives. The Foreign Office was in a dilemma. After six months' deliberations it was decided to send Hormuzd Rassam, a Mesopotamian Nestorian who was employed on the staff of the British administration in Aden, to act as envoy and carry a personal letter from Queen Victoria to the emperor. Rassam's reward was to be thrown into prison together with two other British officials who accompanied him. It was now the turn of Theodore to send an emissary to Queen Victoria to request technical aid in the form of skilled craftsmen who could teach his people. He also asked for a gift of guns, pistols and gunpowder with the necessary equipment to enable the Ethiopians to manufacture their own armaments. The British Government was inclined to agree to these requests provided the prisoners were released. Artisans as well as materials were dispatched to Massawa to await there until the captives were brought to the coast. In the absence of a satisfactory settlement, the Foreign Office warned, an armed expedition would be dispatched. Theodore treated these threats with disdain and, not trusting the British to fulfil their side of the proposed bargain, he allowed matters to take their own course. Public opinion in Britain, not surprisingly, was becoming impatient and, though the Government was genuinely reluctant to become involved in a war, it eventually found that it had no alternative. The final decision was taken by the Cabinet on 19 August 1867 and the wheels of the military machine were set in motion.

If the reports of travellers such as Bruce, Salt, Beke and d'Abbadie had failed to arouse more than a cursory interest among the Jews of the West, the accounts which began to be published in London and elsewhere of the activities of the missionaries, and especially of the apostate Stern, at last produced some reaction. Dispatches from their representatives in the field were published with pride in the C.M.J.'s monthly magazine, *The Jewish Intelligence*, and were reproduced frequently from the mid-1850s onwards in the *Jewish Chronicle* combined with urgent pleas that something should be done to assist the Falashas to withstand the attentions of the missionaries.

The mid-nineteenth-century was a period when great efforts were made by the Jewish communities of Western Europe, and especially of Britain under the energetic leadership of Sir Moses Montefiore, to succour their less fortunate brethren in other parts of the world. Philanthropy was in the air. It might have been expected, therefore, that the plight of the hard-pressed and impoverished Ethiopian Jews would attract widespread and sympathetic notice. That this did not occur can be attributed principally to the uncertainty which existed among the orthodox as to whether the Falashas should be considered as part of the Jewish people. The Ethiopian Jews' ignorance of the Oral Law and the rules of conduct contained in the *Halacha*, their retention of certain practices such as the sacrifice, and their adoption of some non-Jewish customs combined to put doubts into the minds of rabbis and laymen alike. Besides, with their adherence to the notion of a Jewish race, descended from the white-skinned children of Israel, how was it possible that there could be Jews who were very nearly black?

The methods adopted by Stern and his colleagues had been made quite clear in their writings and speeches. In the past Christians and Muslims had often attempted to convert Jews by forcible and brutal methods. The new style of missionary adopted persuasion which sometimes amounted to sheer deceit. Bringing to bear sophisticated theological arguments, Stern and his friends sought to discredit the faith of the simple and primitive people. 'We informed them', wrote Stern, 'that we were also Falashas who, moved by compassion for their hopeless and deplorable condition, had crossed seas and deserts, dreary swamps and unsightly wilds to communicate to them those tidings of mercy which alone can secure peace to the troubled conscience and fill the soul with love to a sin-hating God.'[1]

Stern knew what the consequences of his preaching might be and at times his callousness was staggering. He foresaw that conversions might provoke serious trouble for, he wrote, 'it may rouse the slumbering demon of persecution, and subject the newly-gathered converts to a baptism of fire, and a trying and sifting ordeal of their faith. An eventuality of this kind we must be prepared to expect, whenever the great truth which is at present moving the heart of the unbelieving Falasha shall come into collision with the pride, ignorance, and superstition of the corrupt

[1]*Wanderings among the Falashas in Abyssinia*, p. 200.

Amhara.'¹ This passage brought down on his head the impas-
sioned denunciation of the *Jewish Chronicle*, which said that while
Stern and his colleagues 'imperilled the lives of the poor defence-
less Falashas they have evinced all the feelings of cowards and
sneaks'.²

Fortunately, a blood-bath did not follow but the real damage
done by the missionaries – even greater than the number of
conversions – was to undermine the stability of a settled and
closely-knit society. They raised doubts among the faithful and
encouraged assimilation for the sole benefit of what Stern himself
called 'that dead church', for which the missionaries admitted they
had nothing but contempt.

By 1864, the year that saw the flogging and imprisonment of
Stern, the Falashas at last found a religious champion in the person
of the German rabbi Israel Hildesheimer of Eisenstadt (1820–99).
No one could dispute the learned and greatly respected Hildesheimer's qualifications for giving a religious ruling. His
orthodoxy was beyond question and he became the founder and
leader of the community known as *Adath Israel*. He was the first
religious leader of stature since Rabbi David ben Abi Zimrah in
the sixteenth century to declare unequivocally that the Falashas
were Jews and, further, that it was the duty of their co-religionists
to come to their assistance. His declaration took the form of a very
urgent appeal addressed to leaders of Jewish opinion in several
countries. In England, Abraham Benisch, the editor of the *Jewish
Chronicle*, published it in full under an introductory paragraph in
which he observed that all the information about missionary
activities which Hildesheimer condemned so emphatically had
originally appeared in his columns.³ He would have appreciated a
word of acknowledgement.

The rabbi had thoroughly examined the credentials of the
Falashas and had satisfied himself, on the basis of Rabbi David ben
Abi Zimrah's 'responsum', the writings of Filosseno Luzzatto and
inquiries he made in Jerusalem, that they were authentic members
of the House of Israel. He urged that a mission should be
dispatched as soon as possible to make contact with them and
concluded his appeal with these words:

> Since long my heart longed to give vent to my emotions. Have
> pity, dearest fellow-believers; save, deliver, aid this holy matter
> in the name of God; organise committees, offer yourselves as

¹ibid., p. 301.
²*J.C.*, 6 December 1867.
³*J.C.*, 4 November 1864.

members thereof... contribute abundantly and frequently, and what seems to be so difficult will be accomplished in a comparatively short time.

It cannot be said that the appeal created much more than a ripple of interest on either side of the English Channel. Apart from a single letter of support in the *Jewish Chronicle* from 'A British Jew', little stirred until, over two years later, it was announced that the Alliance Israélite Universelle of Paris was prepared to send a mission to Abyssinia. It was only when the damage caused by the missionaries was eventually recognised that any positive action was contemplated. Even this did not become a matter for real concern until the imprisonment of Stern and his companions generated popular excitement and Britain found herself drifting into a state of war to vindicate national pride and honour.

The Falasha problem was brought to the attention of the Alliance Israélite, then under the presidency of Adolphe Crémieux, who was later to become French Minister of Justice, by the delegate from Adrianople. Joseph Halévy had been born in Galicia (southern Poland) in 1827 and had moved to Turkey when he was young. Two years older than Filosseno Luzzatto, he too had studied Hebrew and Semitic languages. At the meeting of the central committee on 9 January 1867 he announced that, after profound investigation of the subject, he was prepared to undertake a mission to the Falashas and invited the support of the Alliance. Two months later the central committee accepted the proposal, allocated the sum of 5,000 francs for the project and agreed to seek the co-operation of English Jews.

In London, a committee was formed under the chairmanship of the Chief Rabbi, Dr Nathan Adler, which, by May 1867, had raised 10,000 francs on condition that half the sum should be earmarked for a similar expedition to go to Kaifeng-Fu in China after the return of the Abyssinian mission. The Alliance gladly accepted the London committee's offer with the proviso that it reserved its position in regard to the proposed visit to China until the result of the Abyssinian venture could be assessed. Halévy lost little time in making his preparations and, by the first week of October, after the rainy season, he reached Massawa just a few weeks before the advance party of General Napier's forces landed at Zula, some forty miles further south and near the site of ancient Adulis. With the country in a state of acute unrest and preparing to be invaded, it was not the most propitious moment for Halévy's visit but he intended to strike while the iron was hot and before the Alliance's enthusiasm cooled off.

It had been Halévy's intention to penetrate into the interior of the country by following the British forces, 'but', he wrote in a letter to the Alliance from Massawa, dated 7 October 1867, 'I must wait a long time in view of the slowness of the English. However, there is no other way because the country is in full insurrection and all communication has become impossible.' He went on to recount his difficulties – food, heat and expenses – 'but I am content and happy because I hope to resolve the problem of my journey during the winter. I am well in spite of everything.' Nor did he omit to inquire whether the London committee had come to a decision about his mission to China. He also reported that he had been informed at the Catholic mission in Massawa that when they wanted to build their church they were obliged to bring Falasha masons from the interior because the local Christians and Muslims were incapable of undertaking the work. The priests could not speak too highly of the honesty and deep religious feelings of the Falasha craftsmen.

It is not surprising that Halévy found it difficult to understand why the British military expedition took so long to get going. General Napier was a careful commander and he was amassing a considerable force, comprising 12,000 British and Indian troops, 15,000 followers and thousands of transport animals, including forty-four elephants. Halévy lived in the army camp and, assiduous linguist that he was, and with the possibility of going to China in his mind, he seized the opportunity to learn both Hindustani and Chinese from coolies employed by the navy. Among the soldiers of the Indian Army he was delighted to find three Jewish sappers from Cochin with whom he observed the Day of Atonement.[1] But his impatience could not wait on the army's timetable and he decided to make his own way into the interior. Besides, he discovered that Napier's route to engage Emperor Theodore would not take him to those parts of the country where the Falashas lived, and so he set off northwards for Keren, in the country of the Bogos, where he arrived on 24 November, and thence travelled west to Kassala in the Sudan. Here he turned south and, crossing the Takkaze river near Kir Labanos, he made for the Falasha villages in the mountainous Wolkait region. He traversed wild and lawless country, mounted on a camel and pretending to be a rhinoceros trader, and one can but admire the courage of the Alliance's 'intrepid envoy'. When he arrived at the first Falasha village he was hard put to it to convince the inhabitants that he was a co-religionist until a 'more intimate

[1] *Travels in Abyssinia*, p. 16.

encounter' dispelled their doubts. He spent about three months visiting many villages in the Wolkait, Armachoho and Djanfancara districts, including the monastic settlement at Mount Hoharwa which had provided Luzzatto with so much of his material.

Owing to the activities of various warring factions he could not reach Gondar or Kwara province with its considerable Falasha population. He therefore headed for the Sudanese border at Metemma and thence returned via Gedaref and Kassala to Massawa to embark for Suez. In July he reached Alexandria, where, accompanied by a Falasha lad whom he was taking to France to be educated, he proudly announced that 'my journey has been successful'. Soon he reached Paris – to the relief, one may suppose, of his family and friends, who, at one time, had thought that he had perished. Before the month was out he presented his report to the central committee of the Alliance, before whom he appeared in an elated mood, convinced that his labours would bear fruit.

He introduced the young Falasha whom he had brought with him and whom he would entrust to the care of the Alliance so that he might eventually return to his country as 'the teacher and the civilizing agent of myriads of men avid for the light'. All too soon, Halévy's high hopes were disappointed. The Alliance, having lost their early enthusiasm, instead of keeping the young man in France sent him to Cairo, where he died shortly afterwards.

In vivid language Halévy described his journey to the ancient land of Ethiopia and to the Falashas, about whom, he said, practically nothing was known but their name; who, despite disasters, have remained faithful to the sublime truths enshrined in the code of Sinai. He had no doubt that, notwithstanding their colour, they were Jews who worshipped the One God whom they acknowledged as the God of their ancestors, Abraham, Isaac and Jacob. They were dedicated to love for the Holy Land. Moreover, Halévy claimed, the name 'Falasha', 'which they give themselves', proves that in their own eyes they are strangers on Ethiopian soil.

He described the distribution of the Falashas, mentioned that they spoke both Agau and Amharic, and sketched their way of life. In a corner of each Falasha village, he said, 'is found the place of worship or "mesgid", which is more like the sanctuaries of old than is the modern synagogue, and in the courtyard the sacrificial altar is built of undressed stone. The prayers of the faithful rise from the sacred area in praise of the Everlasting God for the well-being of Israel, in love of Jerusalem, in expectation of a happier future for all humanity, mixed with sighs and lamentations and cries of joy and hope.'

Halévy reported that commerce was unpopular among the Falashas because it interfered with religious observances, while slave trading, which was prevalent in his day, was abhorred. Falashas had a high reputation as farmers, artisans and soldiers. They were well known for their bravery and many thousands had enlisted in the Emperor Theodore's army. While he found that there were no religious differences among them, Halévy noted that each community was independent and that it was only when danger threatened their religion that they united against a common foe. In this way, he said, the weak and ignorant Falashas had succeeded in paralysing the efforts of the missionaries. Halévy was certain that the Falashas formed a distinct sect within Judaism. He recognised the difficulty of distinguishing between myth and fact in disentangling their history and mentioned that in the Semien mountains, in his day, there was an old man called Abba Gideon who was generally regarded as being a direct descendant of the former royal house. Falashas considered the restoration of Jewish nationality a principal article of faith, and set great store on the expectation of the coming of the Messiah.

A few years before Halévy's visit the conjunction of Emperor Theodore's accession to the throne and the message preached by the missionaries had deceived many Falashas into believing that a new era was dawning. Imbued with a strong sense of Ethiopian tradition, they recognised Theodore as the name of the expected Messiah. When Kassa assumed that name on his coronation and declared that he was the heaven-appointed Saviour of the nation, many simple folk imagined that the Messiah was at hand. Added to this, the missionaries declared that the Messiah had arrived long ago in Jerusalem and had been accepted by the Jews and it was only their abysmal ignorance which had prevented the Falashas from accepting the glad tidings. Many people began to think that the prophecies were at last being fulfilled.

A letter was even written, in Ge'ez, by a certain Abba Sägga in 1862, addressed to the chief priest of all the Jews in Jerusalem, inquiring whether the time had come for them to return to the Holy City. The message was mentioned in Rabbi Hildesheimer's appeal and was printed in the *Journal Asiatique* of Paris in 1867.[1] The translation reads as follows:

God be praised, Lord of Israel, Lord of all spirit and of all that is flesh; this letter is sent by Abba Sägga; may it reach the priest of Jerusalem, Kaka Yusef, the chief priest of all the Hebrews; Kaka

[1] Vol. 9, February–March.

Yusef, may it reach you by the hand of Buronkosä. Peace to you, our brother Hebrews! The first letter which you sent by the hand of Daniel son of Ananya, father of Muse. . . . Has the time arrived that we should return to you, [to] our city, the holy city of Jerusalem? For we are a poor people and have neither prince nor prophet and if the time has arrived send us a letter which will reach us, because you are in a better position than us. Tell us and inform us of all that will happen to us. But as for us, a great agitation has disturbed our hearts, for they say that the time has arrived; the men of our country say, 'Separate yourselves from the Christians and go to your country, Jerusalem, and reunite yourselves with your brothers and offer up sacrifices to God, Lord of Israel, in the Holy Land. As for you, Bironkos, man of God, as we love you, so go take for us that letter to our brother Hebrews. Peace to you, peace to you, with much peace, our brother Hebrews, you who are in the Law of the Torah which God gave to Moses his servant on Mount Sinai! I who have sent this letter, Abba Sägga, . . . I sent it to you in seven thousand, three hundred and fifty-four, year of the world [i.e. 1862], in the second month. The letter is finished.[1]

The addressee of this poignant letter has not been identified[2] nor is it known whether any reply was sent. The bearer, whose name also appears, in a different context, spelt Berinkos, in Halévy's *Travels in Abyssinia*[3] is probably Bronkhorst, one of the missionaries from Jenda. According to Wurmbrand[4] the letter was handed to Bishop Gobat, who did not deliver it, and it eventually came into the hands of Rabbi Jacob Safir of Jerusalem, the author of '*Even Sappir*', who communicated it to Hermann Zotenberg by whom it was published.

The original Ge'ez text of the sentence referring to 'Daniel, son of Ananya, father of Muse' is defective and it is therefore unclear whether Daniel brought a letter from Gondar or took one there. What we know from Safir is that Daniel came to Jerusalem in 1855 bringing his son Moses. They stayed a few months and then Daniel returned to Ethiopia, leaving his son behind to receive a Jewish education. The leaders of the community in Jerusalem gave Daniel a letter addressed to Itzhak ha Cohen in Gondar in which they expressed their sorrow that the Falashas had forgotten Jewish tradition, as a result of their prolonged wars and troubles, and begged them to recognise the interpretation of Judaism which

[1] I am indebted to Dr David Appleyard for this translation.
[2] Kaka Yusef has since been identified as Rabbi Joseph Schwartz.
[3] p. 41.
[4] Postscript to Hebrew edition of *Quer durch Abessinien*.

they had taught Daniel. They also suggested that three or four
intelligent Falashas should go to Jerusalem to be educated. Daniel
is said to have made a second journey to Jerusalem, perhaps to
fetch his son, but it is not known whether he carried a second letter
with him from Gondar. In any case, Daniel's journeys seem to
have done little to lift the Falashas' veil of ignorance though they
do indicate that the Jews of Palestine were made aware of the
existence of the Falashas before Halévy's journey.

While some waited for an answer to their letter others could not
restrain their impatience to reach Jerusalem. In his report to the
Alliance Halévy had written that about five years earlier an
immense multitude of men, women and children abandoned their
homes and, singing hymns and waving flags, set forth eastwards.
Uncertain of the route and ill prepared, they expected the waters of
the Red Sea to divide when they arrived at its shores and give them
a safe passage to the Holy Land. By the time they reached Axum,
in Tigrai province, the pilgrims were already in a desperate plight
and could go no further. Many died from starvation and sickness
but the remainder held on for three long years before abandoning
the ill conceived project. Those who eventually returned found
their huts in ruins, taken over, said Halévy, by hyenas and
scorpions, but with one great consolation – the missionaries had
disappeared, having been imprisoned by the emperor while they
were away.

After this catastrophe the Falashas suffered all the hardships of
the anarchy which devastated the country. Those in utter poverty
were obliged to beg for charity from those slightly better off. The
herds of cattle which formed their sole wealth disappeared and, in
his day, wrote Halévy:

... the Falasha harnesses himself to the plough with his wife and
children in order not to die of hunger. Fearing that he will not
harvest what he has sown, he abandons his field and attempts to
gain a livelihood by handicraft which brings in little in view of
the poverty of the country. He visits the markets and risks going
as far as the Sudan but he will be fortunate if, on his return, he is
not robbed by the soldiers or the outlaws who infest the
highways. He returns home as poor, but more miserable than
before, bringing back nothing for his children except a fatherly
kiss.

Halévy was writing as an eyewitness, perhaps a little sentimen-
tally, but there is no need to suppose, keen observer that he was,
that he was exaggerating.

He attempted an estimate of the Falasha population and, basing himself on an average of five persons to a family, concluded that the total was in the region of 150,000 to 200,000 souls, or 10 per cent of the population. This figure compares with the quarter of a million estimated at the same period by Henry Stern, with whose writings Halévy was acquainted, and coincides with Martin Flad's estimate in his book *Abessinischen Juden*, published in 1869. Bruce's figure, a century earlier, had been twice this number. The reduction no doubt reflected the losses resulting from the chaotic state of the country in the intervening period as well as the demoralising effect of the Protestant missions in breaking down the cohesion of the community. The missionaries claimed that by 1881 they had performed at least 800 baptisms.[1] In 1922, after nearly seventy years' endeavour, their figure for the total number of conversions over the whole period did not exceed 2,000[2] or an average of under 30 per annum. These were relatively modest figures but the proselytes represented a nucleus in the villages and by degrees whole communities transferred to Christianity and were accepted by the Orthodox Church.

Though it is impossible to arrive at reliable figures for the Falasha population, both Bruce's and Halévy's estimates reflect the importance of the Jewish presence in Ethiopia. Its dramatic decline began with the coming of the Europeans and accelerated as their influence increased. By the beginning of the twentieth century the estimated population was reduced to a quarter of Halévy's estimate and today it is only slightly more than half the former figure. Under the dual impact of the forces of disillusion and discrimination, the trend towards assimilation inevitably gathers strength. There is not much time left if the remnant is to be saved from extinction.

Halévy ended his report to the Alliance with a moving plea for European Jewry to come to the aid of the Falashas on the grounds that they were Jews, that they were miserably depressed, and that they showed a great yearning to rehabilitate themselves. It would redound to the glory of the Alliance, he said, to put the Falashas in permanent contact with their European brothers. It is noteworthy, and greatly to their credit, that the Falashas, both then and later, did not beg for material aid but always emphasised their need for spiritual and educational regeneration.

In 1869 Halévy wrote a longer and more scientific article on his journey for the *Bulletin* of the French Geographical Society,

[1]Payne, *Ethiopian Jews*, p. 62.
[2]ibid., p. 69.

entitled *Excursion chez les Falasha, en Abyssinie,* which aroused so much interest that he was promptly asked by the Académie des Inscriptions et Belles Lettres to undertake a mission to south-west Arabia to investigate the remains of the ancient civilisations in that region. He accepted the invitation and in 1870 accomplished an extensive and hazardous tour in the Yemen, disguised as a Jerusalem rabbi collecting alms for the poor, and brought back an invaluable collection of inscriptions. His reputation as a Semitist was established but the projected mission to the Jews of China – which failed to kindle the enthusiasm of the Alliance Israélite while it engaged the interest of the English Chief Rabbi Nathan Adler – went into limbo. His interest in and sympathy for the Falashas, however, did not wane. Although he did not return to Abyssinia he made an important contribution to Falasha studies by translating and editing some of their writings, including Falasha prayers in 1877, *Te'ezaza Sanbat* or Commandments of the Sabbath in 1902, and also the royal chronicle of the war of Sarsa-Dengel against the Falashas, which he published, in 1907, in the original Ge'ez text together with translations in French and Hebrew. In 1877 the Society of Hebrew Literature of London published his *Travels in Abyssinia,* a slim volume translated by James Picciotto, based on notes of his journey.

In contrast to Luzzatto, who saw the origin of the Falashas in the Jewish settlements of ancient Egypt, Halévy considered that Judaism was introduced into Ethiopia by the Himyarites of the Yemen. He thought that Jewish captives brought to Ethiopia after the defeat of Dhu Nuwas (in AD 525) had converted some of the Agau tribes among whom they settled. This theory, however, is scarcely tenable for a variety of reasons, which have already been explained,[1] and, in particular, because it brings the introduction of Judaism into Ethiopia to a date long after it is known to have existed there.

By the time that Halévy returned to Paris in 1868 the Abyssinian war was over. Emperor Theodore had committed suicide after his defeat at Magdala, the captives had been released and the army had returned, or was on its way, to its barracks in India and Britain. The British army's withdrawal immediately its mission was achieved came as a surprise to some who regarded the operation as an imperialist adventure but it had been part of the original plan, for occupation of the country had not been seriously envisaged. The war had not been particularly popular but, allowing for the normal number of military muddles, it was executed with skill

[1] See above, p. 63.

and, whatever the Abyssinian casualties, with a minimum of loss to British and Indian troops in extremely difficult conditions. Lord Stanley, the Foreign Secretary, entered in his diary that it was 'a war on which we embarked with extreme reluctance and only from a sense of the impossibility of doing otherwise'.[1] There was, of course, a more romantic side to the picture which was not lost on Disraeli, who was then Prime Minister. In proposing a vote of thanks in the House of Commons to General Napier and his men for the successful conclusion of the campaign he proudly proclaimed that the standard of St George had been hoisted on the mountains of Rasselas.[2] Whatever his attitude may have been towards the object of a war to liberate missionaries who were intent on converting Jews, he was delighted by the outcome which gave his administration a much needed fillip. Criticism came principally from those who objected to the cost of the expedition which, as is in the nature of such operations, had risen steeply from the original estimate of £3½ million to nearly £9 million. This was one aspect which also worried the *Jewish Chronicle*, which, in a long leading article at the beginning of the war, inveighing against the missionaries, objected that British Jews, in common with their fellow citizens, would be called on as taxpayers to foot the bill for rescuing 'those whom they consider the enemies of their eternal welfare to recommence their detestable practices – of course, if not in Abyssinia, elsewhere'.[3] Even *The Times* allowed itself to refer to 'the Abyssinian missionaries to whose silly and misguided zeal the present trouble is in part owing'.[4]

After the war was over the Alliance Israélite suggested that Sir Francis Goldsmid, one of the handful of Jewish Members of Parliament, should be asked to intercede with the British Government on behalf of the Falashas. It was a sensible suggestion for Sir Francis, like his uncle, the venerable Sir Moses Montefiore, took a keen interest in his persecuted co-religionists and assiduously advocated their cause in Parliament. It is unlikely that anything came of this proposal but it would have been ironical if Her Majesty's Government had found themselves at one and the same time rescuing the missionaries and succouring their victims.

The death of Theodore and the aftermath of the war left Abyssinia in a state of great confusion with rival *rases* once again vying for supreme power. Eventually the question was resolved

[1] Bates, *The Abyssinian Difficulty*, p. 213.
[2] Hansard, 2 July 1868 (522–9).
[3] *J.C.*, 29 November 1867.
[4] ibid., 1 November 1867.

when Kassa of Tigrai defeated his main rival, Gobazye the ruler of
Lasta, and, in 1872, was proclaimed Emperor under the name of
John IV (Yohannes). The new King of Kings proved to be a
fanatical supporter of the Ethiopian Orthodox Church and
tolerated neither other Christians nor infidels. He forbade the
missionaries to re-establish themselves and engaged in a series of
wars against the encroaching Muslims on his borders. He ordered
all Kemants – whose religion is a mixture of pagan, Jewish and
Christian beliefs – and Muslims in his dominions to be baptised
and, according to Payne,[1] he intended to include the Falashas in
this decree. It is not clear how far he was able to implement this
proposal but news of it eventually reached the Board of Deputies
of British Jews, the senior representative body, whose conjoint
Foreign Committee in 1881 included an item on their agenda to
consider 'an endeavour on the part of King John of Abyssinia to
compel his Jewish subjects to embrace Christianity'.

Throughout his reign John was beset with problems on his
borders. At the time that the Italians, as their contribution to the
scramble for Africa, occupied Massawa and the coastal strip his
western frontier was overrun by an invasion of Mahdists from the
Sudan. These fanatical Muslim dervishes penetrated nearly as far
as Debra Tabor, burning much of Gondar on the way, destroying
Christian and Jewish villages and converting the inhabitants to
Islam by the edge of the sword. John believed this threat to be
even greater than the arrival of the Italians and planned to dispose
of the dervishes first. A great battle was fought at Metemma in
1889 which halted the Muslim advance but caused the death of
the emperor.

Such conditions were not conducive to further contacts
between the Falashas and their new-found friends abroad. The
early interest generated by Halévy's mission was allowed to
subside and other preoccupations, especially the worsening condition of Jews in eastern Europe, engaged the attention of Jewish
leaders. Halévy had not only brought the plight of the forgotten
Falasha tribe to the attention of the western world but he had also
emphasised, like Luzzatto, the importance of a study of its
religion, language and customs for a fuller understanding of the
early history of both Judaism and Christianity. If his report did not
produce the results for which he ardently hoped his enthusiasm
succeeded in firing the imagination of one of his ablest pupils.
Jacques Faitlovitch came forward to take up the cause initiated by
his master and to prove that his labours had not been in vain.

[1]*Ethiopian Jews*, p. 60.

7

Jacques Faitlovitch

FOLLOWING the death of Emperor John while fighting against the dervishes in 1889, the imperial crown passed to Menelik, the King of Shoa. The new emperor had already shown that he was a strong and enterprising ruler and his accession heralded many important developments. His empress, a woman of strong character, called Taitu, who, like her husband, belonged to the Solomonic line, was said, according to Faitlovitch,[1] to be a descendant of the Falasha royal family of Gideon.

Both before and after he became Emperor, Menelik II had greatly extended the frontiers of his territory and, by moving his seat of government to the newly-founded city of Addis Ababa ('The New Flower', built, it is said, at the request of the Empress), his capital became the centre of an enlarged, united Ethiopian Empire. The Italians, meanwhile, consolidated their possessions on the Red Sea coast and pressed further inland. By means of the Treaty of Uccialli of 1889 they gained a nominal protectorate over all Abyssinia and received formal recognition of their colony which, in 1890, by royal decree was given the name of Eritrea, from the Greek word for red to signify its association with the Red Sea. Italian ambitions, however, were not satisfied and soon war broke out, culminating in the Italian disaster at Adowa in 1896, when Menelik gained a decisive victory. Any further encroachments on Abyssinian territory were halted for forty years until Mussolini sought to avenge the defeat by his conquest of Ethiopia, which lasted only until 1941.

Menelik was prepared to co-operate with the Western powers and welcomed a considerable number of foreign advisers. He also took steps to modernise his country by such measures as granting a concession for building a railway from Djibouti to Addis Ababa

[1] *Quer durch Abessinien*, p. x.

and by constructing a telephone and telegraph system. Foreigners were allowed to settle in the country in search of trade.

Under the previous Emperor, John, the Protestant mission to the Falashas, which had established its headquarters at Jenda in Dembea province just north of Lake Tana, was obliged to operate under considerable difficulties. Flad was not allowed in the country and had to be content with meetings on the frontier, where he saw some of the converts and gave them encouragement and guidance for furthering the work of the mission. With Menelik's accession there was some hope of improvement but, on the contrary, conditions became so difficult that in 1892 there was talk of closing down the mission. It struggled on and in 1908 the historian of the C.M.J. reported that:

... famine, war, bloodshed, imprisonment, ecclesiastical jealousy, civil strife, the Dervish invasion, the failure of the Italians have been potent hindrances, powerful enough to harass and impede but not to stop the work. Indeed, it has flourished beyond expectation and, since 1869, without the aid of any direct European guidance on the spot. In spite of all opposition and in spite of ignorance and want of freedom the Gospel has spread among the Falashas 1513 of whom have been baptized in the Abyssinian church through the agency of the Society and from 200 to 300 not in immediate connexion with it.[1]

One man's meat is another man's poison. The success claimed by the C.M.J. was, understandably, anathema to the Jewish organisations in Europe who were receiving reports of Falashas being forced to convert. Pressed by Joseph Halévy, whose visit to Abyssinia thirty years earlier had been sponsored by them, and influenced by the tales of Italian Jewish officers returning from the war, the Alliance Israélite now decided to send another emissary to investigate the position. Their choice fell on a Dr A. Rapaport but he got no further than Cairo before the Alliance changed their mind and he was recalled. The nineteenth century drew to its close and no effective steps had been taken to aid this isolated outpost of the Jewish religion.

Halévy's original report with its call for action failed to attract the attention it deserved. Perhaps because his story was so remarkable and so strange, the leaders of the Alliance themselves began to mistrust their representative. Some even went so far as to question

[1]Gidney, *The History of the London Society for Promoting Christianity amongst the Jews*, p. 616.

whether he had been to Ethiopia and claimed that the young man whom he had brought back with him with such high hopes was a negro whom he had bought in a slave market of the Sudan. This suspicious attitude is oddly reminiscent of the experience of Bruce, who was similarly calumnied. Halévy even found himself obliged to call on Munzinger, the French Consul in Massawa, to speak on his behalf and deny the allegations.

Among his pupils at the École des Hautes Études in Paris, Halévy was fortunate to find one who was inspired by his ardour for the Falasha cause. Jacques Faitlovitch, fifty-four years his junior, coming from a rabbinic family in Lodz, in Poland, was imbued with a crusading spirit and a taste for adventure. Halévy had little difficulty in persuading him to study Amharic and Tigrinya and to place his talents at the service of the Ethiopian Jews. It was a happy collaboration which set the course for the young man's life's work and he lost no time in seeking support for what he regarded as his mission. He was not yet twenty-three when he succeeded in arousing the sympathy of Baron Edmond de Rothschild, an outstanding member of the French banking family, whom he persuaded to finance his first visit to Abyssinia.

It is not difficult to imagine with what sense of excitement he set out from Paris in January 1904 to follow in the footsteps of his master. The spirit of adventure which, ten years earlier, had led him, with a friend, to leave his home in secret with the intention of studying abroad to become a rabbi and a doctor stood him in good stead on this exploit. His boyish escapade had taken him no further than Breslau but on this occasion, with the support of one of the principal leaders of French Jewry, he would fulfil his aim to bring a message of hope to his hard-pressed and neglected brethren in Ethiopia. After landing at Massawa he made his way to Asmara and thence to Adowa and on to Axum. Here he met his first Falasha, a carpenter who came to repair his bed and who gladly put him in touch with members of his community. In the face of considerable difficulties he travelled to Gondar – which Halévy had been unable to reach owing to the disturbed state of the country – and visited many Falasha villages in Dembea, living with the people for eighteen months, gaining their trust and affection and studying their religion and customs.

In August 1905 he was back in Paris, well satisfied with his adventure, and presented his report to Baron de Rothschild.[1] In October, in a long interview with the Paris correspondent of the

---

[1]Subsequently published in Paris under the title *Notes d'un Voyage chez les Falachas*.

Jewish Chronicle, he related his experiences and explained how he had succeeded in overcoming the suspicions of the Falashas. 'Every time a European comes to see us,' he was told, 'he proclaims himself a Jew; but that is only in order to deceive us and to convert us'.[1] It was four decades since Halévy had been among them and as he had not returned they thought he must be dead and, once again, they felt neglected and decided that they must be the only Jews left in the world. It was Faitlovitch's task to reassure them. In some ways he presented a less depressing picture than Halévy, who had visited the country at a particularly bad time. He did not suggest that the Falashas were being persecuted and he reported that 'they live very happily in the country where they maintain cordial relations with the other inhabitants when these are not incited against them by the chiefs and the missionaries. I may say, however, that the Negus Menelik shows them much goodwill.'[2] What worried him was their isolation, their poverty, their lack of education in anything but the simplest religious instruction and, above all, the activities of the missionaries. He saw clearly, as Halévy had done, that only by overcoming their ignorance would the Falashas be able to counteract the influence of the evangelists whose resources, though strictly limited, seemed immense to these simple folk.

They were eager for assistance and Faitlovitch reported that 'in the midst of the ignorant populations among whom they dwell they form an elite desirous of emerging from their degraded condition, burning with idealism, full of love for the faith of their ancestors, which they would not abandon except if compelled to do so by violent methods. These brothers', he declared, 'must be retained in the religion of Israel; and with this object the Jews in our country must interest themselves in these Israelites who are so worthy of their sympathy and solicitude.'[3]

With the object of forming a cadre of teachers and leaders who would be trained in Europe, Faitlovitch brought back with him to France two young men, Tamrat Emanuel, whom he had met in Asmara, and Getie Jeremias, from Fendja, who were placed in the care of the Alliance Israélite. He also brought a pathetic message from the Falashas, written in Amharic, begging for help, which throws a revealing light on the state of the community at that time. It reads, in translation,[4] as follows:

[1] *J.C.*, 27 October 1905.
[2] ibid.
[3] ibid.
[4] *J.C.*, 13 October 1905.

May the Lord God of Israel be praised. Letter sent from Abyssinia by Israelites called Falashas in order that it may reach our brethren in Jewish communities, to the great doctors in Jerusalem as well as in the land of the Franks, and in countries where there are Jewish communities. Peace! Peace! How are you? We are in a state of profound misery. Have pity on us. In the time of the Kings Theodore and John attempts were made forcibly to convert us. We gave our hearts, and the God of Abraham, Isaac and Jacob has saved us. Thanks to your prayers, a small number of us still remain. Formerly we were very numerous; formerly there were 200 synagogues, now only 30 remain. In the time of the Dervishes a frightful number of people died from famine. Thanks to your prayers, we have today a good King. Menelik has said to us: 'Remain like your fathers.' May God grant him long life! Nevertheless, the disciples of Flad are travelling all over Abyssinia, and are urging us to be baptised. They say that whoever is not baptised will be condemned to perdition. He who is baptised will be saved. But we are fighting for the laws of Moses. In the name of the Lord of Israel help us by your prayers. The present letter has been written by Abba Areien, Abba Theim, High Priests and by the Scribe Debtera Teka, in order that it may reach Israelite communities and the great doctors, through the hand of Jacob, son of Moses, who has come to see us. This has given us great pleasure. When an Israelite comes to us we are pleased. Peace! Peace! Much peace to you sons of Israel, our brothers who are in the law of Moses. Oh! our brethren do not forget us. We are in great misery. Our books have been destroyed; the Dervishes burnt them by fire. We have no longer any schools; they are destroyed. Pray to God for us. Written at Gouraba-Sekelt on the 18th day of the month in the 12 month.

Of the two youths who entered the Alliance teachers' training college, Tamrat Emanuel was by far the more gifted. Both withstood the shock of the sudden leap virtually from the Iron Age into the sophistication of Western civilisation, to say nothing of the rigours of a northern climate, and returned to Ethiopia to serve their people. Jeremias was twenty-three when he came to Europe and, after studying in Paris and Jerusalem, returned to his village near Gondar where he resumed his life as a farmer by day and a teacher of Hebrew and religion at night. He died in 1946.

Tamrat Emanuel became a leader and a scholar. He was five years younger than his companion and more adaptable. He came originally from Jenda, where his parents had fallen under the influence of the missionaries and had been baptised. He had a Christian education and, as his friend, Dr Israel Ben Ze'ev, has written,[1] he would surely have been lost to the Jewish community had it not been for Faitlovitch's intervention. After the teachers' training college in Paris he spent seven years at the rabbinical seminary in Florence, one year in Frankfurt, and completed his studies in Paris and Switzerland. The First World War intervened but he returned to Ethiopia in 1920 to teach.

On his return to Europe in 1905, Faitlovitch set about writing his doctoral thesis at the Sorbonne and organising assistance for the Falashas. From this period can be dated the beginning of the first concerted aid programme. Having studied the condition of the Ethiopian Jews on the spot, Faitlovitch was determined to arouse the conscience of his co-religionists. He was convinced that the missionaries had to be opposed by the creation of new schools which would provide education and prove to the Falashas that they had not been abandoned by their white brethren. Little could be achieved without money and his first task was to found pro-Falasha committees in Europe and the United States. Originally, he made Germany the headquarters of his movement but soon it was moved to Florence, to be presided over by the Polish-born rabbi Dr Margulies, who was head of the rabbinical seminary there. 'The ultimate object of our endeavours', the rabbi said in an interview, 'is to found a Jewish school in Eritrea', and to introduce western methods and knowledge.[2]

Faitlovitch was indefatigable in pursuit of his aims though he realised that besides money he also needed the moral support of the rabbinate. He had to demonstrate that his protégés were Jews and to persuade the religious authorities to recognise them as such. An orthodox Jew himself, he had examined the beliefs and customs of the Falashas with understanding and sympathy and was in a strong position to enter into debate with the rabbis. Already before his first visit he had secured the encouragement of the highly respected Chief Rabbi of France, Zadok Kahn. Now he extended his range and Rabbi Margulies eagerly became an enthusiastic ally. In just over a year after his return to France, Faitlovitch secured the signatures of forty-four leading orthodox rabbis to an open letter, written in Hebrew, and addressed to 'our brethren, sons of Abraham, Isaac and Jacob who dwell in Abyssinia'. The signatories were from many countries and included Hermann Adler and Moses Gaster, respectively the Ashkenazi and Sephardi chief

[1]Preface to the Hebrew edition of *Quer durch Abessinien* (1958). Ben Ze'ev died in Israel in 1980.

[2]*J.C.*, 10 January 1908.

rabbis in Britain, Salis Daiches of Sunderland, Isaac Jacob Reines, the first head of the Mizrachi (orthodox Zionist) movement of Russia, Moritz Güdemann, the Chief Rabbi of Vienna and Raphael Meir Panigel, the Sephardi Chief Rabbi of Jerusalem and the head of the Jewish community of Palestine. Faitlovitch could scarcely have collected a more representative cross-section of orthodox Jewish opinion, though Zadok Kahn's signature was missing as he had died shortly after Faitlovitch's return from Africa. The rabbis referred to the Falashas as 'our flesh and blood' and assured them that we 'want to do all we can to prepare teachers and books for you, so that your children shall learn to fear only God all their days, and to keep his law which is changeless'. They ended with an expression of hope that one day the Almighty 'will gather us from the four corners of the earth and bring us to Zion'.[1]

No doubt this unequivocal declaration of support and involvement helped Faitlovitch to establish a string of pro-Falasha committees in Europe and America and to spread knowledge of the black Jews. Nevertheless, a degree of scepticism remained and not least in the circles of the Alliance Israélite Universelle, which not only controlled large sums of money but was very effective in founding and maintaining many excellent schools for Jewish communities, especially in Muslim countries. This powerful organisation was almost ideally suited to bring educational aid to a backward Jewish community but the plight of their Ethiopian co-religionists failed to excite the worthy French Jews who presided over its destinies. It has been suggested that a touch of colour prejudice may perhaps have played a part. Be that as it may, under pressure from growing public concern the Alliance was eventually persuaded once more to examine the problem.

This time they decided that their representative would be Rabbi Haim Nahum, a teacher in the rabbinical seminary at Constantinople, who was soon to be nominated Chief Rabbi of Turkey and, in 1925, became Chief Rabbi of Egypt. He was to be accompanied by a young doctor of Russian origin called Eberlin. The two-man mission arrived in the new capital, Addis Ababa, in February 1908, forty years after Joseph Halévy, representing the same organisation, had entered the north-west area of the country from the Sudan. Forty years which had seen big changes, though the wretched condition of the Falashas, like that of the majority of the inhabitants of the empire, had scarcely altered. Those four decades had seen – besides the foundation of Addis Ababa and the consolidation of the imperial government – the establishment of

[1] A translation in German is included as an appendix in *Quer durch Abessinien*.

the Italian colony in Eritrea, the infiltration of foreign merchants, adventurers and concessionaires, the incursion and withdrawal of the dervishes, the introduction of a telegraph system and the building of a railway from Djibouti as far as Diredawa, which would have to wait another ten years before it reached the capital. There was considerable improvement in the standard of public security but the impact of Western civilisation had scarcely impinged on the lives of the impoverished peasants and artisans.

Nahum and his companion were punctilious in presenting an address on behalf of the Alliance to Emperor Menelik, who favoured them with a most friendly reception and provided them with a safe conduct for their journey. On 26 April the expedition set forth from the capital comprising 15 men, 3 riding mules and 12 baggage mules. They spent four days at Debra Tabor, the capital of Begemeder province, as honoured guests of Ras Gugsa, the emperor's son-in-law and the empress's nephew, and reached Atshera, on the east bank of Lake Tana, where they met their first Falashas.

Three years earlier Faitlovitch had been in the same region collecting material on which to base his report for Baron de Rothschild. The difference in the attitudes adopted by the two emissaries helps to explain why Faitlovitch had not seen fit to join forces with Nahum. The Alliance were at best lukewarm on the whole subject. They had done nothing to follow up Halévy's findings and they had shown little interest in Faitlovitch's proposals. Indeed, they seemed to be searching for an excuse not to get involved. They were anxious to show that the Falasha problem was marginal and that the numbers involved were minimal. To be fair, they did not, like subsequent Jewish leaders, try to show that the Falashas were not Jews. The Alliance instructed their mission to discover the size of the Falasha population, to investigate its social and economic situation and to assess its needs and state of mind. Faitlovitch had been invited to join the expedition in a subordinate position but, in view of his experience and knowledge of the country, he considered this an affront and declined. Instead, the pro-Falasha committee in Florence, piqued by the way the Alliance had behaved, decided to act independently and dispatched Faitlovitch on his second visit to Ethiopia.

As Nahum made his way northwards, Faitlovitch set off to the south from Massawa, where he had landed on 1 May 1908. The two expeditions crossed at Adi Shoa, in Tigrai province, on 21 June where, wrote Faitlovitch curtly, they greeted one another and exchanged a few words. There was little love lost between them. Faitlovitch considered that the rabbi had queered his pitch in the Falasha villages where he had stopped and later he reported that Nahum had caused him a lot of unpleasantness by his behaviour, especially because he had travelled on the Sabbath and thereby undermined the Falashas' confidence in foreign Jews.[1]

Faitlovitch wanted to show the Falashas that the white Jews cared about them and would bring them books and education. He distributed a leaflet he had written in Amharic containing the open letter signed by forty-four rabbis and he made preparations for opening the first schools. Nahum, on the other hand, was not going out of his way either to find Falashas in remote areas or to raise their expectations.

He returned to Paris at the end of July and left almost immediately to take up his new post in Constantinople with the result that his report was not ready until the following March. His conclusions were simple: firstly, that the Falasha population was at most six or seven thousand (about one eighth of Faitlovitch's estimate) scattered over a wide area and, secondly, that they were primitive people for whom the educational methods employed by the Alliance in such places as Morocco or Turkey were not appropriate. It was essential that any programme should be considered with the greatest care. Elsewhere he had said that 'it does not seem to me desirable that anything should be done. In view of their small numbers and wide distribution the creation of schools seems to me impossible.'[2] The Alliance were let off the hook and they naturally followed the advice of their trusted and distinguished representative. Faitlovitch, however, has explained how Nahum, who did not speak Amharic, was intentionally deceived by local Ethiopian officials into underestimating the size of the Falasha population.

During his journey Nahum made a close study of the religious customs of the Falashas and concluded that they were 'Mosaists' or followers of Moses, but that in many respects they contravened the Mosaic Law. As to their origins, he believed that they were converted by a 'judaised group' who came from Egypt about the second or third century BC and probably at the time of Ptolemy Euergetes. He thought that the immigrants followed the river Atbara and established themselves on the left bank of the river Takazze, in western Abyssinia. Is it for this reason, he asked, that the Falashas of that district are called Kaylas, those who have not crossed the water? Thus, he approximated to Luzzatto's position,

[1]*Quer durch Abessinien*, p. 47.
[2]*J.C.*, 7 August 1908.

which was adopted by Faitlovitch in his later writing, and he did not share Halévy's theory that they came from Arabia.

Irked by the indifference of the Alliance, Faitlovitch nevertheless pursued his aims relentlessly. He had spent just over a year on this expedition, returning to Europe in June 1909, and immediately began writing his account of the journey, which was published in Berlin the following year under the title *Quer durch Abessinien*, intended as a response to the views of the Alliance.

While the latter were apparently not prepared to oppose the work of the missionaries, Faitlovitch was determined to do his utmost to preserve the integrity of the tribe. He reported that, as a consequence of his presence among the Falashas, he had brought the number of conversions to a halt and he was gratified to learn that the missionaries themselves were acknowledging the effectiveness of what they called the 'counter mission'. They admitted that, following Faitlovitch's first visit, no more baptisms took place until 1909, 'by which time', wrote Payne, 'of the 1,600 Falashas who had been baptised by the mission, over 700 were still alive, scattered in many villages'.[1] The latter included some of the converts whom Faitlovitch had found were anxious to return to the fold but were frightened to do so for fear of the punishment reserved for those who left the Church. In effect, these proselytes, like many in other parts of the world, found themselves in the invidious position of being rejected by their old community and not being fully accepted by the new. It has frequently been asserted that a great many converted Falashas would return to their community if they were given the necessary encouragement and safeguards.

Once he had overcome the initial suspicion of the Falashas for all foreigners ('ferengis', or Franks, as they were called) and of 'white Falashas' in particular, Faitlovitch gained their wholehearted trust and co-operation. This was nowhere more forcefully demonstrated than when, in defiance of all warnings about the dangers of the route, he visited the remote Jewish monastic community on the slopes of Mount Hoharwa, where he was following in the footsteps of Antoine d'Abbadie and Joseph Halévy. The area became a battleground for rival political armies and was infested by *shiftas* or bandits. According to tradition the synagogue was erected in the fifteenth century by Abba Sabra, who was responsible for converting Abba Saga, the son of Emperor Zar'a Yaqob and the author of several books. Together they introduced monasticism to the Falashas and compiled prayers

[1]*Ethiopian Jews*, p. 68.

for them,[1] thereby introducing some few elements of Christian practice into Ethiopian Judaism. Faitlovitch described the synagogue at Loso on Mount Hoharwa as the most beautiful Falasha prayer house, an imposing building in the characteristic shape of a temple with a corrugated iron roof, visible from far off. There were remains of other synagogues nearby.

The reception which he received from the priests and people brought tears to Faitlovitch's eyes. They greeted him in festive garb, dancing, singing, praying and reciting psalms accompanied by musical instruments. His reputation had gone before him and they imagined that they were greeting the Messiah. It took quite a while before he was able to convince the multitude that he was simply a white Falasha, a European Jew who wanted to help them.

He found the community was in a sad state of decline but he noticed many relics of a more prosperous past. Only small pieces of land still belonged to the Falashas who had once been the freeholders. As elsewhere, since losing their independence in the seventeenth century, they had gradually been deprived of their lands by the conquering Amharas.

On his return to his base at Amba Gualit, in Dembea, Faitlovitch decided to undertake the arduous journey to Addis Ababa which Nahum had recently made in the reverse direction. He had been so deeply impressed by the sincerity and the sufferings of the Falashas that he acceded to their request to plead their cause with the emperor in person. He considered that this was a matter of such urgency that he abandoned his original intention of visiting some of the remote villages to the south and west of Lake Tana.

On his arrival in the capital he immediately sought an audience, which was granted ten days after he reached the city. His task was facilitated by his fluency in Amharic, which pleased both the emperor and his courtiers. When he handed Menelik a copy of his book, *The Death of Moses*, with the Ethiopic text and translations in French and Hebrew, the Emperor asked him to read a few words of the latter as he said that he wanted to hear the language of his forefathers.[2]

In a grandiloquent speech, Faitlovitch explained the object of his visit. On behalf of his brothers, the Falashas, he said that they suffered from the calumny of being labelled *budas*, sorcerers, who eat the flesh of living people and at night turn into hyenas who kill

[1] See p. 95 above and Leslau, *Falasha Anthology*, p. xxv.
[2] *Quer durch Abessinien*, p. 133.

their neighbours' cattle. Faitlovitch had himself witnessed an example of this accusation, brought by a local chieftain against a villager at Amba Gualit while he was there. On that occasion a Christian mother had dreamt that a respected leader of the Falasha community, Debtera Finhas, who happened to be an uncle of Tamrat Emanuel, had drunk the soul of her child and caused its death. The chieftain had come to the village with an armed band to seek revenge and to demand the surrender of the Debtera. The presence of Faitlovitch in the village helped to save the situation. Faitlovitch told the emperor how the Falashas sometimes saw their wives and children carried away and their goods stolen as a result of such outrageous accusations. He also appealed for help for the Falashas who had been brought to the capital as craftsmen. They became, he said, the victims of unscrupulous officials, forced to break the Sabbath, confined to the kingdom of Shoa and treated almost like slaves. Menelik, according to the account, was deeply affected by the speech and replied that he would immediately issue a proclamation forbidding these abuses.

How far the edict penetrated we do not know and, in any event, ingrained prejudices and superstitions are not easily eradicated by decree. It was significant, however, that a European had come to defend the rights of one of Ethiopia's oppressed minorities and had secured a promise of redress on behalf of the emperor's Jewish subjects which they could never have achieved for themselves.

His mission to the capital accomplished, so far as was possible, Faitlovitch set out for the coast and his return to Europe, not by the comparatively easy way to Djibouti but by the far more strenuous route through Eritrea. First, he went to Debra Libanos, at the request of the emperor, who had taken up his quarters there, to complete arrangements for the book on Abyssinia which he had been asked to write and to obtain the royal *laisser-passer* for his homeward journey through Tigrai. From there he went to Ankober, the former royal capital of Shoa, in order to visit the villages in the neighbourhood belonging to the Tabibans. He found the members of this community deeply suspicious and reluctant to answer his questions. He concluded, however, that they were a breakaway sect who had become completely separated from the Falashas of Dembea and now lived ostensibly as Christians. He believed that they were the descendants of Falashas who had been brought to Shoa towards the end of the seventeenth century to be employed as craftsmen. They had retained a number of Falasha customs, including observance of the Sabbath, purification and circumcision on the eighth day after birth.

As he made his way northwards, Faitlovitch came across a small settlement of Falashas at Yedju, three days' march beyond Dessye, living as crypto-Jews, in fear of not being considered Christians like the marranos of Spain. If he had had time, he would have visited some of the scattered settlements in Lasta district and he reported that in Makale, one of the principal cities of Tigrai, there were only two Falashas, from Amhara, who, however, had been baptised.

After two adventures with robbers in his camp, he arrived in Asmara at the beginning of March and immediately called on the Governor-General of the colony. He was anxious to express his gratitude for the Governor-General's help, to report to him on his journey and, above all, to obtain the assurance of the Italian authorities that they viewed with favour the proposal to found a Falasha school in Eritrea and that any report to the contrary was without foundation. This assurance – which was willingly given – was requested in order to counteract Rabbi Nahum's assertion that the Italian authorities were opposed to the scheme.

Nahum had reported to the Alliance that the Governor-General, Marquis Salvago Raggi, had told him that he did not see the use of establishing a school for Falashas at Asmara. He considered that such a project would meet with the disapproval of the 'natives' and would only encourage hatred of the Falashas. Nor was he impressed by a suggestion that an agricultural colony should be founded at Asmara since there was no suitable land available. It is not clear whether the difference between those two versions of the Italians' attitude was due to Faitlovitch's proposal to build a school in Eritrea, whereas Nahum spoke about a school in Asmara, but, in any case, the Nahum report was obviously the one which the Alliance wanted to hear.

The feast of Passover was approaching and Faitlovitch had promised to spend the holiday at a Falasha village in Eritrea called Tucul, near the Mareb river, and just inside the border with Ethiopia. He considered that this might be a suitable site for the school, having the advantage of being under Italian protection and also accessible to the Jews of Tigrai and the Gondar area.

On his return to Asmara he found that he had nearly a month to spare before he could sail for home, and he therefore decided to visit the Jews of Aden to whom he carried a letter of introduction from Elkan Adler, the brother of the English Chief Rabbi. He went in the expectation of raising support for the Falashas but was sadly disappointed. He found the community desperately in need of help from abroad and he was particularly horrified by the abject poverty and misery of the immigrants from the Yemen who had recently arrived in the neighbouring town of Sheikh Othman. He came to the colony, he wrote, to seek help for the Falashas but left as the bearer of the hopes of the Jews of Aden.

Back in Eritrea he made the final preparations for his return journey to Europe, calling at Palestine on his way. Getie Jeremias, who had been with Faitlovitch during the whole of this tour, had been joined at Amba Gualit by a friend, Solomon Isaac, and when they reached Jerusalem both young men were put in the care of the school of the Hilfsverein der Deutschen Juden, a German Jewish philanthropic institution operating on the same lines as the Alliance Israélite, which had been founded in 1901.

Faitlovitch had been deeply suspicious of the Alliance and the Nahum mission before he set out for Abyssinia but it was only when he reached Florence that he learned from the pro-Falasha committee of the damage which had been inflicted by the rabbi. Months before his official report was published in the *Bulletin* of the Alliance Nahum had been giving interviews to the press and insisting that educational aid for the Falashas was unnecessary. In reply, Faitlovitch hastened to publish his account of his travels with the object of refuting Nahum's recommendations, which were based, he considered, on inaccurate information and gave the philanthropists whom the pro-Falasha committee approached an excuse for refusing their help.

Faitlovitch was scathing in his attack on the rabbi. He contrasted the latter's opinion with the plea of an Abyssinian scholar contained in a letter to Charles Singer, written in July 1904, before Faitlovitch had published the report of his first journey, and, therefore, uninfluenced by the latter's 'missionary zeal'. 'What educated man', asked Wolda Haimanot, 'could be found without being touched with sympathy when he heard the story of these people who stick to their marvellous religion for so long a time in the midst of wild African people?' He went on to urge Christians and Jews 'to assist in teaching them agriculture, arts, trades, elementary education etc. according to modern views'.[1]

Despite opposition encouraged by the Nahum report, which placed serious obstacles in his way, Faitlovitch pursued his objective with immense energy. He succeeded in establishing pro-Falasha committees in a number of countries, including one in the United States which attracted a fair measure of support in influential quarters. In 1913 he paid his third visit to Ethiopia. This time he was able to establish his first village school and appointed

[1] *Jewish Quarterly Review*, vol. 17, 1905, pp. 142–7.

Getie Jeremias as its teacher. On his return he visited England and formed a pro-Falasha committee with the new Chief Rabbi, Dr J. H. Hertz, as president. But by then the war clouds were gathering, schemes were abandoned or postponed and when the storm broke Faitlovitch went to Geneva where he lectured on Ethiopian languages at the university. He had to wait until 1920 before he could travel again to Ethiopia for his fourth visit. The Falashas had not forgotten him and had not abandoned hope. He has left this description of his reception on this visit:

The news of my arrival in Abyssinia spread among all the Falasha settlements and hundreds of people came from all parts of the country to visit us in the province of Dembea where we pitched our camp. The joy of the Falashas to see me again in their midst was indescribable. My pamphlet inspired them and made a profound impression upon all. From many quarters I received requests for the booklet and words of appreciation from those who read it. From all points delegates of various Jewish communities came to greet me, to confer with me, and to report the needs of their people. In the fall of 1920, a large group of Falasha notables gathered in the village where I had my quarters to pass the high Holy Days with me, and when the Days of Awe were over they presented me with a letter to be communicated to the Jews throughout the world.[1]

He had brought Tamrat Emanuel and Solomon Isaac back to Ethiopia after completing their education and when he left, after three months, he again took with him four young boys to be placed in schools. Among them was Yona Bogale, then aged thirteen, who was destined to play a leading role in the fortunes of his people.

After the First World War Faitlovitch transferred the centre of the pro-Falasha movement to the United States. In 1921 he secured a declaration of more than usual importance from a leading orthodox rabbi. This was an appeal, dated 4 December, from Abraham Isaac Kook, the highly respected Chief Rabbi of Palestine, to the Jews of the world 'to save our Falasha brethren from extinction and to rescue 50,000 souls of the House of Israel from oblivion. A holy obligation', he wrote, 'rests upon our entire nation to raise funds with a generous hand to improve the lot of the Falashas in Ethiopia and to bring their young children to

[1] American Pro-Falasha Committee leaflet, 1922.

Jewish centres in Palestine and the Diaspora.' Although this forceful declaration must have helped Faitlovitch to raise funds it failed to create more than a ripple in the Jewish world where other pressing matters were demanding urgent attention – such as the pogroms and confusion following the end of the war and the birth-pangs of the Jewish National Home.

Back again in Ethiopia in 1924, Faitlovitch arranged to open the first Jewish boarding-school in Addis Ababa with Tamrat Emanuel as the headmaster. Many years later Yona Bogale gave the present writer this account of the school, which is reproduced in his own words:

The building was a hired house with several tukuls [huts] which served as classrooms and dormitories for the students. The first students were children of Falasha families who were forcefully brought to Addis Ababa by Emperor Menelik II in the 1890s, to build palaces and churches. The Emperor settled these workers in a special quarter not far from the Imperial Palace, which they gave the name Avuare in memory of the village Avora near Gondar where they came from. The opening of a Jewish school in Addis Ababa was received by this people with enthusiasm and regarded as a providence of God to keep them and their children from complete disappearance. The news of this school was received by the Falashas of Begemedir and elsewhere as a fairytale. Young men and grown-up people did not hesitate to walk the several hundred kilometres by foot to reach the school. In the following years the school compound became unfit for a great number of students. In this situation a new school compound has been granted by the Emperor Haile Selassie I in the Gulale area. In the same year a provisional building with several rooms was built with wood and mud and the school transferred to it. On one occasion the emperor himself visited the school.

The school had eighty boarding students and the greatest part of them came from different parts of the country. The grown-up students, after two years study, were sent to the interior to open schools in the central Falasha villages. The younger and gifted ones, after a certain preparation, were sent abroad. On this basis, in the following villages schools were opened: Wokerdiba in the Woggera region; Wachgedebge in the Belessa region; Beluha in the Kwara region; Yadeva in the Kwara region, and Wolkait in the Wolkait region.

From 1924 to 1935, about forty students were sent to Eretz Israel, France, Germany, England and other countries. On their return, part of them became teachers in the school and others employees in government offices.[1]

The opening of Jewish schools in Addis Ababa as well as in Falasha villages in the interior did not fail to create a strong reaction by the Ethiopian clergy and local officials. The clergy, pushed and encouraged by the different missionaries, especially by the Protestant ones, used all their efforts and influence on the emperor and provincial governors to prevent Jewish schools opening in Addis Ababa as well as in the provinces. In several cases the teachers in the provinces were put in prison and the students dispersed. The governors of the provinces treated the Falasha population with inhuman harshness. The craftsmen of all kinds were liable to compulsory work for the officials and the church. The Falashas were under the unlimited power of the governors. The first director of the school, Tamrat Emanuel, backed by Dr Faitlovitch, resolved to undertake the dangerous fight against the powerful masses for better treatment of his oppressed brothers. Unfortunately, the success was interrupted by the conquest of the Fascist Italy.

In 1936, pursued by the Fascist authorities, Tamrat had to leave the country secretly. Following this the school was closed by order of the authorities and the students were dispersed. At this time the following teachers and students were imprisoned by the Fascists and never seen again: Makonen Levy, studied six years in England[2] and was a teacher in the school; Yonathan Wizkims, studied six years in Germany and France, and was a teacher in the school; Yohanan Gobau, an outstanding student, who was preparing to leave for Europe and Telahun Telelo and Mellesse Kassa, who were students.

The Italian invasion, followed three years later by the outbreak of the Second World War, spelled disaster for the educational programme which was just getting into its stride, creating a body of Falashas with a good grounding in general and Jewish education. The dire consequences of this catastrophe have never been repaired nor the victims compensated.

---

[1] A list of these students was published in the *Ethiopia Observer*, vol. vi, no. 3 (1962).
[2] At Townley Castle school, Hampstead (see *J.C.*, 15 February 1929).

8

The Struggle for Recognition

THE liberation of Ethiopia by the Allied army in 1941 was achieved by a three-pronged attack: from the north into Eritrea under General Platt, from the south under General Cunningham, and from the west, from Er Roseires, by a much smaller force commanded by Colonel Orde Wingate, who was accompanied by the emperor. By one of those odd quirks of fate it seems to have been decreed that the thrust along the Blue Nile valley should be led by that brilliant and dedicated Christian Zionist who never ceased to demand the establishment of a Jewish army to join the Allied war effort. Though it is probably safe to say that he was unaware of the historical connection, as he led his column into the Agau country south of Lake Tana, Wingate was almost certainly following one of the routes by which the Jewish religion entered Ethiopia in the far-off days of the Axumite empire. It was also the ancient caravan route which carried gold from Fazugli, near Roseires, and ivory from Sennar in the days when the overland track was used to bring merchandise to Adulis on the Red Sea coast. This may have been the gold land of Havilah of Hebrew mythology, watered by the raging Sambatyon river,[1] surely a reference to the swirling Blue Nile racing through its mile-deep gorge. When, by a series of dashing exploits, reminiscent of his distant kinsman T. E. Lawrence (whom he did not admire), Wingate secured the passage for the Emperor to regain his throne, little did he seem to have realised that his contingent, called Gideon Force after his favourite biblical hero, bore the name of the last Jewish king in Ethiopia. Nevertheless, it was perhaps as well that he was unaware of the damage which the Amharic dynasty of the line of Solomon had inflicted on the Jewish population. Although Wingate went out of his way to enlist

[1] See above, p. 75.

Palestinian Jews to serve in Gideon Force there appears to be no
evidence that he was conscious of the existence of a native Jewish
population in the country he was liberating. In a military sense
Wingate's previous experience in Palestine proved invaluable for
he applied the lessons learnt from his special night squads with
devastating effect in the guerrilla war he fought against the
Italians, as he did again when he led the Chindits in Burma.
Politically and emotionally his service in Palestine had left an
indelible mark, with the result that, as Christopher Sykes has
written, 'throughout the whole of the [Ethiopian] campaign, and
in the period immediately after it, Wingate never lost sight of his
ultimate aim; to achieve an overwhelming personal success which
he could put to the service of Zion. This did not mean that his
devotion to the Ethiopian cause was qualified, but that he found
himself ardently devoted to two causes which he saw as closely
related',[1] namely, Judea for the Jews and Ethiopia for the
Ethiopians.

The Fascist colonial regime had been harsh on the Falashas. The
school in Addis Ababa had been closed in the wake of the Italian
invasion, never to reopen. Tamrat Emanuel, the headmaster, fled
the country and many of his former students lost their lives. After
the war he returned and took up a position in the Ministry of
Education. Later he settled in Jerusalem, where he died on the last
day of 1963. Tamrat's nephew, Tadessa Yacob, whom Faitlovitch had taken with him to Cairo in 1931 to be educated,
returned with the emperor's entourage in 1941 and rose to high
office in the government. But he fell a victim of the amharaisation
policy and was converted to Christianity, only to be imprisoned
when the emperor fell. His son became ambassador in Rome
under the Provisional Military Government but was not re-
employed by the post-revolutionary regime. Tadessa Yacob was
released from prison and visited Israel but took up residence
in Ethiopia. Yona Bogale, another of Faitlovitch's protégés emigrated to Israel in 1979 and settled in Petach Tikvah where he died
in 1987.[2]

During the war of liberation Falashas served in the under-
ground movement and as soldiers with the guerrillas. They claimed
to have lost thirty-two men killed in one battle alone at
Madowa.[3] Naturally, they looked forward to an amelioration of
their lot as soon as victory was gained but, once more, they
were bitterly disappointed. 'After the war,' they wrote in a

[1] *Orde Wingate*, p. 261.
[2] See Obit in *JC* 4.9.87 and *The Jerusalem Post* 14.9.87.
[3] Petition submitted to the emperor in 1958.

memorandum addressed to world Jewry in 1960, 'to our great sorrow, our condition deteriorated to an even worse state than it had been previously.'

Throughout the war Faitlovitch had tried to remain in touch with Ethiopian affairs. He had formed a good relationship with the emperor who as the Regent, Ras Tafari, had given him as long ago as 1922 a written assurance that any persecution of Falashas would be punished. The Regent had also, in the same letter, expressed his pleasure at hearing that some Falashas were being educated abroad as they 'will bring benefit to the whole country'.[1] In 1944, as a mark of appreciation, the emperor appointed Faitlovitch to be an advisor in his embassy in Cairo. When the war was over Faitlovitch resumed his work on behalf of the Falashas and made his home in Israel. In 1946 he paid his last visit to Ethiopia and then concentrated on enlisting support for his educational schemes and devoting himself to research.

The times could hardly have been less propitious. In the aftermath of the war the attention of world Jewry was concentrated on helping the survivors of the holocaust in Europe and establishing the State of Israel. Few were prepared to concern themselves with the isolated remnant of the black Jews of Africa. With the creation of the Jewish State Faitlovitch considered that it should now assume responsibility for redeeming the exiled tribes and he looked to the new government and the Jewish Agency, which was responsible for the absorption and education of immigrants, to undertake this task. After protracted discussions, and guided by the report of a representative who had been sent to Ethiopia, the Jewish Agency decided to set up a teacher-training boarding-school in Asmara, the capital of Eritrea, and to restart some of the village classes in the Gondar region. It was none too soon. The missionaries had been busy in the Falasha villages for some years for one of Haile Selassie's first acts after his return had been to encourage their activities. At last, it seemed, a link was being forged connecting the Ethiopian Jews with their brethren in Israel. The school in Asmara opened in January 1954 with fifty-seven students of both sexes including seven kohanim, or priests. A year later twenty-seven boys and girls were sent to the children's village of Kfar Batya at Ra'anana in Israel, most of whom eventually returned to Ethiopia to teach. One group of students, after spending three years in Israel, was invited by Haile Selassie

[1] Quoted in Preface to Hebrew edition of *Quer durch Abessinien*.

to his palace in Asmara to give him a verbal report of their experiences.[1]

When the first party of children arrived in Israel Jacques Faitlovitch, by now infirm and almost blind, was nearing the end of his life. A few days before his death, in October 1955, he had the great satisfaction of receiving a representative group at his house in Tel Aviv. At his funeral, attended by twelve Falasha children from Kfar Batya, his lifelong friend Professor Nahum Sloushz, an authority on oriental Jewry, praised his long struggle, often in the face of great difficulties arising out of prejudice, to help the black Jews.[2] Faitlovitch had dedicated his whole life to their cause and he bequeathed his library of books and manuscripts dealing with Ethiopia to the municipality of Tel Aviv, from which it has now passed to the city's university. By his endeavours, over a period of fifty years, he saved the Falashas from extinction, though their struggle for full recognition had yet to be won.

With the death of their great champion even the mild support for the Falashas in the Jewish Agency immediately waned. No more children were sent to Kfar Batya and two years after Faitlovitch's death the school in Asmara was closed. The Jewish Agency pleaded shortage of funds. The students and equipment in Eritrea were transported the 300 odd miles to Wuzaba, in the mountains near Gondar, where the Falashas themselves established a boarding-school. But all this unwonted activity deep in the countryside aroused the suspicion of their neighbours. According to Yona Bogale, who meantime had become the spokesman and leader of the villagers in the Gondar region, the Christian population suspected that the Falashas intended to usurp their land. On the night of 24 January 1958, one of the dormitories and the dining-hut were set on fire. Fortunately, there were no casualties but it was decided to close the simple boarding accommodation and, once more, the school was moved; this time to the neighbouring but safer village of Ambober, which thenceforward became the centre of Falasha educational activity, staffed by teachers who had been trained at Kfar Batya.

Other schools were started, scattered over a very wide area from Semien in the north to Gojjam in the south and Kwara to the west of Lake Tana. Altogether twenty-seven schools were opened, employing thirty-six teachers who had received their training at Addis Ababa, Asmara or Kfar Batya. The teaching did not rise above the elementary level except at Ambober but it was a

[1]*J.C.*, 13 December 1957.
[2]*J.C.*, 21 October 1955.

beginning and enabled contact to be maintained between some of the far-flung villages. But even this brave attempt was not to last long for, by the end of 1958, the Jewish Agency, which had been paying the teachers their meagre salaries, once more reduced its financial support and ordered all the schools except Ambober to be closed. Only the teachers from Kfar Batya were retained on the Agency's pay-roll.

Once again, the Falashas were in a mood of despair but now they were fortunate to have in Yona Bogale, European-educated with a talent for languages, an able and impressive spokesman who could bring their plight to the attention of Jews abroad. The missionaries were increasing their efforts and were bringing medical aid to reinforce the influence of their schools. Accusations of sorcery had not been eliminated and had led to instances of murder and arson, and the desecration of cemeteries. The tribe's economic situation was deteriorating as a result of increasing pressure on tenant farmers from greedy and unscrupulous land-lords, while the craftsmen were meeting severe competition from factory-made utensils. In desperation, though with little hope, they presented a petition to the Emperor three times, in 1958 and 1959, in which they reported their grievances. They listed the names of thirteen of their number who had been murdered accused of sorcery, three instances of arson, including the school at Wuzaba, eight attacks on cemeteries, innumerable examples of eviction and details of outrageous rents and tithes. They com-plained that in some areas, in addition to government taxes, they had to pay the landlords half of the harvest, as well as five Ethiopian dollars for a permit to use the land, 25 kilogrammes of wheat to the landlord's agent and 15 kilogrammes of wheat as tithes for the church. In addition, they wrote, 'we are not allowed to erect houses of stone nor to plant fruit trees nor any other kind of trees. We must pay for the clay we use for pottery, for river water and the trees of the forest, which was not the practice previously.' The petition continued on this pathetic note:

We are falsely accused of sorcery, in that we transform ourselves at night into wild beasts such as hyenas, and that not only do we kill our neighbours and their cattle, but that we also exhume the bodies of their dead and eat them. It is by means of such false accusations that your servants are persecuted like wild animals, and many of us have been murdered in the most barbarous manner.

We, your servants, Beth Israel, have been living in this country since time unknown, yet nevertheless, we are viewed by the Christian population as a foreign race. We, your servants, are in such bad plight that were we to find a ladder reaching to heaven we would ascend it, or would submit ourselves to being swallowed up by the earth should it open under us.

If, through their own fault, our forefathers were removed from their lands, surely it is within the power of the king to revoke the orders of his predecessors, and we, your servants, prostrate ourselves before the flag of Ethiopia and the throne of your exalted Majesty in supplication that you will deign to make an order for the protection of your servants and trust that such an order will be faithfully executed.

Signed on behalf of all Beth Israel living in Ethiopia, the delegates

> Debtera Gata Amra
> Enrano Magabi

About the same time, in February 1960, an open letter was addressed to Jewish organisations abroad explaining their difficulties. After detailing their grievances in terms similar to those in the petition to the emperor, they explained what they believed to be the attitude of the monarch towards their community. They said they were deeply offended because their delegation had been refused an audience when the emperor visited Gondar in 1959. They were bitterly disappointed that the promise which he had given them in 1946 – and which was a repetition of the assurance which, when Regent, he had given to Faitlovitch in 1922 – had not been fulfilled. They had reached the conclusion that the emperor favoured the missionaries and wished to encourage assimilation and, therefore, the merging of the Falasha community into the Amhara majority. This would correspond with Haile Selassie's well-known policy of amharisation, which meant ensuring the continuing dominance of the ruling people over the other nations and tribes of the empire. They believed, too, that this was one of the reasons why the emperor opposed emigration to Israel, as it would reduce the number of his supporters in relation to the non-Christian and especially the Muslim population. The emperor, like his successors, was obliged to deal with grave problems in maintaining the unity of his diverse realm.

The same open letter from the Falashas complained 'that World Jewry has cast us forth from the fold of Judaism and is far from willing to help us in this last stand against overwhelming factors.' It was with disappointment and despair that they had heard about a discussion in the office of the Chief Rabbinate in Jerusalem from which they concluded that 'we are not considered to be Jews at all.

Have we not suffered and are we still not suffering similarly to the entire Jewish race on account of our religion? And why should our tribe be considered less than the rest of Jewry?' The document ends with an appeal for help and, once again, one cannot fail to be struck by the dignity of the plea. As on many previous occasions this is not a begging letter, a request for alms, although it came from a desperately impoverished community, but a request for help in negotiating with the monarch about emigration, for medical assistance 'in order to render us independent of the Mission', for improvement in Hebrew education 'by the establishment of a school and boarding-school for thirty young teachers in Addis Ababa', and for technical instruction through the ORT organisation.

The document reached two of the leading Jewish institutions, the American Joint Distribution Committee (AJDC) and the World Jewish Congress (WJC), who decided to invite Professor Norman Bentwich to visit Ethiopia and report. Bentwich, then a spry seventy-eight, paid his first visit to the Falasha villages in 1961. He came from a well-known Anglo-Jewish family which followed a tradition of combining the best in English and Jewish culture, and, in his words, devoting themselves to public service and humanity. A lifelong Zionist, with a fine record in the First World War, he had been Attorney-General in Palestine in the Mandatory Government and subsequently became Professor of International Relations at the Hebrew University of Jerusalem. His home was in England though he travelled frequently to Israel, 'a wanderer', as he called himself, 'between two worlds'. During the Second World War, after a short spell in the Royal Air Force, he had acted as consultant on international relations to Haile Selassie and, in 1943, on a visit to Addis Ababa, he had met Tamrat Emanuel, who was then working in the Ministry of Education. All his life Bentwich had been a fearless champion of the oppressed and a tireless seeker after peace. During and after the war, among his multifarious activities, he had worked ceaselessly on behalf of the victims of the Nazis and was no less indefatigable in his quest for reconciliation between Jews and Arabs, while, in Israel, he had fought the orthodox rabbis for the rights of the dark-skinned Jews from India. He was well suited to become an advocate for the Falashas but, after nine years of endeavour and three more visits to Ethiopia, in 1963, 1966 and 1970, he was appalled by the continuing Jewish neglect of the community. He was still struggling on their behalf when he died, in London, in April 1971 at the age of eighty-eight.

Bentwich recognised that the great danger to the continued

existence of the Ethiopian Jews lay in the activities of the missionaries, now busier than ever, and in the forces of assimilation. If the community was to be saved it needed substantial help from abroad and a reinforcement of the tenuous links connecting it with world Jewry and especially with the State of Israel. The paltry aid supplied by the Jewish Agency, which paid the miserable salaries of half a dozen teachers in one or two village schools, though better than nothing, had to be augmented. Bentwich threw his considerable prestige and authority behind the attempt to stimulate interest in the subject. He carried weight in the Jewish community and had been an official member of the Ethiopian delegation to the peace conference in Paris in 1946. He supported the claims of Ethiopia for reunification with Eritrea and had gained the high regard of the emperor. He had also been chairman and vice-president of the Anglo-Ethiopian Society in London. But it was an uphill struggle.

If it had been difficult to overcome the objections of the rabbis to the recognition of the Jews of India, who at least followed the precepts of the *Halacha*, or Oral Law, it was a great deal harder to meet their prejudices in regard to the Falashas, who were not only ignorant of all rabbinic teaching but, quite obviously, did not conform with the popular notion of so-called 'racial purity'. In addition, an influential section of the world of Jewish scholarship gave its support to the rabbis by declaring that the Falashas represented a Judaised sect which followed many non-Jewish practices but was not a Jewish tribe. The Israeli Government found it convenient to accept these arguments in order to justify it in discouraging immigration from Ethiopia, or *Aliyah*, to use the Hebrew term. The word was put about that the Falashas were not Jews; both rabbis and scholars had said so, therefore it must be true. In such a climate it was difficult to persuade the great Jewish charitable organisations to part with their funds. The 'Responsum' of Rabbi David ben Abi Zimrah in the sixteenth century, the declaration of Rabbi Hildesheimer in the nineteenth, the appeal of the forty-four Orthodox rabbis and of Rabbi Kook in this century, to say nothing of the opinions of such scholars as Luzzatto, Halévy or Faitlovitch, were ignored or disregarded.

By sheer persistence Bentwich made some progress. He gained the support of Lady Henriques (the widow of Sir Basil Henriques), the dynamic head of the British OSE Society, an organisation whose function was to bring medical aid to impoverished Jewish communities abroad. The Jewish Colonisation Association (JCA), which encourages Jewish agricultural settlements in various parts of the world, and was then presided over by Sir

Henry d'Avigdor-Goldsmid, M.P., agreed to assist the educational work. A fresh start, though a modest one, had been made.

At the end of May 1967 Bentwich called a conference, with Lady Henriques in the chair, of those organisations and individuals who had displayed some interest in the fate of the Falashas. He reported on the situation and called for an increase in financial support. He said that OSE had enlisted the services of an Israeli doctor who had set up three health centres in villages in the Gondar region which were available to all, irrespective of creed. The ICA contribution had enabled the number of schools supported by the Jewish Agency in Israel to be increased to seven, all of them under the supervision of Yona Bogale, who maintained a regular correspondence with the donor organisations. The total annual budget for the whole of this operation was well below £10,000. All the funds were raised in Great Britain, apart from occasional contributions from individual well-wishers, a promise of US $2,500 for each of the three following years from the American Joint Distribution Committee, and the small Jewish Agency contribution. In relation to the size of the problem only the surface had been scratched, but a lifeline had been thrown to the beleaguered community and, in addition, a Standing Conference of the various organisations was established, with Bentwich as chairman.

No one connected with this minimal programme had any illusions that it would solve the problem but it represented a fresh start and it would help to raise the Falashas' morale. Besides, it was generally recognised that the real solution lay in creating a living and continuing bond with Israel by means of a well organised plan for emigration. But these expectations could not be realised for, on the one hand, the emperor would not allow a mass exodus and, on the other, the Government of Israel was not prepared to admit an Ethiopian *aliyah* under the Law of Return.

For the Israelis the question of Falasha immigration had become a matter of Government policy. Until the Yom Kippur war of 1973, when Ethiopia, under strong Arab pressure, broke off diplomatic relations with Israel, the Jewish state had established very close ties with the kingdom of the Lion of Judah. A strong diplomatic mission had been created in Addis Ababa, as in a number of other countries of black Africa, trade relations developed and, above all, technical assistance, with the financial help of the Americans, was provided on a considerable scale. Israeli experts were active in helping to train the army and police, in providing doctors, geologists and university administrators and teachers, in supervising agricultural development and highway schemes and in other ways. Israel appreciated that Ethiopia occupied a key strategic position, with good harbour facilities on the Red Sea, and represented a non-Muslim state almost surrounded by countries belonging to the Arab League. Personal relations between the emperor and Israel were excellent and needed to be safeguarded. The government of Israel was well aware that there was a demand for *aliyah* – both President Ben Zvi and his successor, Zalman Shazar, had advocated founding a Falasha village in northern Israel – but it also knew that it was a delicate subject with the emperor.

The Government found allies among both religious and lay leaders who doubted whether the Falashas qualified to join the Jewish brotherhood. The rabbis insisted that their failure to observe the Oral Law and their tendency to bring outsiders into the community justified their non-recognition. The secular point of view was expressed by such academics as Professor S. D. Goitein of the Hebrew University, an expert on the Jews of the Yemen, who spoke of the Falashas as 'the so-called Jews of Ethiopia. Their beliefs and practices have very little to do with Judaism.'[1] Edward Ullendorff, the professor of Ethiopian studies at London University and a graduate of the Hebrew University, doubted whether the Falashas should be 'dubbed' the Jews of Ethiopia. Indeed, his reading of history had led him to assert that 'in fact, not until the Christian and Jewish missionary activities of the nineteenth century have the Falashas learnt to regard themselves as Jews'. They 'have never,' he maintained, 'until the Italian occupation of 1936–41, suffered as *Jews* but as the occasional victims of tribal warfare – a fate they have shared with many other Ethiopians.'[2] Clearly, if they were not Jews they could not suffer as such! This is a remarkable doctrine for, as the numerous examples cited in this book have shown, the Falashas have suffered precisely because they adhered strictly to the teaching of the *Torah*, the Five Books of Moses, and refused to accept the doctrines of Christianity. The logic of his thinking led Ullendorff to the conclusion, in 1967, that

the Israeli Government ... has wisely refrained from all involvement in Falasha affairs. Anyone familiar with the Ethiopian scene will question the wisdom of pro-Falasha activities – however well-meaning and noble the motives may be. The Ethiopian Government is extremely sensitive to the

[1] *Religion in the Middle East*, ed. A. J. Arberry, vol. 1, p. 228 (1969).
[2] *J.C.*, 6 January 1967.

encouragement of any tribal forces which might conceivably disturb the delicate fabric of African nationhood. Any activity by outside bodies on behalf of the Falashas can only weaken their position and lay them open to discriminatory measures. Whether the Israeli Government would cherish, in those circumstances, the ingathering of an artificially Judaised diaspora, I have no means of assessing. Is it either wise or politic (and against all the historical evidence!) to create a Jewish problem where none exists and thus to extend gratuitously the range of those liable, at some time or other, to become subject to repressive measures?[1]

Opinions such as these coincided neatly with the Israeli Government's view of the requirements of *haute politique*. In the interests of harmonious Israeli–Ethiopian relations no attempt was made to open the doors to *aliyah*; the discussion of emigration, even of small numbers, with the emperor was practically taboo. In the minds of most Israeli officials the Falashas were not considered to be Jews. Israeli ambassadors were embarrassed by a discussion of the problem, and only a tiny fraction of the massive aid programme which passed through their hands, running into millions of American dollars, was spent on giving assistance or encouragement to the Falashas. At a time when strenuous efforts were being made to bring Jews from the Soviet Union to Israel one may sympathise with Yona Bogale's despairing cry: 'If our skin would be only a little lighter, I am sure World Jewry would take a greater interest.'[2]

How far the Israeli interpretation of the emperor's views was justified may be open to question. Bearing in mind the attitude expressed by the late President Shazar, the present writer, in an audience in May 1970, asked Haile Selassie whether he would favour the establishment of a Falasha village in Israel to act as a link between the two countries. He replied that 'this may be questionable but there will be no objection. We question the importance of this proposal for there are other ways to help the Falashas. For example, education and farms should be improved within their own community. Nevertheless, the choice lies with the Falashas and there are many ways to help them, for example with financial aid.' Bentwich, too, recorded that at each of the audiences he had with Haile Selassie he had mentioned the desire of some of the Falasha youth to go to Israel and the emperor replied that he had

[1]ibid.
[2]In a letter dated 10 May 1973.

no objection. Some years later a senior official of the Israeli Foreign Office confessed his regret that he had not objected when his Government decided to subordinate the plight of the Falashas to what were regarded as the country's wider interests.

About the time when the Standing Conference was being formed in London Yona Bogale, in Ethiopia, was presented with an opportunity which he seized with enthusiasm. The Ethiopian Government, with the assistance of the Food and Agriculture Organisation of the United Nations and the World Bank, had drawn up an agricultural scheme in the area to the north-west of Gondar, adjoining the Sudanese border, which was known as the Setit–Humera Development project. The intention was to provide holdings for landless peasants and to develop a potentially rich but practically uninhabited area. The stretch of land, similar to the cotton-growing country on the other side of the frontier, ran from Humera (Um Hagar) on the Setit (or Takazze) river in the north to Metemma in the south and was not too far from the Falasha villages in the Wolkait and Armachoho districts, though, as it lay in the lowlands, the climate was much more torrid.

In the absence of any prospect of an organised *aliyah* Yona saw in this scheme the possibility that his people could once again secure farming land in their own right, free from the oppression of greedy landlords, where they could found their own settlements. The chance was too good to be missed and he realised that squatters' rights must be established without delay if the Falashas' claims were to be favourably considered by the authorities. Schemes of this kind demand adequate preparations but the impoverished Falashas had virtually no resources at their disposal. Nevertheless, with high hopes and a determination to succeed, a gallant attempt was made which deserves a place in Falasha history. For five years, in the face of great hardship and in strange and inhospitable surroundings, some one hundred young men struggled to clear and cultivate over 2,000 hectares (5,000 acres) of tropical bush with mechanical equipment to which they were unused, and to bring unaccustomed crops to harvest. They succeeded in marketing cotton, sesame and sorghum (millet), which made a small but welcome contribution to the incomes of the families they left behind in the mountains. At one point, owing to the absence of frontier demarcation, they clashed with an armed patrol of the Sudanese Army and withdrew in good order. Later they were harassed by tribesmen who claimed that they were infringing their customary grazing rights, while at all times they had to guard against *shiftas*, or armed bandits. And then, in September 1974, the emperor was deposed and the country was

thrown into a state of turmoil. Counter-revolutionary pro-
Royalist forces of the Ethiopian Democratic Union appeared from
across the Sudanese frontier and the little settlement which had
grown up in the neighbourhood of Abderafi, near the Angareb
river, caught between rival gangs, was forced to abandon its lands,
leaving its equipment behind.

Meanwhile, the Standing Conference in London, though it
suffered from the deaths of Norman Bentwich in 1971 and of Rose
Henriques in the following year, continued its efforts to increase
the aid programme. The British OSE Society had managed to
send a succession of three Jewish doctors, of whom two were
Israelis, to work in the Gondar area where they set up a mobile
medical unit to supplement the three health centres. This operation was helped for a few years by the international co-operation
branch of the Israeli Foreign Office. The seven village schools
were also maintained, of which only one, at Ambober, which
received some support from the Ethiopian Government, taught
up to the sixth standard.

About the same time a committee was formed in Israel under
the chairmanship of Professor Arieh Tartakower, the Jerusalem
representative of the World Jewish Congress. Among its members was Ovadia Hazzi, a regimental sergeant-major in the Israeli
Army, popularly known as 'the father of the Israeli soldiers', a
Yemeni Jew by origin, who had been brought up in Asmara
where his father had been employed by the local Jewish community. It was he who reported that there were neglected Falasha
villages in the Shire district of Tigrai whose existence had not
been notified by Yona Bogale, despite the fact that some of them
had been visited by Faitlovitch and Nahum and were known to the
English missionaries. Hazzi visited these Tigrinya-speaking settlements in December 1971 and was deeply impressed by their
strong attachment to the Mosaic laws and their ardent desire to be
united with the Jews of Israel. He considered that they had a
slightly higher standard than the Jews of the Gondar area and he
noticed that some of them owned their land. They had elected
Mikhail Admass Eshkol, a Falasha from near Gondar who, having
visited Israel, knew some Hebrew, as their spokesman. He had
received the blessing of Uri ben Baruch, the High Priest at Waleka,
near Gondar, but was involved in a bitter quarrel with Yona
Bogale, who alleged that he was a Kemant and not a Jew. The
Falashas of Tigrai, having heard of the assistance which was
arriving from abroad, could not understand why they had been
forgotten and, with encouragement from ben Baruch, they
vented their wrath on Bogale, the representative of the Jewish

organisations, who was responsible for the distribution of aid.

Problems such as these – which are by no means uncommon in the field of charitable endeavour – together with the recognition that Bogale, no longer a young man, was becoming overwhelmed by the difficulties facing him convinced the Standing Conference that it had to send a non-Ethiopian administrator to help supervise its programme. Since there was no money to be saved from the exiguous budget, funds had to be raised for the purpose. Fortunately, a fairy godmother appeared in the unlikely shape of Lord Goodman, who, at the end of 1972, made himself responsible for providing £10,000 to enable the Falasha Welfare Association (as the successor organisation of the Standing Conference was called) to recruit a suitable representative. The choice fell on an Israeli who had spent some years in Ethiopia in a senior position with his country's military mission. He visited a number of Falasha villages at the beginning of 1973 but failed to complete his report and resigned his assignment without explanation. By now hopes had been raised and the gap had to be filled. Nearly a year passed before the Association was able to find a suitable replacement in Julian Kay, an English Jew who had taught for four years in the Wingate School in Addis Ababa. For the next fifteen months he worked devotedly, despite mounting difficulties, to bring educational and medical assistance to the remote and widely separated villages and to demonstrate that they were not forgotten.

In the disturbed conditions which followed the overthrow of the emperor and the establishment of the Provisional Revolutionary Government Kay remained at his post until March 1975, when the authorities refused to renew his temporary visa. He was never given a satisfactory explanation for the refusal though he knew that he had been falsely denounced for organising Jewish emigration to Israel. Possibly the views of the Falasha leaders may have had some influence with the authorities. Whereas the High Priest, Uri ben Baruch, had expressed the opinion that Kay had done 'a lot for the Falashas', Yona Bogale was saying that he was 'friendly with the English missionaries, the enemies of the Falashas, and is no longer welcome among us'.

In Israel, on the other hand, the picture was beginning to look brighter. Ovadiah Hazzi's constant appeals to the Sephardi Chief Rabbi, Ovadia Yossef, were bearing fruit. On 9 February 1973 the rabbi wrote him a letter which is of historic importance. Basing himself on the *responsa* of Rabbis David ben Abi Zimrah (the Radbaz) and his pupil Yaacov Castro he ruled categorically that the Falashas were Jews. He also mentioned 'a number of prominent sages', including Rabbis Hildesheimer, Kook and Isaac Herzog, who had shared this opinion and concluded

that the Falashas are descended from the tribes of Israel who travelled southwards to Ethiopia. There is no doubt that the above sages, who ruled that they (the Falashas) are of the tribe of Dan, investigated and searched and came to this conclusion on the basis of the most trustworthy evidence and testimony. I also, a young man among the tribes of Israel, investigated and searched thoroughly in the matter after their leaders turned to me with a request to be joined to our people, the House of Israel, in the spirit of the Torah and the *Halacha*, the Written Law and the Oral Law, without any restriction, and to carry out all the precepts of the Holy Torah in accordance with the instructions of our great rabbis of blessed memory, by whose utterances we live. I have decided that, in my humble opinion, they are Jews who must be saved from absorption and assimilation. We are obligated to speed up their immigration into Israel and to educate them in our Holy Torah, making them partners in the building up of our land. And the sons shall return to the Holy Land.

I am certain that Government institutions and the Jewish Agency, as well as organisations in Israel and in the Diaspora, will help us to the best of their ability in this holy task that you have taken upon yourself – the *mitzva* [good deed] of redeeming the souls of our people. For whoever saves a single soul in Israel, it is as though he had saved a whole world.

He ended with a reference to Isaiah's plea that God will 'bring back our brethren from Assyria, from Egypt, from Ethiopia and from the isles of the seas and that the scattered ones of Israel and the dispersed ones of Judah may all be gathered together from the four corners of the earth. May they all come and bow down before the Lord on the sacred mount in Jerusalem.'[1]

The ruling – even though it was based on the somewhat problematic descent from Dan – was clear enough. The Chief Rabbi of the largest religious community in Israel had dissipated the doubts of the orthodox as to the claim of the Falashas to be considered part of the Jewish people and had unequivocally called for their return to Zion. Nevertheless, it took a good two years before the Ashkenazi Chief Rabbi Shlomo Goren, Ovadia Yosef's constant rival, could somewhat reluctantly bring himself to express a similar opinion. It was only then that the Ministry of

[1]Isaiah 11:11, 12.

Interior, in April 1975, on the recommendation of an inter-
ministerial committee, converted the religious statement into a
legal measure and decreed that the Falashas were entitled to
automatic citizenship under the Law of Return, which declares
that every Jew has the right to settle in Israel. The rabbinic
authorities demanded, however, that the Falashas should undergo
a token re-circumcision known as *Hattafat Dam B'rit* before they
would regard them as Jews. At first the Falashas did not demur.
One hundred and thirty years after Filosseno Luzzatto, who had
been the first to appeal to western Jewry to accept their Ethiopian
brethren, recognition had been achieved. Now, thought the
Falashas, reunion in the Holy Land was bound to follow, but,
unfortunately, it was not so simple.

The instability in Ethiopia caused by the revolution was
aggravated by the effects of famine and counter-revolutionary
movements, compounded by the invasion of the Ogaden by the
Somalis and the mounting pressure of the liberation movement in
Eritrea. At the same time the introduction of Soviet and Cuban
military assistance, at the invitation of the revolutionary government, militated against the re-establishment of normal relations
with Israel. Conversely, the support which their enemies in the
north and east were receiving from Arab countries gave the
Ethiopians a common interest with Israel. Unofficial contacts
were established. The Ethiopian authorities acquired a small
supply of arms and, in return, turned a blind eye to a limited
emigration of Falashas. Two groups of between fifty and sixty,
mostly young people, reached Israel by air during 1977. Others
would have followed if the authorities in Addis Ababa had not
suddenly clamped down on the traffic following an ill considered
reply which Moshe Dayan, then Israeli Minister of Defence, made
to a newspaper reporter who inquired whether Israel was
supplying arms to Ethiopia. This gaffe has effectively prevented
any further *aliyah* up to the time of writing.

The sense of frustration and disappointment can be imagined. It
expressed itself in noisy demonstrations against the Government
of Israel in January 1979 by Falashas who had settled happily in
the country and demanded that their families should join them. In
Ethiopia attempts to promote emigration were thwarted while
suspected organisers were thrown into jail and, in one case,
summarily executed.

Four of those imprisoned were teachers from the Ambober
school who had been trained at Kfar Batya. After spending many
months in Gondar jail, where one of them was severely beaten,
three were released in June 1980. The revolution brought much

hardship in other ways. Security deteriorated, arbitrary arrests were commonplace, economic activity declined. In addition, many of the Falasha villages in the Gondar area found themselves in the line of advance of the army of the Ethiopian Democratic Union, a Sudanese- and Arab-supported anti-Marxist counter-revolutionary organisation which tried to recover the lands which had belonged to the landlords until they were redistributed to landless peasants. In the course of the fighting some villages were destroyed, cattle stolen, atrocities committed and women and children held for ransom and occasionally sold as slaves. At the same time, further north, the extreme left-wing Ethiopian Peoples' Revolutionary Party, equally opposed to the Government and with a reputation for ruthlessness, attacked and looted a number of Falasha villages in the Woggera region. In Tigrai the Falashas found themselves caught up in the struggle of the Tigrai Peoples' Liberation Movement, which had connections with the similar liberation movement in Eritrea. Their villages continue to be completely isolated from the Jews of the Gondar district and the western world.

On balance, there was little evidence to show that the Falashas were specially selected for persecution. According to an investigation carried out on the spot in 1978, the number of casualties could be counted in tens rather than in hundreds. A considerable number of people were, however, rendered homeless and at the end of 1978 there were 262 Falasha refugee families in Gondar province. News of the disasters naturally spread and, in doing so, became greatly exaggerated so that by the time it reached Israel it had assumed catastrophic proportions.

The funds which were put at the disposal of the Falasha Welfare Association at the beginning of 1973 served their purpose well. They acted as a pump-primer to encourage other supporters and they enabled the Association to put a representative in the field. In 1974 the American Joint Distribution Committee, taking its courage in both hands, reversed its previously aloof policy and decided to participate in the task of saving the Falashas. Together with the Jewish Colonisation Association, who agreed to equal the American contribution, the Joint Distribution Committee promised to subscribe US $25,000 per annum for the following three years and also brought in their United Kingdom colleagues, the Central British Fund, who accepted responsibility for OSE's commitment for medical aid. By now the annual budget had been quadrupled and the operation was beginning to assume a professional look.

Thus, when Julian Kay, having worked hard to develop the

programme, was obliged to leave his post the organisation was sufficiently firmly established to attract a replacement. Six months after Kay's departure, Gershon Levy, an Israeli agronomist with previous experience in Ethiopia and other developing countries, was ready to step into his shoes. He lost no time in enlarging the educational and medical programme and starting a revolving credit fund for farmers, besides cultivating good relations with the civil authorities.

One of his first tasks – one which had never previously been undertaken – was to organise a census of the Falasha population. While not claiming that it was complete, it nevertheless gave a more accurate picture than anything hitherto obtained by guess-work. With the help of agents Levy investigated 490 villages and found that they were inhabited by 6,092 Falasha families having a total Falasha population of 28,189. He discovered that most of the villages contained a mixed population, of which the Falashas represented anything from 10 to 50 per cent. Half the Jewish population was represented by children up to eighteen years of age, indicating a very high mortality rate. The census covered a wide area but it almost certainly omitted some remote settle-ments, more especially as it was undertaken while the state of the country was disturbed and communication was even more difficult than usual. The unsettled conditions impeded the aid programme but a score of primary schools and two health centres, as well as the 8th grade school at Ambober, were kept in operation.

The progress which had been made by the Falasha Welfare Association (F.W.A.) and the recognition of its importance as a means of meeting the threat to the survival of the Falashas had by now drawn the major Jewish body concerned with technical training into the field. In July 1977, after a thorough investigation, the World ORT Union, which has achieved an international reputation for its educational work in many parts of the world, adopted a resolution 'to implement a broad-gauged programme of community development, education, artisanal improvement and related technological advancement' in Ethiopia in conjunction with the American Joint Distribution Committee. The pro-gramme, which was designed to benefit all sections of the people while paying special attention to the educational and religious needs of the Jewish population, would be based in the Gondar region to be easily accessible to the Falasha villages.

Building on the foundations laid by the F.W.A. and furnished with adequate resources provided partly by several governments from their overseas aid funds and partly by special contributions to meet the needs of the Falashas, the ORT organisation under the leadership of Max Braude, its Director-General, took up the challenge with vigour and enthusiasm. At last it was possible to build an infrastructure capable of dealing with the problems of health, education and rural development while at the same time assuring the Falasha population that their particular interests would be safeguarded. In spite of the difficulties of working in an underdeveloped country emerging from a violent revolution, weakened by famine and harassed by war on two fronts, schools and classrooms were built or repaired and furnished, synagogues and health clinics constructed, credit provided for farmers, and teachers recruited.

Any project of this kind is bound to meet many problems but ORT were surprised to discover that they had to overcome opposition from quite unexpected quarters. They soon came under fierce attack both from Falashas who had reached Israel and were desperately anxious to see further immigrants brought in and also from the American Association for Ethiopian Jews, led by Graenum Berger. The latter had long maintained that the only positive way to help the Falashas was by *aliyah*. All else, in his view, simply led to assimilation and, therefore, hastened the extinction of the community. This view was shared by Yona Bogale, whose long years of frustration and disappointment had led him to the same conclusion.

To his chagrin, Braude found his operation denounced by the very people whom he was aiming to help. This was all the more astonishing because ORT enjoyed an unequalled reputation in both Jewish and non-Jewish circles and had been engaged by the governments of many countries in Africa and elsewhere to provide technical education. Such a situation had never occurred before and for a time it threw the organisation off balance, while some members even advocated closing down the Ethiopian programme.

Sensational and ill informed articles appeared in the American and Israeli press during the first half of 1979. Vicious attacks were made on ORT personnel and, in an apparent attempt to force the Israeli Government to organise an immigration scheme similar to that which had been effective in bringing in Soviet Jews, vastly exaggerated accounts of Ethiopian atrocities were spread around under such titles as 'The Falashas: A Black Holocaust Looms'. More distressing were subversive reports which were addressed to international donor organisations and governments insinuating that their funds were being misused. The charges were disproved but they caused a temporary interruption of the programme.

By the end of 1979 the project was back on course and early in the following year ORT were able to report that they had charge of nineteen village schools with 1,663 pupils in 56 primary and 2 secondary classes. However, when this is compared with Levy's census figures showing 490 villages with a population of 14,000 Falasha children under eighteen years of age it will be seen that only the fringe of the problem had so far been tackled. ORT decided to concentrate their efforts where they could be most effective without attempting to spread their resources too far afield. Moreover, they had been constrained by the continuing lack of security in parts of the country, which had prevented them from reopening six of the former F.W.A. schools, including one in Tigrai. Funds were made available to provide scholarships which were awarded to 187 pupils to enable them to attend other schools, including secondary and higher institutions.

The Revolving Credit Fund, up to mid-1980, assisted 384 heads of families, both Falashas and others. It has enabled 223 farmers to buy seeds and oxen and 161 artisans to purchase tools and materials. This scheme has been carried far into the Semien mountains and it is hoped to penetrate to remote villages in the Lasta district of Wollo province, where up to two thousand Falashas are living.

Since their arrival in Ethiopia ORT have been able to improve greatly the medical and health programme. The old, and quite inadequate, clinic at Ambober has been rebuilt on a different site. At Tedda, by a stroke of irony, ORT have taken over the clinic which had been built by the Church Mission to the Jews and which had been such a thorn in the flesh to the Falasha leadership until it was vacated when the mission was closed, in 1978.[1] No distinction is made at the clinics between Jewish and gentile patients who number on average 80 per day at Ambober and 120 at Tedda.

Considerable attention has been paid to the religious needs of the Falashas. ORT have put 26 kohanim, or priests, on their pay-roll who are expected to undertake religious instruction as well as synagogal duties and, if possible, to teach Hebrew. Fifteen synagogues, some newly built and others repaired, come under ORT's care. Hebrew night classes have been started at Ambober by the light of camping-gas lanterns. An expatriate teacher has been recruited to bring a modern interpretation of Jewish culture to the Falasha villagers. This is a delicate subject and needs to be

---

[1] In June 1980 the C.M.J. reported that there were no longer any Anglican missionaries in Ethiopia.

handled with much care in order to avoid confusion in the minds of people who are steeped in ancient traditions which conflict with many modern ideas and practices. The Falashas, however, have constantly requested that they should be given an opportunity to bring their religion into harmony with rabbinic Judaism. In the interests of scholarship it is to be hoped that steps will be taken to make a thorough study of traditional practices before they are swept away by the introduction of western ideas.

Nor has ORT neglected its usual role of providing technical education adapted to the needs of the country in which it operates. Carpentry, metalwork, pottery, sewing and weaving – trades with which the Falashas are familiar – are being taught in the villages near Gondar. Standards will be raised in conformity with today's requirements by methods which are reminiscent of Schumacher's intermediate technology, based on the philosophy of 'small is beautiful'. Here, too, a study is required of traditional arts and crafts – such as the pottery figurines made by the Falasha women at Waleka – before all is changed.

Under the new regime the Ethiopian people are being taught not to despise the craftsman and his product. Clearly, any improvement in the quality of locally made goods for sale in the country markets will benefit the whole region. Other projects undertaken by ORT which are no less beneficial to all the inhabitants include the supply of clean drinking water and the provision of a flour mill at Ambober to which farmers in the region can bring their grain for milling instead of trekking all the way to Gondar. A factory has been erected to manufacture hollow-block bricks which may eventually be handed over to a co-operative society as part of the revolving credit funds, and ORT have built a road into the mountains which is capable of taking lorry traffic where previously only a track, just suitable for a Land-Rover or for mules, existed. This runs for twelve kilometres from Tedda, past Ambober, to Wuzaba where, twenty-two years ago, the Falasha school was burnt by ill disposed neighbours. The new road will enormously improve communications with Gondar.

In view of the criticisms which have been voiced in some quarters it may be asked whether this programme will help or harm the Falasha cause. It certainly conforms with the ideas of earlier champions of Ethiopian Jewry – Halévy, Faitlovitch and Bentwich. None of them saw a conflict between aid brought to the Falashas and the age-old call of the Holy Land. On humanitarian grounds alone it behoves world Jewry to come to their assistance, and it is obvious that unless the political climate changes there is no chance of mass emigration and that no more than a trickle of settlers will be able to reach Israel. To bring aid and succour to those on the spot is the least that world Jewry can do.

There is little difference as regards emigration between the policy of the revolutionary government and that of its imperial predecessor. Tight control is exercised now, as it was then, over the rights of citizens to cross the frontiers. In former times it might have been possible to strike a bargain with the government. Today it is more difficult. The State of Israel has no diplomatic representation in Ethiopia and no leverage. The Ethiopians, on the other hand, have no incentive to let their people go, more especially if, like the Falashas, they represent an economically valuable, though small, element in the population. Moreover, the present regime has to be cautious not to offend the Russians and Cubans who play a vital role in the defence of the country. Neither of these partners would view with favour any arrangement which they thought would benefit Israel. In addition, Ethiopia must be circumspect in her relations with the Muslim states which practically surround her and who would oppose any encouragement of *aliyah*. The best that can be hoped for at present, and even that seems far off, is an agreement, negotiated perhaps by a neutral party such as the Red Cross, for the reunification of separated families or an appeal under the Declaration of Human Rights for freedom to emigrate.

Meanwhile, benefiting from the good will of the authorities, ORT is bringing as much assistance and moral support as it can. Since the revolution Falashas may own land where previously they were almost serfs, their skills as craftsmen are honoured where formerly they were despised, they are free to exercise their religion and to benefit from foreign aid and instruction. No one can tell how long this will continue but every school or synagogue or clinic which is built or rehabilitated is an asset to the community. Of course, the Government, presided over by Lieutenant-Colonel Mengistu Haile-Mariam, is an avowedly Marxist regime which severely limits the freedom of the individual, but, for a people as impoverished and depressed as the Falashas, freedom is a relative concept. Since the Falashas, like the serfs in Tsarist Russia, had at best a nominal freedom before the revolution the majority had little to lose under the new dispensation and, indeed, quite a lot to gain.

Whether the revolution will hasten or arrest the decline of the community remains to be seen, though doubtless there are dangers ahead. The catastrophic fall in their numbers since the Falashas lost their independence three hundred years ago is a measure of the inroads which have been made by the forces of assimilation. No one can be sure how many would leave if *aliyah* became a possibility – perhaps as many as half of the community, perhaps more – but experience in other countries has shown that not all would emigrate. Even in the Yemen and in other Arab countries isolated pockets of Jews have remained behind when most have departed. The ORT programme, so long as it continues, ensures that some contact between the Falashas and the outside world is maintained. And this, surely, in present circumstances is the best if not the only way to ensure their survival.

At a time when the world is moving constantly towards a greater degree of uniformity, when variety becomes ever more rare, it would be sad if this unique tribe were to disappear. In the course of two millennia the Falashas have made their mark on history and have added their contribution to civilisation. By their strict adherence to the Laws of Moses they have borne witness, in the face of great hardships, to those principles of ethics and morality which form the foundation of the religions practised in the greater part of the world. The Falashas' saga deserves to be granted an honourable place both in Jewish history and in the annals of the Horn of Africa.

Author's Note
It will be appreciated that this chapter, like the Postscript, was written in 1982. The reader will, therefore, recognise the need, where necessary, to adjust the present to the past tense. I have left the text as originally printed since it remains useful as a record of the situation as it appeared at that time.

Postscript

THE year 1980 ended on a note of sober optimism. The ORT aid programme was going well, relations with the central government in Addis Ababa were cordial and the country as a whole was achieving a certain stability despite a critical economic situation and continuing guerrilla activities in Eritrea and Tigrai. Ten months later, though the last of the imprisoned teachers had been released, the Falashas were again in serious trouble. The dangers mentioned in the last chapter were becoming real.

In July ORT received a letter from the Deputy Secretary-General of the Supreme Council praising the organisation and congratulating it on its work, which benefited the whole country. Three months later, without any prior notification, the same official wrote politely and succinctly to say that the government intended forthwith to take over ORT's projects and to assume full responsibility for their administration. Nothing was said either about the financing of the programme, the payment of staff salaries in the future, or how the handover was to be effected. ORT were left with no choice but to suspend their activities, leaving only the clinics in operation.

Since no explanation was given, the government's reason for this sudden change of policy remained a matter for conjecture. In ORT circles it was believed to be the consequence of advice received from the Governor of Gondar Province, where most of the Falashas live. Emigration across the frontier into Sudan, which was illegal, was known to be increasing and reports had been circulating that close on three thousand Falashas, whose ultimate aim was probably to reach Israel, were to be found in refugee camps. It is possible that the Governor suspected that, although ORT was certainly not responsible for this movement, its presence encouraged it and he probably believed that by removing ORT he would stop the traffic. Whatever efforts may have been made by those ministers and the Commission for Relief and Rehabilitation who were known to be sympathetic to the project, they were apparently over-ruled at the highest level. In a country which urgently requires all the assistance it can get the so-called 'politicization of aid' has, naturally, been deplored.

Those observers may have been correct who suggested that the vociferous campaign conducted by certain individuals and organisations, especially in America, had aroused the suspicions of the Ethiopian authorities. Even worse could befall if, as seemed likely, reprisals were meted out against the leaders of the community. The arrest of the teachers in 1978 had been a warning. More recently, the greatly respected chief priest in one of the villages was arrested, imprisoned and ill-treated, while efforts to secure his release proved counter-productive. Those who shout loudest often do not realise the harm they can do to the very people they aim to help.

The suspension of the programme, which affects both Falashas and non-Jews, is all the more tragic in the light of the real progress which was being achieved. The number of pupils in the schools in 1980 had risen by a third since the previous year to 2,244, the agricultural and technical programmes were being extended and new synagogues built. Jean-Claude Nedjar, the field director, had recorded his emotion on seeing villagers in a remote corner of the Semien mountains constructing their own place of worship 'so poor and yet so devoted to the maintenance of their Jewish identity'. During 1980, for the first time, imported *matzos* were distributed at Passover and, also for the first time, a gift of Hebrew prayer books was donated by the Addis Ababa community of Jews from Aden, thereby marking the end of the schism between the Falashas and their co-religionists from the Yemen.

While the anxiety of the Falashas to emigrate to Israel may have been the ostensible reason for the Ethiopian Government's repressive measures, its actions should be seen against the background of the international situation in which Ethiopia has a difficult part to play. On the one hand, she is bound to her Soviet partner, whose anti-Jewish stance is well-known; on the other, she desires to maintain friendly relations with the countries of the West from whom she seeks economic aid to supplement that received from the East. Nearer home she needs to cultivate good relations with Sudan and to dissuade her neighbour from assisting the Eritrean and Tigrean rebels. Meanwhile, in September 1981, she signed a treaty of friendship with South Yemen and Libya at a time when the latter was at daggers drawn with Sudan. In these circumstances Addis Ababa may have concluded that the sacrifice of the Falasha aid programme represented a small price to pay in order to placate simultaneously the Russians, the Arabs, Colonel Gaddafi and Sudan. It is the unfortunate Falashas who suffer as a result and one can only hope that the severance of their life-line to the outside world will be of short duration.

Afterword: Further Thoughts on Falasha Origins and the Nature of the Evidence[1]

The main text of this work contains a number of references to books of the Old and New Testaments which suggest that a Jewish presence existed in Cush (Ethiopia) in ancient times but we are still woefully short of unimpeachable data. In order to try to overcome the difficulty I pleaded in previous editions for the cause of Ethiopian Jewish studies. It is gratifying to record that a beginning was made with the formation in 1991 of the international Society for the Study of Ethiopian Jewry (SOSTEJE) and the establishment of a bursary at the School of Oriental and African Studies (SOAS), while in Israel the authorities have outlined a project for an Institute for Ethiopian Jewish Culture. So far only the surface has been scratched. Little progress has been made in the pre-mediaeval period and Biblical studies have not been extended to include the Meroitic kingdom of Cush, which is virtually a *terra incognita* in that discipline.

Much of the misunderstanding, even in academic circles, in attempts to unravel the early history of the Ethiopian Jews has been caused by uncertainty in defining what is meant by Ethiopia. Even the *Encyclopaedia Judaica* confuses Abyssinia with ancient Ethiopia.[2] As I have explained in the main text, the biblical Hebrew name for the country was Cush (Kush) which was also the Egyptian and Meroitic name. The term Ethiopia was introduced by the Greeks (meaning the land of the burnt faces) but it was also called Meroë, Nubia and, more recently, northern Sudan. Present-day Ethiopia was generally known as Abyssinia (Habash) a name which has gone out of use as it contained, in some circles, a disparaging connotation associating it with an inferior status and slavery.

To add to the confusion, as Professor Martin Bernal has pointed

---

[1]Based on a lecture delivered at the School of Oriental and African Studies, University of London, on 22 November 1994.
[2]Vol. 6, col 943: 'Ethiopia (Abyssinia) – A Christian kingdom in NE Africa under Egyptian rule from 2000 BCE to about 1000 BCE ...' K. A. Kitchen, in *The Third Intermediate Period in Egypt (1100–680 BCE)*, p. xii wrote, 'For the 25th Dynasty I have rejected the thoroughly misleading term "Ethiopian" ... and have preferred to use Nubian.'

out, the ancient Greeks recognised two or more Ethiopias: one
was Elam, the present-day Khuzestan at the head of the Persian
Gulf, and the other was Nubia.[1] Herodotus wrote 'there are two
sorts of Ethiopians ... the eastern Ethiopians had straight hair
while the Ethiopians in Libya had the crispest and curliest in the
world.'[2] The tradition of several Ethiopias is much older than
Herodotus, who lived during the fifth century BC. Mention
of Ethiopians in the Bible could, therefore, also refer either to
Elamites or Midianites or, depending on the context, to Nubians.
Cushite became a generic term used, loosely, for any person of
dark skin, much as it is in Israel today.

For the purposes of this book I accept all indigenous non-white
Jews living or previously living in Abyssinia as Ethiopian Jews.
I do not distinguish between the various names by which they
were called of Ayhud, Kayla, Beta Israel or Falashas provided
they practise the Jewish religion in broad terms, that is to say that
they are monotheists who accept the teaching of the Torah but do
not necessarily observe the rabbinic *Halachah*. I retain the name
Falasha because it is generally understood and not, of course, in
any pejorative sense.

No apology is required for relying heavily on biblical sources
for the Old Testament has extraordinary historical value. The
place of legend and folklore, however, should not be underrated
in contributing to history for, as Jay Spaulding says, a figure such
as the Queen of Sheba should not be dismissed only as a 'biblical
or merely mythical figure'.[3] Historians such as Moses Finlay as
well as anthropologists like Ruth Finnegan have stressed the
significance of myth and legend for the analysis of a people's sense
of history and identity. The amateur, too, has a part to play in this
discussion and may contribute insights which have hitherto been
overlooked or ignored.[4]

To the inhabitants of ancient Israel and Judah, Ethiopia was not a
far-away land of which they knew little. On the contrary, they had
many contacts with the people who lived on the southern border
of their powerful Egyptian neighbour. The biblical references

[1]'While the Biblical name Cush generally referred to Nubia or Ethiopia, it was
also used for two other regions and their peoples: the Midianites in Western
Arabia and the Kassu or Kassites to the east of Mesopotamia (Elamites) who
controlled Mesopotamia for much of the middle of the second millenium.'
Bernal, *Black Athena*, vol. II, p. 253.
[2]ibid., p. 254 and Herodotus vol. III, bk. vii, para. 70, p. 383, translated by
A. D. Godley (Loeb Classical Library).
[3]'The Fete of Alodia' in *Meroitic Newsletter* no. 15 (October 1974), p. 29.
[4]'It will be a sad day when there is no longer any role for the amateur in
scholarship' wrote J. D. Ray in *Journal of Mediterranean Archaeology*, vol. 3, no. 1
(1990), p. 77.

to the country and its people are numerous, beginning with the descendants of Noah enumerated in Genesis 10. The story of Moses' Cushite wife is told in Numbers 12, and was vastly elaborated by Josephus who also described the visit to King Solomon of the Queen of Sheba whom he called Queen of Egypt and Ethiopia. It is conceivable, though less likely, that she came from one of the Sabean colonies which, it has been suggested, were established on the western coast of the Red Sea in the eighth or seventh century BC 'under pressure from the Assyrians'.[1] This idea, while it might help to explain her title of 'Queen of Sheba' (Saba), also lends some support on chronological grounds to the suggestion that the queen visited King Hezekiah rather than Solomon who had reigned two hundred years earlier. These Sabean immigrants or refugees seem to have had an experience similar to that of the four northern tribes of Israel who, as mentioned below, also under pressure, first from the Assyrians and then from the Babylonians, having fled Israel, appear to have moved into Judah and from there to Cush where, according to legend, they settled on the Sambatyon river.

In 2 Samuel 18:21 it is reported that a Cushite messenger brought the news of Absalom's death to King David. The second Book of Chronicles 14:9 describes how Asa, King of Judah (912–872 BC), defeated Zerah the Cushite who had an army 'one million strong and 300 chariots'. It is uncertain who these Ethiopians were and the size of the army which was threatening the borders of Judah is obviously exaggerated. They may have come from Nubia or they may have been nomadic tribes, possibly of Midianite or Elamite origin, seeking fresh pastures. Not many years after this engagement, another raid was reported when 'The Lord aroused against Joram [Jehoram (849–842 BC)] the anger of the Philistines and of the Arabs who live near the Cushites, and they invaded Judah and made their way right through it ...'[2] Whoever these Cushites were they appear to have been firmly established close to the Judaeans and a clear distinction has been drawn between them and the Arabs.

There was constant communication and commerce between the countries of the Levant and Egypt and Nubia both overland and by the Red Sea. Consequently, it is not surprising to find that by the time of the Prophets, especially Isaiah and Zephaniah, there are references to what appear to be Jewish settlements in Cush where their existence has been recorded, probably for the first

[1] Munro–Hay, op. cit. p. 65.
[2] 2 Chronicles 21:16 (NEB).

time in a map of the Jewish world, by Nicholas de Lange.[1] Though there may be some uncertainty about the date when the Book of Isaiah was written, it is quite precise in naming those places, including Cush, from which the Almighty 'will bring back his people, those who are still left'.[2] Zephaniah, the son of Cushi, in the latter part of the seventh century BC,[3] was also unambiguous when he prophesied 'from beyond the rivers of Cush my suppliants of the Dispersion shall bring me tribute.'[4] This may be a later addition to the book, but it indicates that a Jewish diaspora existed in Ethiopia about the time of the Babylonian exile or slightly before it.

In the Prophet Isaiah we have a powerful witness for he lived at the time of the siege of Jerusalem by the Assyrians who in 701 BC, led by Sennacherib at Eltekeh, near Ashdod, defeated a strong Egyptian/Ethiopian army commanded by Tirhaka (Taharqo), a Nubian, who was soon to become a pharaoh of the twenty-fifth (Ethiopian) Dynasty. The Assyrian invasion had been preceded by negotiations between the Judeans and the Egyptian/Ethiopians who tried to inveigle King Hezekiah to join an alliance of Levantine states to oppose the Assyrian threat. An exchange of ambassadors took place which the Book of Isaiah describes in the following graphic poem:

There is a land of sailing ships, a land beyond the rivers of Cush, which sends its envoys by the Nile, journeying on the waters in vessels of reed. Go swift messengers, *to* a people tall and smooth-skinned, *to* a people dreaded near and far, a nation strong and proud, whose land is scoured by rivers ... At that time tribute shall be brought to the Lord of Hosts *from* a people tall and smooth-skinned, dreaded near and far, a nation strong and proud, whose land is scoured by rivers. They shall bring it [tribute] to Mount Zion, the place where men invoke the name of the Lord of Hosts.[5]

Apart from the historical significance of this passage, implying that a close relationship had been established between Judah and the Cushites (who, clearly, from their description, were of the Nubian variety) it also suggests that the Ethiopian envoys were to be made aware of the significance of Mount Zion, the place where

[1] *Atlas of the Jewish World*, p. 25.
[2] Isaiah 11:11.
[3] Peake, op. cit., pp. 640, 560a.
[4] 3:10 (NEB).
[5] Isaiah 18:1–7 (NEB).

the Lord of Hosts was worshipped. It would seem that this encounter provided not only a diplomatic occasion but also an opportunity for a cultural exchange enabling the Nubians to acquire a knowledge of the Hebrew religion which they might share with members of the Jewish community already established in their country.

The Assyrian and Babylonian invasions, with their cruelties and transfer of populations, to be followed shortly after by the Persian conquests, inevitably had a disturbing effect on the whole region when Egypt and Cush provided something of a safe haven for refugees. Among those who fled to Egypt was the prophet Jeremiah and he himself owed his life to a Cushite for it was Ebed Melech, a eunuch in King Zedekiah's service, who rescued him from the prison into which he had been thrown by his master on a charge of treachery. Perhaps it was this experience which inspired Jeremiah's memorable question: 'Can the Ethiopian change his skin or the leopard his spots?'[1]

Two Egyptian pharaohs of this period, Psammeticus III and Nekhtnebf, the last native pharaoh before Alexander's conquest, fled to Ethiopia. Herodotus, who visited Egypt during the Persian occupation and lived only about 100 years after the events he described, reported that, during the reign of Psammeticus II (594–589 BC), disaffected members of the garrisons at Daphne and Elephantine – the latter of which, as described in the body of this book, included a sizeable Jewish element – had crossed the frontier and migrated to Ethiopia. He and subsequent writers, Eratosthenes and Strabo, also reported this incident, which was caused by failure to relieve the guards after three years' duty. The king pursued the deserters but failed to persuade them to return. Herodotus wrote that one of the soldiers 'so the story goes, said, pointing to his manly part that wherever this should be they would have wives and children. So they came to Ethiopia and gave themselves up to the king of the country, who, to make them a gift in return, bade them dispossess certain Ethiopians with whom he was at feud, and occupy their land. These Ethiopians then learnt Egyptian customs and have become milder-mannered by intermixture with the Egyptians.'[2]

There were reported to be 240,000 of these deserters who established themselves on an island far up the river which can be identified tentatively with what is now called the Gezireh, between the White and Blue Niles, where the ancient city of Sennar stands

[1]Jeremiah 13:23 (RV).
[2]Herodotus, op. cit., vol. 1, bk. II, 29–30, p. 309. Translated: A. D. Godley.

and which, significantly, some Falasha traditions associate with their origin (see p. 111 above). They were ruled by a queen who was subject to the kings of Meroë. According to Herodotus they were called 'Asmach, meaning those who stand on the left hand of the king',[1] though Strabo, who included them in his map of the world,[2] called them Sembritae, meaning foreigners, a name remarkably similar to Samaritae (Samaritans).[3] As some of these deserters had come from Elephantine it is possible that members of the Jewish garrison were among them and had moved into the heart of Meroë, little more than 150 miles from the gold deposits of Fazughli on the southern frontier.

The revolt of the garrison seems to have occurred shortly before another group of refugees entered Ethiopia from the north. The Talmud recounts that, after the Babylonian conquest, 'The Israelites went into three different lands of exile, one beyond the Sambatyon river, one to Daphne at Antioch, and one on which the cloud descended and which the cloud covered.'[4] Eldad ha-Dani seems to have elaborated on this story when he reported that four Samaritan tribes from Israel – Dan, Naftali, Gad and Asher – fled from the Babylonian invasion and, instead of travelling eastwards, turned south and made their way to Cush. If this story contains a kernel of historical truth it is conceivable that the tribes found a staging post in the Gezireh, in the company of the deserters from Elephantine, on their journey to the 'gold land of Havilah'[5] tentatively identified with Fazughli on the banks of the river variously designated as the legendary Sambatyon or the Pishon, that is the Nile, and possibly the Ophir of the Bible. There 'they dwelt for many years being fruitful and multiplying exceedingly and grew very wealthy'.[6] There is no reason why this story, like so many legends, should not contain an element of historical truth.

The proposition that there was a Jewish presence in Cush before the Christian era receives additional support from the New Testament story of St Philip and the Ethiopian eunuch whether it is considered either as a symbolic or a realistic account of an event. Either way it indicates that there was a belief in the first century AD that a Jewish community existed at Meroë and this, like the

[1] ibid.
[2] *The Times Atlas of the Bible*, p. 92/3.
[3] See p. 45 above.
[4] Yerushalmi Sanhedrin, ch. 10, paras. 5–6. The reference to Antioch may be questionable since the Daphne at Tahpanhes, in Lower Egypt, where Jeremiah found refuge (Jeremiah 43:7), would appear to be more appropriate.
[5] *Enc. Jud.*, vol. 6, col. 575.
[6] M. Waldman *Jews of Ethiopia*, p. 80.

Sembritae story, could represent an intermediate position between the authenticated Jewish settlement at Elephantine and the legendary Jewish kingdom at Havilah/Fazughli right on the borders of the Axumite kingdom. A seventeenth-century traveller once reported that 'in the land of Habash I found many Jews and they were as black as Ethiopians.'[1] The legend of the Sambatyon river was well defined in Midrashic writing and was mentioned by Josephus. The value of the Danite model as a guide to history must be weighed against the absence of evidence to refute it. Nearly forty years ago an historian wrote 'one of the most difficult lessons which we have still to learn is the right use of negative evidence. In an age which made few written records the absence of records does not necessarily imply the absence of a given institution or of a given tradition . . . it may only mean that the records ceased to be kept or were lost.'[2] The Danite tradition was firmly established by the fifteenth century when it was quoted by the celebrated Cairo rabbi, David ben Abi Zimrah, and his example was followed by his disciples. By the nineteenth century the tradition was recognised by Rabbi Israel Hildesheimer and western rabbis recruited to the Falasha cause by Jacques Faitlovitch. Finally, in 1973, the Sephardi Chief Rabbi of Israel, Ovadia Yossef, declared unequivocally, that 'the Falashas are descended from the tribes of Israel who travelled southwards to Ethiopia'. It was largely on the basis of this declaration, followed by a similar announcement by the Ashkenazi Chief Rabbi, that the government of Israel accepted the Beta Israel as citizens under the Law of Return.

The Danite tradition deserves close attention by students of Jewish historiography and of the Ethiopian Orthodox church for it is questionable whether Christianity would have established itself and with it the capacity to oppose the advance of Islam, if, as in the Mediterranean basin, there had not already been a Jewish substratum on which to build. There is no distinction to be drawn, as Professor Richard Pankhurst has observed,[3] either ethnically or anthropologically, in the racial sense of the words, between their Ethiopian neighbours (whether Agaw, Tigrean or Amhara) and the Beta Israel who, as a consequence of miscegenation and acculturation shared the same physical features.

However, in enumerating the characteristics which the Falashas and Christians shared in common, Pankhurst, with his great knowledge of Ethiopia, has omitted to describe what divides

[1]N. Ansubel, *A Treasury of Jewish Folklore* (1964), p. 529.
[2]N. K. Chadwyck (ed.), *Studies in the Early British Church* (1958).
[3]R. Pankhurst 'The Falashas, or Judaic Ethiopians, in their Christian Ethiopian Setting' in *African Affairs* (1992), 91, 567–82.

them. He underestimates their deep religious differences, the Falashas' refusal to accept the New Testament as well as their longing to bring their exile to an end by migrating to Israel. He overlooks the discrimination they suffered precisely in that 'Ethiopian historic and cultural context' into which he places them, nor does he recognise their humble status as a disadvantaged minority who were deprived of their lands and their independence by their Christian Amhara overlords and endured the obloquy of their superstitious neighbours for allegedly practising sorcery. It is these experiences, which are so often ignored or denied, which entitle the Falashas to claim common cause with Jews in other Christian and Muslim countries. Like Jews elsewhere they suffered from the syndrome designated by Zangwill as 'the dislike of the unlike'. The Falashas were a religious, social and to some extent an economic minority group whose observance of the Jewish religion, omitting the Oral Law, developed certain traditional practices which did not obtain in normative Judaism. Their description by some writers as a 'caste' seems to me doubtful and is suitable only in the widest possible meaning of the word. Their variations in religious observances, however, should in no way exclude them from the concept of *Klal Israel*, the brotherhood of Jewry. The spread of Judaism from Egypt to Abyssinia, by way of Meroë, was far more a peaceful march of ideas in which proselytisation no doubt played a significant role than a movement of people and may be compared with the diffusion of other great world religions which have adapted themselves to a multiplicity of geographical, ethnic and cultural surroundings while retaining the essential elements of their faith. Nor did Jewish influences necessarily halt at the borders of Ethiopia. The existence, today, of African tribes, particularly in Central and Western Africa, who claim to have a Jewish background and who still observe certain Jewish rites, is testimony to the penetration of Hebraic ideas which may well have originated with the Beta Israel of Ethiopia.[1]

[1] See T. Parfitt, *The Thirteenth Gate*, p. 149, *passim*.

Select Bibliography

d'ABBADIE, A., 'Notice sur les Falacha' in *Journal des Débats* (Paris, 1845).
ABRAHAMS, I., Bevan, E. R., and Singer, C. (eds), *The Legacy of Israel* (Oxford, 1944).
ADAMS, W. Y., *Nubia* (London, 1977).
AESCOLY, A. Z., 'The Falashas; a bibliography' in *Kiryath Sepher*, xii, xiii (1935–7) Sefer Hafalashim (Jerusalem 1943).
ANFRAY, F., Caquot, A., Nantin, P., 'Une Inscription Grecque d'Ezana' in *Journal des Savants* (Paris, 1970).
APPLEYARD, D. L., 'A Descriptive Outline of Kemant' in *Bulletin of S.O.A.S.*, vol. xxxviii. pt 2 (London, 1975).
ARBERRY, A. J. (ed.), *Religion in the Middle East* (Cambridge, 1969).
ARKELL, A. J., *A History of the Sudan* (London, 1961).
BARON, SALO W., *A Social and Religious History of the Jews* (New York, 1952).
BATES, DARRELL, *The Abyssinian Difficulty* (Oxford, 1979).
BECKINGHAM, C. F., and HUNTINGFORD, E. W. B., *The Prester John of the Indies* (London, 1961).
BEKE, C. T., 'The Samaritans' in *Jewish Chronicle*, 5 February 1847.
BEKE, C. T., 'Remarks on the Matshafa Tomar' in *J.C.*, 31 March 1848.
BENTWICH, N., *My 77 Years* (London, 1962).
BEN-ZVI, I., *The Exiled and the Redeemed* (London, 1958).
BEVAN, EDWYN, *A History of Egypt under the Ptolemaic Dynasty* (London, 1927).
BRUCE, JAMES, *Travels to Discover the Source of the Nile* (Edinburgh, 1790).
BUDGE, E. A. WALLIS, *The Queen of Sheba and her only son Menyelek* (London, 1922).
BUXTON, DAVID, *Travels in Ethiopia* (London, 1957).
DORESSE, JEAN, *Ethiopia* (London, 1959).
EICHHORN, D. M., (ed.), *Conversion to Judaism* (New York, 1965).
FAITLOVITCH, JACQUES, *Notes d'un Voyage chez les Falachas* (Paris, 1905).
FAITLOVITCH, JACQUES, *Quer durch Abessinien* (Berlin, 1910).
GAMST, F. C., *The Qemant* (New York, 1969).
GARDINER, A. L., *Egypt of the Pharaohs* (Oxford, 1964).
GIDNEY, W. T., *The History of the London Society for Promoting Christianity amongst the Jews* (London, 1908).
GINZBERG, L., *Legends of the Bible* (Philadelphia, 1956).
GOITEIN, S. D., *Jews and Arabs* (New York, 1970).
GRANT, M., *The Jews in the Roman World* (London, 1973).
HABER, L., 'The Chronicle of the Emperor Zara Yaqob 1434–68' in *Ethiopia Observer*, vol. v, no. 2 (Addis Ababa, 1961).
HALÉVY, J., 'Rapport concernant la Mission auprès des Falachas' in *Bulletin de l'A.I.U.* (Paris, 1868).
HALÉVY, J., 'Excursion chez les Falacha, en Abyssinie' in *Bulletin de la Société de Geographie* (Paris, March–April 1869).
HALÉVY, J., *Travels in Abyssinia* (London, 1877).
HALÉVY, J., *La Guerre de Sarsa Dengel contre les Falachas* (Paris, 1907).
HAY, M., *The Foot of Pride* (Boston, 1951).

HERODOTUS, *History*, ed. A.J. Evans (London, 1941).
HESS, R. L., 'An outline of Falasha History' in *Proceedings of the Third International Conference of Ethiopian Studies*, vol. 1 (Addis Ababa, 1969).
HUDSON, G., 'Language Classification and the Semitic Prehistory of Ethiopia' in *Folia Orientalia*, vol. xviii (1977).
JESMAN, C., *The Ethiopian Paradox* (London, 1963).
JONES, A.H.M. and MONROE, E., *A History of Ethiopia* (Oxford, 1960).
JOSEPHUS, FLAVIUS, *The Antiquities of the Jews*, transl. W. Whiston.
KAHANA, Y., *Among Long-Lost Brothers* (Hebrew) (Tel Aviv, 1977).
KEDOURIE, E. (ed.), *The Jewish World* (London, 1979).
KIRWAN, L. P., 'The Christian Topography and the Kingdom of Axum' in *The Geographical Journal*, vol. 138 (London, 1972).
KIRWAN, L. P., 'Rome beyond the Southern Egyptian Frontier', in *Proceedings of the British Academy*, vol. lxiii (London, 1977).
KOBISHCHANOV, Y. M., *Axum* (Pennsylvania, 1979).
KOESTLER, A., *The Thirteenth Tribe* (London, 1976).
LANDSHUT, S., *Jewish Communities in the Muslim Countries of the Middle East* (London, 1950).
LESLAU, W., *Falasha Anthology* (New Haven, Connecticut, 1951).
LESLAU, W., *Coutumes et Croyances des Falachas* (Paris, 1957).
LEVINE, D., *Greater Ethiopia* (Chicago, 1974).
LUZZATTO, F., 'Mémoire sur les Juifs d'Abyssinie ou Falashas' in *Archives Israélites* (Paris, 1851–4).
MARCUS, M. L., *Notice sur l'Époque de l'Établissement des Juifs dans l'Abyssinie* (Paris, 1829).
MENDELSSOHN, S., *The Jews of Africa* (London, 1920).
MOOREHEAD, A., *The Blue Nile* (London, 1962).
MURRAY, A., *The Life and Writings of James Bruce* (Edinburgh, 1808).
NAHOUM, H., 'Mission chez les Falachas d'Abyssinie' in *Bulletin de l'A.I.U.*, no. 33 (Paris, 1908).
NORDEN, H., *Africa's Last Empire* (Philadelphia, 1930).
PANKHURST, R., *An Introduction to the Economic History of Ethiopia* (London, 1961).
PARKES, J., *The Foundations of Judaism and Christianity* (London, 1960).
PARKES, J., *A History of the Jewish People* (London, 1962).
PAYNE, E., *Ethiopian Jews* (London, 1972).
PEAKE's Commentary on the Bible (ed. by M. Black and H.H. Rowley London 1962).
PHILBY, H. ST. JOHN, *The Queen of Sheba* (London, 1981).
PORTEN, B., *Archives from Elephantine* (Berkeley, 1968).
PRITCHARD, J. B. (ed.), *Solomon and Sheba* (London, 1974).
QUIRIN, J., 'The Process of Caste Formation in Ethiopia: A Study of the Beta Israel (Falasha), 1270–1868' in *International Journal of African Historical Studies*, 12, 2 (1979).
RAJAK, T., 'Moses in Ethiopia' in *Journal of Jewish Studies*, vol. xxix, no. 2 (Oxford, 1978).
RAPOPORT, L., *The Lost Jews* (New York, 1980).
RATHJENS, C., *Die Juden in Abessinien* (Hamburg, 1921).
REID, J. M., *Traveller Extraordinary* (London, 1968).
SANCEAU, E., *Portugal in Quest of Prester John* (London).
SCHNEIDER, R., 'Les Débuts de l'Histoire Éthiopienne' in *Documents Histoire Civilisation*, RCP 230, CNRS, fasc. 7 (1976).
SHINNIE, P. L., *Meroë, A Civilization of the Sudan* (London, 1967).

SINGER, C., 'The Falashas' in *Jewish Quarterly Review*, vol. xvii (London, 1905).
STARK, F., *The Southern Gates of Arabia* (London, 1936).
STERN, H.A., *Wanderings among the Falashas in Abyssinia*, 2nd edn with Introduction by R. L. Hess (London, 1968).
STRABO, *Geography* (Loeb Classical Library, 1966).
SYKES, C., *Orde Wingate* (London, 1959).
TADESSA TAMRAT, *Church and State in Ethiopia, 1270–1527* (Oxford, 1972).
ULLENDORFF, E., *The Semitic Languages of Ethiopia* (London, 1955).
ULLENDORFF, E., *The Ethiopians* (Oxford, 1965).
ULLENDORFF, E., *Ethiopia and the Bible* (London, 1968).
VITERBO, C. A., *A Program for the Falashas* (Rome, 1967).
WURMBRAND, M., 'Falashas' in *Enc. Jud.*, vol. 6 (Jerusalem, 1971).
ZOTENBERG, H., 'Un Document sur les Falachas' in *Journal Asiatique*, vol. ix (Paris, 1867).

Addenda

BETH HATEFUTSOTH, *The Jews of Ethiopia: a people in transition* (Tel Aviv, 1986).
BETH HATEFUTSOTH, *Beyond the Sambatyon: the myth of the ten lost tribes* (Tel Aviv, 1991).
FRIEDMANN, DANIEL, *Les Enfants de la Reine de Saba* (Paris, 1994).
FREND W. H. C., *The Early Church* (London, 1982).
HANCOCK, GRAHAM, *The Sign and the Seal* (London, 1993).
KAPLAN, STEVEN, *Les Falashas* (Ed. Brepols, 1990).
KAPLAN, STEVEN, *The Beta Israel (Falasha) in Ethiopia* (New York, 1992).
MESSING, SIMON D., *The Story of the Falashas* (New York, 1982).
MUNRO-HAY, STUART, *Aksum* (Edinburgh, 1991).
OLIVER, ROLAND, *The African Experience* (London, 1991).
PARFITT, TUDOR, *Operation Moses* (London, 1985).
PARFITT, TUDOR, *The Thirteenth Gate* (London, 1987).
QUIRIN, JAMES, *The Evolution of the Ethiopian Jews* (Philadelphia, 1992).
SHELEMAY, K. K., *Music, Ritual and Falasha History* (Michigan, 1986).
SHELEMAY, K. K., *A Song of Longing* (Urbana & Chicago, 1991).
TAYLOR, J. H., *Egypt and Nubia* (London, 1991).
TREVISAN SEMI, EMANUELA, *Allo Specchio dei Falascia* (Florence, 1987).
VERMES, G., *The Dead Sea Scrolls in English* (London, 1990).
WALDMAN, MENACHEM, *The Jews of Ethiopia* (Jerusalem, 1985).
WARNER, MARINA, *From the Beast to the Blonde* (London, 1994).
YELMEH, SHMUEL, *The Road to Jerusalem* (Hebrew) (Tel Aviv, 1995).

Index